Harnessing AI for Multigenerational English Language Learning

Christina Nicole Giannikas
CG Education and Research Consultancy, Cyprus

IGI Global
Scientific Publishing
Publishing Tomorrow's Research Today

Vice President of Editorial Melissa Wagner
Director of Acquisitions Mikaela Felty
Director of Book Development Jocelynn Hessler
Production Manager Mike Brehm
Cover Design Jose Rosado

Published in the United States of America by
IGI Global Scientific Publishing
701 East Chocolate Avenue
Hershey, PA, 17033, USA
Tel: 717-533-8845
Fax: 717-533-7115
Website: https://www.igi-global.com E-mail: cust@igi-global.com

Library of Congress Cataloging-in-Publication Data

Names: Giannikas, Christina Nicole, editor.
Title: Harnessing AI for multigenerational English language learning / edited by Christina Giannikas.
Description: Hershey, PA : IGI Global, 2026. | Includes bibliographical references and index. | Summary: "This publication will significantly impact the research community by presenting a nuanced exploration of the intersection between AI and language learning"-- Provided by publisher.
Identifiers: LCCN 2024051496 (print) | LCCN 2024051497 (ebook) | ISBN 9798369354773 (hardcover) | ISBN 9798369354780 (paperback) | ISBN 9798369354797 (ebook)
Subjects: LCSH: English language--Study and teaching--Technological innovations. | Artificial intelligence--Educational applications. | LCGFT: Essays.
Classification: LCC PE1128.A2 H345 2025 (print) | LCC PE1128.A2 (ebook) | DDC 428.0078/563--dc23/eng/20241214
LC record available at https://lccn.loc.gov/2024051496
LC ebook record available at https://lccn.loc.gov/2024051497

British Cataloguing in Publication Data
A Cataloguing in Publication record for this book is available from the British Library.

Table of Contents

Detailed Table of Contents

In response to the demand of engaging preschoolers in an English learning environment, the creation of the Enspire Online mobile application arises as a cutting-edge solution. This app is specifically designed for Vietnamese preschoolers and provides a complete and interesting platform using generative AI for learning the English language. Enspire Online uses a variety of interactive games, activities, and multimedia content to establish an engaging learning environment that captures the interest of young learners and encourages their inquisitiveness. This book chapter examines the design concepts and language acquisition methodologies used in the creation of the Enpsire Online app. It aims to enhance the comprehension of early childhood language education and provides insights for future design strategies in educational technology by examining and analyzing the app's developmental stages through discussion and reflection.

This chapter explores the interesting and challenging world of gamified language learning. It focuses on how game mechanics and design principles can be utilised to transform language acquisition into an engaging and effective experience. It examines the benefits of gamification and specific game elements suitable for language learning. After exploring leading language learning platforms and applications, it provides practical strategies for educators and language learning platforms to effectively implement these elements to create immersive and motivating experiences for learners. Finally, it addresses the challenges in gamifying language learning and discusses the prospects of language learning, including the potential integration of AI-enhanced gamification to further enhance the learning experience.

This chapter examines the integration of artificial intelligence (AI) in education, particularly ChatGPT. It provides an overview of the historical use of computers in education and the recent advancements making AI tools more accessible. ChatGPT's applications in writing support, assessment, personalized learning, and language learning are explored, highlighting its potential to enhance educational experiences. The chapter addresses concerns regarding academic integrity, ethical use, and the need for clear policies on AI integration. It emphasizes the benefits for teachers, including lesson planning, grading assistance, and fostering student engagement. The chapter concludes that responsible AI use can significantly improve personalized learning, provide timely feedback, and support diverse educational needs, suggesting a shift towards a process-oriented approach in education. The authors argue for a balanced approach that utilizes AI as a supportive tool while preserving the essential role of human teachers in fostering creativity, critical thinking, and ethical use of technology.

The impact of the unpredictable spread of artificial intelligence in education is also seen in language learning or language use. The use of AI to overcome or eliminate problems / challenges encountered in language learnings is getting more interest. This idea is also becoming more and more common. AI applications that focus on the problems faced in language learning can provide personalized learning environments. Through personalized learning models learning can be effective. In this study the problems encountered in terms of language learning will be mentioned. Then, the methods, techniques and applications based on AI which can be used to solve these problems will be mentioned. Besides theoretical approaches used to explain AI usage in language learning are presented. Popular AI based apps focusing on different language learning skills are described. Also limitations and suggestions for future work presented.

The integration of artificial intelligence (AI) and virtual reality (VR) into education is growing, expediting the optimization of personalized adaptive language learning (PALL). This chapter discusses the foundations of personalized adaptive learning, explaining its importance for language learners. The potential of AI in language learning and an overview of VR–assisted language learning are presented with a particular focus on the potential of AI embedded into VR, which enables PALL experiences. The role of AI-enhanced high-immersion VR is explained with examples of providing language learners with individualized and contextualized learning environments through immersive real-world based scenarios and simulations. The chapter pinpoints current challenges and future avenues for exploration.

The paper underscores the significance of incorporating Artificial Intelligence (AI) literacy into English language instruction to adapt to the changing educational landscape. Utilizing a comprehensive mixed-methods research design, a survey was administered among 115 English Language Teaching (ELT) educators from various geographical locations worldwide. The findings indicate a high level of self-reported AI literacy among educators, with strong competencies in detecting, understanding, and applying AI. The findings further reveal that a small percentage of educators have received training in AI application in ELT, and among those who have, perceived benefits were reported as low. Although a number of teachers expressed concern about the reliability, transparency, and potential negative impacts on teaching quality and student outcomes when considering the use of AI in ELT, the findings confirmed that utilizing AI tools in language education, such as customized feedback and automated assessment, can offer various benefits for learners.

Preface

INTRODUCTION

Artificial intelligence (AI) is revolutionizing the field of language learning and teaching by providing tools and strategies that cater to learners of all ages (Tiwari, 2024). Through the integration of AI technologies, both language educators and learners are discovering new opportunities for personalized, efficient, and dynamic language education (Mananay, 2024). The continued advancement of AI promises even greater innovation, including:

- **Advanced virtual reality (VR) and augmented reality (AR)** applications for creating immersive language-learning environments.
- **Improved real-time translation tools** that support bilingual and multilingual education.
- **Enhanced integration of AI** into traditional classrooms, combining the strengths of human educators with AI technologies.

AI's impact in language learning has transformed it for a wide range of language learners, enhancing their proficiency and improving their linguistic skills. This gradually empowers learners and could potentially prove to bridge global communication gaps (Wei, 2023). The authors who have contributed in this edited volume attempt to explore AI's potential in language education, contributing valuable insights into its applications, benefits, and challenges.

"The bottom line is, if we want to stay ahead of technological developments, we have to find and refine the qualities that are unique to our humanity, and that complement, not compete with, capacities we have created in our computers; schools need to develop first-class humans, not second-class robots." — Andreas Schleicher, as quoted in The Impact of AI on the Future of Education

A key area of exploration is AI's role in personalizing language learning. AI-powered platforms use adaptive algorithms to tailor content to individual learner needs, which improves engagement and educational outcomes (Kabudi, 2021). For younger learners and adolescents, gamification has been shown to increase engagement. AI-driven gamified learning platforms that incorporate educational content and interactive elements have demonstrated positive effects on motivation and learning outcomes (Cheah, 2021). In terms of pronunciation and speaking skills, Natural Language Processing (NLP) has made significant advancements, enabling more effective pronunciation training. AI-powered conversational agents simulate real-world dialogues, helping learners develop their speaking skills by encouraging spontaneous responses in English (Xaio, 2023). Additionally, AI-driven tools support writing development by offering personalized feedback, allowing learners to refine their writing skills outside traditional classroom settings (Ghorbandordinejad, 2024; Marzuki, 2023).

The present edited volume delves into the transformative role of artificial intelligence in revolutionizing language learning across diverse age groups. This comprehensive guide explores the integration of cutting-edge AI technologies into language education, providing educators, learners, and researchers with valuable insights, strategies, and practical applications. The book covers a wide range of AI-driven tools, from personalized learning platforms to natural language processing, offering a roadmap for enhanced language acquisition and proficiency.

This publication will significantly impact the research community by presenting a nuanced exploration of the intersection between AI and language learning. It provides a synthesis of current research findings, identifies emerging trends, and offers a critical analysis of the effectiveness of AI applications in language education. Scholars and researchers in the fields of linguistics, education, and technology will find this book to be a valuable resource, stimulating further inquiry and discussions on the evolving landscape of AI-assisted language learning.

The book caters to a diverse audience, including educators, language learners, researchers, and professionals interested in using AI for language acquisition. Teachers will discover practical strategies for integrating AI tools into their classrooms, while learners of all ages will find guidance on utilizing these technologies for personalized and efficient language learning experiences. Researchers will benefit from a thorough examination of the current state of AI in language education and potential avenues for future exploration. Ultimately, "Harnessing AI for Multigenerational English Language Learning" serves as a bridge between theory and practice, empowering individuals and institutions to harness the power of AI for a more effective and engaging English language learning journey.

CHAPTER OVERVIEW

Each chapter of this edited volume is significant to the growing literature in AI in language education.

Chapter 1, with the title Designing and Developing Enspire Online - A Mobile APP for Vietnamese Preschoolers to Learn English by Tuan Nhat Nguyen and Huong Thi Bao Dinh, responds to the demand of engaging preschoolers in an English learning environment, the creation of the Enspire Online mobile application arises as a cutting-edge solution. This app is specifically designed for Vietnamese preschoolers and provides a complete and interesting platform using generative AI for learning the English language. Enspire Online uses a variety of interactive games, activities, and multimedia content to establish an engaging learning environment that captures the interest of young learners and encourages their inquisitiveness. This book chapter examines the design concepts and language acquisition methodologies used in the creation of the Enpsire Online app. It aims to enhance the comprehension of early childhood language education and provides insights for future design strategies in educational technology by examining and analyzing the app's developmental stages through discussion and reflection.

Chapter 2, with the title Levelling Up Language Skills: gamified elements for language learning by Richa Srishti, explores the interesting and challenging world of gamified language learning. It focuses on how game mechanics and design principles can be utilised to transform language acquisition into an engaging and effective experience. It examines the benefits of gamification and specific game elements suitable for language learning. After exploring leading language learning platforms and applications, it provides practical strategies for educators and language learning platforms to effectively implement these elements to create immersive and motivating experiences for learners. Finally, it addresses the challenges in gamifying language learning and discusses the prospects of language learning, including the potential integration of AI-enhanced gamification to further enhance the learning experience.

Chapter 3, with the title Leveraging AI Tools to Enhance Writing Skills and Assessment in Language Education by Christina Kitson and Nabat Erdogan, examines the integration of artificial intelligence (AI) in education, particularly ChatGPT. It provides an overview of the historical use of computers in education and the recent advancements making AI tools more accessible. ChatGPT's applications in writing support, assessment, personalized learning, and language learning are explored, highlighting its potential to enhance educational experiences. The chapter addresses concerns regarding academic integrity, ethical use, and the need for clear policies on AI integration. It emphasizes the benefits for teachers, including lesson planning, grading assistance, and fostering student engagement. The chapter concludes that responsible AI use can significantly improve personalized learning, provide timely feedback, and support diverse educational needs, suggesting a shift towards a process-oriented approach in education. The authors argue for a balanced approach that utilizes AI as a supportive tool while preserving the essential role of human teachers in fostering creativity, critical thinking, and ethical use of technology.

Chapter 4, with the title Overcoming Language Barriers with Artificial Intelligence by Hümeyra Yener, looks at the impact of the unpredictable spread of artificial intelligence in education is also seen in language learning or language use. The use of AI to overcome or eliminate problems / challenges encountered in language learnings is getting more interest. This idea is also becoming more and more common. AI applications that focus on the problems faced in language learning can provide personalized learning environments. Through personalized learning models learning can be effective. In this study the problems encountered in terms of language learning will be mentioned. Then, the methods, techniques and applications based on AI which can be used to solve these problems will be mentioned. Besides theoretical approaches used to explain AI usage in language learning are presented. Popular AI based apps focusing on different language learning skills are described. Also limitations and suggestions for future work presented.

Chapter 5, with the title Personalized Adaptive Language Learning in AI–Powered High-Immersion Virtual Reality by Eunkyoung Elaine Cha and Yongluan Ye, discusses the integration of artificial intelligence (AI) and virtual reality (VR) into education and how it is growing, expediting the optimization of personalized adaptive language learning (PALL). This chapter discusses the foundations of personalized adaptive learning, explaining its importance for language learners. The potential of AI in language learning and an overview of VR–assisted language learning are presented with a particular focus on the potential of AI embedded into VR, which enables PALL experiences. The role of AI-enhanced high-immersion VR is explained with examples of providing language learners with individualized and contextualized learning environments through immersive real-world based scenarios and simulations. The chapter pinpoints current challenges and future avenues for exploration.

Chapter 6, with the title Preparing for Tomorrow: AI Literacy in English Language Teaching by Ivana Krsmanović and Dagmar Anna Archan, underscores the significance of incorporating Artificial Intelligence (AI) literacy into English language instruction to adapt to the changing educational landscape. Utilizing a comprehensive mixed-methods research design, a survey was administered among 115 English Language Teaching (ELT) educators from various geographical locations worldwide. The findings indicate a high level of self-reported AI literacy among educators, with strong competencies in detecting, understanding, and applying AI. The findings further reveal that a small percentage of educators have received training in AI application in ELT, and among those who have, perceived benefits were reported as low. Although a number of teachers expressed concern about the reliability, transparency, and potential negative impacts on teaching quality and student outcomes when considering the use of AI in ELT, the findings confirmed that utilizing AI tools in language education, such as customized feedback and automated assessment, can offer various benefits for learners.

Chapter 7, with the title The Role of Artificial Intelligence in Linguistic Corpus Analysis by Hélder Fanha Martins, explores the transformative role of artificial intelligence (AI) in linguistic corpus analysis within applied linguistics. It begins with an overview of applied linguistics and the significant methodological development of corpus analysis, emphasizing its applications in teaching, language use analysis, and lexicography. The integration of AI in linguistic research is examined, focusing on advancements in natural language processing (NLP) and machine learning, which enhance the depth and accuracy of language analysis. The chapter highlights how AI-driven tools, such as deep learning models and neural networks, facilitate complex tasks like speech recognition, sentiment analysis, and text classification. It also discusses the evolution of corpus analysis tools and the impact of AI innovations on language teaching and translation research. The chapter concludes by addressing the challenges and future trends in AI and corpus analysis, underscoring the potential for interdisciplinary collaboration and the ethical considerations involved in AI applications in linguistics.

The edited volume, *Harnessing AI for Multigenerational English Language Learning*, represents a significant contribution to the rapidly evolving discourse on the intersection of technology and language education. The chapters included in this book display ways in which artificial intelligence reshapes language learning, this book not only highlights the potential of AI-driven tools but also establishes a framework for understanding their practical applications, theoretical underpinnings, and societal implications.

The volume impacts the field of language education by bringing together diverse perspectives from educators and researchers. This multidisciplinary approach enables readers to gain a comprehensive understanding of AI's transformative role in education. By addressing learners across diverse age groups, the book underscores the adaptability of AI technologies to meet the unique needs of children, adolescents, adults, and lifelong learners. Such inclusivity fosters a deeper appreciation of how AI personalizes and democratizes access to high-quality language learning experiences, bridging gaps in traditional educational systems.

One of the volume's central contributions is its focus on practical applications of AI in language learning. Through detailed explorations of learning platforms, natural language processing tools, conversational AI, and automated assessment systems, the book equips educators and learners with actionable strategies for enhancing English language acquisition. This practical focus not only empowers stakeholders to integrate AI effectively into education systems but also provides a roadmap for navigating the challenges that accompany its adoption, such as data privacy, ethical considerations, and technological inequities.

Equally important is the volume's emphasis on innovation and forward-thinking. By discussing emerging technologies and more sophisticated machine learning models, the book positions itself as a forward-looking resource that anticipates the future trajectory of AI in education. This perspective inspires both researchers and practitioners to think creatively about how AI can further enrich language learning, while also prompting critical reflection on the evolving roles of educators and learners in AI-enhanced environments.

The book also makes a critical scholarly contribution by addressing the ethical and societal implications of AI in English language education. Its discussions on algorithmic bias, the digital divide, and accessibility challenges broaden the dialogue, ensuring that technological advancements are contextualized within broader considerations of equity and inclusion. By doing so, the volume not only highlights the potential of AI but also fosters a more balanced and reflective approach to its integration into language education. The edited volume, *Harnessing AI for Multigenerational English Language Learning*, represents a significant contribution to the rapidly evolving discourse on the intersection of technology and language education. By showcasing the myriad ways AI reshapes language learning, this book not only highlights the potential but also establishes a framework for understanding their practical applications, theoretical underpinnings, and societal implications of AI.

Looking forward, the volume inspires readers to envision the future of language education in a rapidly changing world. It calls upon researchers, educators, policymakers, and stakeholders to collaborate in developing AI-driven solutions that not only enhance language learning but also address global challenges such as linguistic diversity and cross-cultural communication. By doing so, the book positions itself as a catalyst for innovation and a guide for navigating the complexities of AI-assisted education.

CONCLUSION

In conclusion, *Harnessing AI for Multigenerational English Language Learning* is a scholarly resource and a call to action. By offering a comprehensive exploration of AI's role in language education, the authors of this book provide a roadmap for stakeholders seeking to embrace the opportunities and navigate the challenges of this transformative era. Through its blend of theoretical insights, practical applications, and visionary perspectives, the volume enriches academic discourse, empowers practitioners, and inspires learners to harness AI's potential in building a more connected and linguistically proficient world. This edited collection will undoubtedly serve as a cornerstone for future research, innovation, and progress in the field of AI-driven language education.

Chapter 1
Designing and Developing Enspire Online:
A Mobile App for Vietnamese Preschoolers to Learn English

Tuan Nhat Nguyen
https://orcid.org/0009-0007-7757-4319
Hanoi University, Vietnam

Huong Thi Bao Dinh
https://orcid.org/0009-0009-6002-5668
Phenikaa University, Vietnam

ABSTRACT

In response to the demand of engaging preschoolers in an English learning environment, the creation of the Enspire Online mobile application arises as a cutting-edge solution. This app is specifically designed for Vietnamese preschoolers and provides a complete and interesting platform using generative AI for learning the English language. Enspire Online uses a variety of interactive games, activities, and multimedia content to establish an engaging learning environment that captures the interest of young learners and encourages their inquisitiveness. This book chapter examines

DOI: 10.4018/979-8-3693-5477-3.ch001

the design concepts and language acquisition methodologies used in the creation of the Enpsire Online app. It aims to enhance the comprehension of early childhood language education and provides insights for future design strategies in educational technology by examining and analyzing the app's developmental stages through discussion and reflection.

1. INTRODUCTION

Vietnam has made significant strides in early childhood education, recognizing its crucial role in shaping a child's cognitive, social, and emotional development. As of 2022, the nation boasts a robust network of 15,334 kindergartens and nursery schools, catering to over 5 million preschoolers aged 1.5 to 5 (MOET, 2022). At the same time, demand for English language instruction among preschoolers in Vietnam has also significantly increased. A survey by the National Foreign Language Project of Vietnam in 2022 reveals that over 75% of public preschools and most of non-public schools in the country implemented activities to familiarize children with English at school. This represents a significant increase of 20.3% compared to 2017, 26.4% compared to 2016, and 30.5% compared to before 2015. Despite the increasing quantity, the need to guarantee the high standard and uniformity of English language teaching in various preschool environments presents a significant challenge for both educators and policymakers. Besides, teacher training and learning resources also pose several issues. Insufficient teacher training can impede educators' capacity not only to effectively teach but also to successfully incorporate technology into the classroom. Additionally, a lack of access to up-to-date learning resources may impede preschoolers' opportunities for engaging with digital tools and materials, which play an important role in the development of this "digital" native generation. In response to these challenges, the creation of the *Enspire Online* mobile application appears to be one of the solutions. This program is specifically designed for Vietnamese preschoolers and provides a complete and interesting platform using generative AI for learning the English language. *Enspire Online* uses a variety of interactive games, activities, and multimedia content to establish an engaging learning environment that captures the interest of young learners and nurtures their language acquisition process.

The *Enspire* learning app was developed in 2021 and launched in 2022. This app has been approved to be used in English language teaching for preschoolers by the Hanoi Department of Education and Training, Vietnam. It is now used in almost 120 schools, with almost 15,000 users. The app was designed based on an insightful analysis of the learning needs of preschoolers and the utilization of technology to cater to those needs.

2. EARLY CHILDHOOD EDUCATION IN VIETNAM

Prior to 1945, traditional Vietnamese family structures emphasized childcare responsibilities residing with mothers and grandmothers, leading to a delayed focus on formal early childhood education (ECE) (Pham et al., 2006). The Democratic Republic of Vietnam (DRV) marked a turning point with significant educational reforms following the August Revolution of 1945. Decree 146, issued in 1946, established the Infantile Education Level for children under seven under the purview of the Ministry of Education (Democratic Republic of Vietnam, 1946; Vasavakul, 2000). Despite rapid expansion, this initial phase of ECE was hindered by a lack of structure, resulting in low quality (Pham et al., 2006). The first national kindergarten conference in 1949 addressed these concerns by outlining two key objectives: fostering responsible citizens and alleviating childcare burdens on women (Pham et al., 2006). Notably, Deputy Minister Nguyen Khanh Toan's 1949 book (cited in Pham et al., 2006; Vasavakul, 2000) advocated for female kindergarten teachers due to their perceived maternal qualities. This concept influenced the rebranding of ECE as "Nursery Education" (M u giáo) in 1950. Decree No. 404 of July 1950 established the Nursery Division, tasked with curriculum development, teacher training, parental education on child-rearing, and supporting local governments in establishing kindergartens.

Following reunification in 1975, ECE adopted a teacher-centered approach aimed at preparing children for primary school. Kindergartens were managed by agricultural cooperatives, factories, or state farms, with a focus on developing practical skills, intellectual capacity, moral values, and health (Vu, 2021). Since 1986, ECE policy has undergone significant transformations to reflect societal changes. The goals of ECE were redefined through policy reforms in 1998 and 2006-2009, emphasizing its role in national modernization and globalization (Dang & Boyd, 2014). The Education Law mandated pre-primary education, contributing to Vietnam's impressive growth in ECE enrollment rates, reaching nearly 90% by 2019 (General Statistics Office of Vietnam, 2020). This expansion is driven by government investment and a growing recognition of the crucial role ECE plays in shaping children's cognitive, social, and emotional development (Vu, 2021).

The aforementioned review of ECE development in Vietnam reveals a dynamic interplay between historical influences and curriculum development. Traditionally, Vietnamese ECE reflected a teacher-centered approach aligned with Confucian values emphasizing respect for authority (Dang & Boyd, 2014). However, the nation's evolving socio-political landscape has impacted ECE practices. Notably, Vietnam's exposure to Western educational philosophies have contributed to a shift towards child-centered learning. A significant milestone in this shift was the introduction of the Innovative Curriculum (1998P) in 1998 (Phan, 2012). This curriculum, guided by principles of child-centered education, encouraged educators to tailor learning activities to children's interests and developmental needs (Pham et al., 2006; Phan, 2012). It granted teachers greater autonomy in selecting lessons and topics, and advocated for diverse pedagogical approaches (Phan, 2012). Furthermore, the 1998P emphasized creating a child-centered environment with open play areas fostering individual and collaborative learning. Building upon the 1998P's foundation, the 2009 Curriculum (2009P), initially piloted between 2006 and 2008, was adopted nationwide in 2009 (Phan, 2012). This curriculum further strengthens the child-centered approach and integration of learning experiences. The Ministry of Education and Training (2009) highlights the program's emphasis on child progress evaluation, enabling teachers to adapt lesson plans to cater to individual capabilities. This flexibility allows educators to incorporate children's interests and local contexts into their instruction (Ministry of Education and Training, 2009).

In short, Vietnamese ECE has undergone a significant transformation, moving from a teacher-centered approach to a child-centered one. This shift reflects the nation's evolving socio-political landscape and the influence of Western educational philosophies. The 1998P and 2009P curricula stand as key milestones in this ongoing development, promoting greater autonomy, flexibility, and child-centered learning within Vietnamese ECE.

A recent development marking Vietnam's progress towards internationalization and globalization of ECE is the introduction of English language learning programs. In late 2020, the Ministry of Education and Training launched an "English familiarization program" for preschool children (MOET, 2020). This initiative gained further momentum in 2022 with MOET approving 39 sets of English language textbooks specifically designed for preschool use (MOET, Circular No. 50/2022). Schools with adequate facilities and qualified teachers can offer English classes with parental consent, primarily aimed at familiarizing young children with the language. The program's learning objectives focus on basic comprehension and repetition skills. Children are expected to understand and repeat simple words, phrases, and sentences. They should also be able to respond to basic requests and comprehend the content of short, simple stories, poems, and rhymes. Additionally, singing simple songs is included in the curriculum (MOET, 2020). According to the Vietnam Institute of Educational Sciences, by the end of the previous school year, over half (53 out of 63) of Vietnamese localities had implemented the English familiarization program (Vietnam Institute of Educational Sciences, 2023). This translates to nearly 267,000 children (out of approximately 472,000 preschoolers) having access to the program, representing a significant participation rate of 56.5% (Vietnam Institute of Educational Sciences, 2023). In the context of globalization, Vietnamese parents increasingly seek to expose their children to international academic environments. This desire stems from a belief in the benefits of early English language acquisition and fostering a global citizen mindset. Despite the influx of free international educational resources like Duolingo and Khan Academy in Vietnam, English language learning programs remain highly sought-after Notably, locally developed products like Monkey Junior and Kidsup have also gained parental trust and this is a reason leading to the development of Enspire Online.

3. INTELLECTUAL AND LANGUAGE DEVELOPMENT OF PRESCHOOLERS

Maria Montessori and Jean Piaget, two pioneers in the field of child development, provide unique viewpoints on the intellectual development of children between the ages of three and six. Montessori (1967) underscores the notion of the "absorbent mind," which posits that children possess an inherent drive to acquire knowledge and information from their surrounding environment. Her method is centered on the provision of self-directed activities in prepared environments that are tailored to the specific developmental requirements of the child (Liu & Tian, 2023). By means of investigation and manipulation of these materials, children enhance their comprehension of the world, thereby cultivating independence, critical thinking, and problem-solving skills (Lillard, 2016). On the other hand, Piaget advocates for a cognitive development theory that is founded on stages (Piaget, 1970). According to Piaget, children progress through a series of distinct stages, each characterized by specific ways of thinking and understanding the world. Through active exploration and interaction with their environment, children build upon their existing knowledge and mental frameworks. In Piaget's perspective, children between the ages of two and seven exhibit egocentrism and encounter challenges with logical reasoning during the preoperational stage. It is crucial to note that the preoperational stage is anything but inert, despite the presence of egocentrism and difficulties with logic. This period is also distinguished by a blooming imagination. Children engage in elaborating scenarios and using objects as symbols to represent something else, resulting in complex pretend play. This play enables them to explore a variety of roles and scenarios, thereby indirectly developing their problem-solving abilities and social comprehension. The capacity to comprehend logical principles and anticipate alternative perspectives will gradually develop as children progress through the preoperational stage and engage more with the real-life world. They are capable of performing duties such as conservation and thinking more logically about the world around them by the time they reach the concrete operational stage, which typically occurs around the age of 7. As a result, their ability to symbolically represent the world through language is significantly improved (Gelman, 2002). In general, it is clear that both theories recognize the importance of play and exploration in the formation of the mind. During this mind formation process, language acquisition plays a central role for development. Piaget's (1952) theory suggests that children's language development is linked to their cognitive stage. During the preoperational stage, children engage in egocentric speech, primarily focusing on their own thoughts and experiences. As their symbolic thinking develops, their use of language becomes more social and collaborative (Gelman, 2002). Montessori (1967) observed a "sensitive period" for language development, where children actively listen, mimic what they hear, and readily experiment with forming their own words and sentences, which later fuels their understanding of the surrounding world. Both Montessori and Piaget highlight the crucial role of adults in language development. Montessori educators act as facilitators, providing rich language experiences and modeling correct grammar. Piaget emphasizes the importance of social interaction for language development, suggesting that children learn through conversations and play with peers.

As can be seen, understanding these perspectives set a solid foundation for educators who are responsible for designing and developing language curriculum for young learners as it allows them to create inviting environments that cater to the specific learning needs of young children, fostering their intellectual and linguistic growth.

4. LANGUAGE LEARNING NEEDS OF PRESCHOOLERS IN TRADITIONAL AND DIGITAL ENVIRONMENT

Theories from eminent educators like Montessori and Piagets can be used to analyse the language learning needs of preschoolers. Montessori's approach emphasizes a child-centered environment and hands-on exploration, fostering language acquisition in a natural and holistic manner. According to Montessori (1967), "the environment must be rich in motives that lend interest to activity and invite the child to conduct his own experiences" (p. 101). The use of tactile materials like sandpaper letters to facilitate language development and simultaneously enhance fine motor skills plays a vital role in this process. Piaget's cognitive theory complements this perspective, emphasizing the importance of sensorimotor experiences in language acquisition. Piaget (1952) asserts that "children construct their understanding of the world through their actions on objects" (p. 17), highlighting the active role of children in their own learning process. Both Montessori and Piaget underscore the significance of experiential learning and self-discovery in preschoolers' language development. By providing rich linguistic environments and opportunities for exploration, educators can effectively assist preschoolers in developing language skills.

In our modern era, the language surrounding mentioned by Montessori and Piaget can expand to the digital environment. It is noticed that social connection is essential for acquiring language, and digital platforms enable children to engage in collaborative learning experiences, even in virtual environments (Marsh, 2018). These digital tools provide a variety of learning experiences that include text, graphics, audio, and video. This allows for different learning styles and preferences to be accommodated (Plowman & McPake, 2013). Children connect with language through interactive applications, games, and multimedia content, which offer dynamic and responsive learning experiences (Golinkoff & Hirsh-Pasek, 1999).

As can be seen, the expansion of language acquisition in digital contexts aligns with ideas promoted by Montessori and Piaget in several ways. Montessori (1967) supported the idea of self-directed learning and the establishment of prepared surroundings that encourage children's innate curiosity. Piaget highlighted the significance of active involvement and tactile investigation in the cognitive advancement of youngsters (Piaget, 1952).. Children in digital environments actively participate in language acquisition through interactive activities and multimedia information, which is consistent with Montessori's and Piaget's views on the importance of active engagement in the learning process (Bibizadeh et al., 2023). Furthermore, digital platforms provide chances for individualized learning experiences and independent investigation, which are fundamental principles of both Montessori's and Piaget's educational ideologies (Sarker et al., 2019). In addition, social connection is essential for acquiring language, and digital environments enable children to engage in collaborative learning experiences, aligning with Piaget's focus on social interaction in cognitive development (Marsh, 2018). In digital environments, the transformation of language acquisition aligns with the ideas of constructivism and child-centered learning promoted by Piaget and Montessori. This transformation highlights the significance of children's active involvement, independence, and social interaction in their learning experiences.

The connection between "traditional" language learning theories and digital environment elucidates that the design and development of an English language learning app for preschoolers should incorporate the principles of language acquisition as were described by Piaget and Montessori and the nature of the digital environment.

5. PARENTAL ENGAGEMENT IN EARLY CHILDHOOD EDUCATION IN THE DIGITAL AGE

Parents play a critical role in shaping their child's development, impacting various aspects of growth. Their influence aligns significantly with the principles outlined in the child development theories of Maria Montessori and Jean Piaget. Montessori (1967) advocated for the creation of a "prepared environment" at home. This meticulously designed space, filled with age-appropriate materials and opportunities for self-directed exploration, mirrors the core tenets of Montessori classrooms. By providing freedom within boundaries and nurturing a child's natural curiosity, parents can cultivate independence, intrinsic motivation, and a love for learning – all of which are cornerstones of the Montessori philosophy. Piaget's theory (Piaget, 1970), on the other hand, emphasizes the importance of active exploration in cognitive development. Parents can facilitate this process by engaging their children in stimulating discussions, encouraging them to ask questions, and offering experiences that challenge their existing understanding of the world. In essence, by creating a stimulating and responsive environment that reflects both Montessori's prepared environment and Piaget's focus on active exploration, parents become crucial partners in their child's cognitive and emotional development.

In the digital age, technology has become a ubiquitous element within family interactions. A recent study by Kapella, Schmidt, and Vogl (2022) employing case studies from Austria, Estonia, Norway, and Romania, highlights how digital tools can contribute to the concept of "doing family" in multiple ways. The study demonstrates that actively experiencing digital technologies together can solidify family identity and cultivate a sense of belonging. Furthermore, co-using technology can act as a springboard for discussions, particularly around sensitive topics, potentially strengthening children's resilience. Parents, in this context, can adopt various roles, including positive role models, online activity guides and supervisors, home educators, and content filters. Research consistently demonstrates a strong correlation between parental engagement, particularly when it fosters high-quality learning experiences at home, and a child's future academic success, socio-emotional development, and societal adaptation (OECD, 2019; Sylva et al., 2004). In an increasingly digital world, digital literacy has become a critical factor in preparing children for future challenges. The rise of mobile technologies presents novel opportunities to leverage technology in promoting family engagement and fostering successful child development (Hall & Bierman, 2015).

Şad et al. (2016) define parental involvement in early childhood digital literacy as the multifaceted role parents play in supporting, facilitating, and monitoring the development of digital skills in their young children. This encompasses a range of actions, including supervising device use, providing guidance, facilitating access to educational digital resources, and maintaining positive communication about technology use. Research consistently demonstrates a significant correlation between parental involvement and early childhood digital literacy. Children with higher levels of parental involvement in their digital literacy development tend to exhibit several key benefits. These include a stronger understanding of online risks, improved digital information processing skills, and a greater propensity for responsible technology use (Livingstone et al., 2015). This positive impact stems from the supportive environment fostered by actively engaged parents (Nikken & Jansz, 2014). Such parents provide essential guidance, supervision, and mitigation of risks associated with excessive use or inappropriate content (Bergert et al., 2020).

In conclusion, parental involvement is a cornerstone of early childhood digital literacy development. By actively supporting their children's digital skills, parents equip them with the necessary tools to navigate the complexities of digital technology in today's society (Prior et al., 2016).

6. PRINCIPLES FOR DEVELOPING MATERIAL AND ACTIVITIES IN LEARNING APP

To develop an effective English language learning app for preschoolers is a challenging task due to a number of reasons. Firstly, preschoolers' cognitive development is still in its early stages, characterized by short attention spans and limited abstract thinking. This necessitates the design of engaging and interactive activities that capture their attention and cater to their developmental level. Secondly, individual differences in learning styles and preferences are significant at this age. The app needs to offer a variety of learning materials and activities to cater to diverse learning needs and preferences. Thirdly, the integration of technology into young children's lives requires careful consideration of developmental appropriateness and potential risks. The app must be designed with safety and child development in mind, ensuring a positive and enriching learning experience. Finally, the app needs to be aligned with early childhood education frameworks and best practices to ensure its educational value and effectiveness. To overcome such challenge, it is essential to establish a set of principles that can be used as guideline for material and activities developers. From the analysis of Montessori and Piaget's theories in previous sections, the following six fundamental principles are determined:

Active Engagement: Interactive activities like quizzes, games, and simulations encourage active participation and exploration, promoting engagement and language practice.

Self-Directed Learning: A variety of resources and materials cater to different learning preferences, allowing preschoolers to choose activities based on their interests and needs, fostering autonomous exploration and self-directed learning.

Prepared Environment: Clear instructions, easy navigation, and accessible resources create a well-organized and supportive learning environment, similar to Montessori's prepared environment.

Personalized Learning: Adaptive learning technologies adjust the level of challenge and content based on individual student proficiency, providing personalized learning pathways for each child.

Social Interaction: Online discussion forums, group projects, and virtual classrooms encourage peer interaction and collaboration, promoting social learning and language development, drawing from Piaget's emphasis on social interaction in cognitive development.

Multimodal Learning: Videos, images, and audio recordings provide diverse stimuli for language learning. Storytelling, virtual tours, and interactive media engage multiple senses, enhancing language acquisition.

As can be seen, the six principles derived from the analysis of preschoolers' intellectual and language development provide a valuable framework for designing an effective online English language learning app. Active engagement through interactive activities fosters participation and language practice. Self-directed learning empowers preschoolers to choose activities based on their interests and needs, promoting autonomy. A prepared environment with clear instructions and accessible resources creates a supportive learning atmosphere. Personalized learning tailors the app to individual needs and proficiency levels, ensuring optimal learning. Social interaction encourages collaboration and social learning, drawing from Piaget's emphasis on social interaction in cognitive development. Finally, multimodal learning utilizes diverse multimedia content to engage multiple senses and enhance language acquisition. By incorporating these principles, the online English language learning app can provide a stimulating, engaging, and effective learning experience for preschoolers.

7. TECHNOLOGY ACCEPTANCE MODEL

The Technology Acceptance Model (TAM) is a widely used theoretical framework that explains how individuals accept and use technology. Developed by Davis (1989) and grounded in the theories of reasoned action and planned behavior, TAM posits that two key factors drive technology acceptance: perceived usefulness and perceived ease of use. Individuals are more likely to adopt and actively use a technology if they believe it will significantly enhance their ability to achieve their goals (usefulness) and if they find it effortless and intuitive to learn and operate (ease of use).

This core framework offers invaluable guidance when designing mobile learning apps. By focusing on the core principles of perceived usefulness and perceived ease of use, developers can create apps that resonate deeply with learners. Perceived usefulness translates to ensuring the app demonstrably aids in knowledge acquisition and skill development. This can be achieved through features like personalized learning pathways, gamified elements that promote engagement, and access to relevant and high-quality learning materials. Perceived ease of use emphasizes intuitive design and user interface. This encompasses clear navigation, seamless integration with existing mobile devices, and minimal learning curve for accessing and utilizing app functionalities. By prioritizing both these aspects, mobile learning apps can foster a positive user experience, ultimately leading to increased adoption, sustained engagement, and successful learning outcomes.

Preschoolers' unique learning characteristics present both challenges and opportunities when applying the TAM model to mobile learning app design. As was discussed, their learning is heavily influenced by play-based exploration. In other words, young children learn best through active engagement and hands-on experiences (Kettler et al., 2019). Mobile apps, therefore, need to be highly interactive, incorporating elements like touch, sound, and movement to stimulate curiosity and exploration. Besides, abstract concepts are difficult for preschoolers to grasp so there are needs for concrete learning. Learning content should be presented in a visually appealing and age-appropriate manner, utilizing relatable examples and real-world connections (Montessori, 1967). It is also important to note that preschoolers have limited attention spans, requiring frequent breaks and varied activities to maintain engagement (National Scientific Council on the Developing Child, 2007). Mobile apps, therefore, should offer bite-sized learning modules, diverse content formats (videos, games, songs), and clear transitions to keep them focused.

Within the context of preschool mobile learning, the TAM model takes on a unique twist. For young children, "usefulness" translates directly to fun and engaging learning experiences. Mobile apps must demonstrably support crucial developmental goals like language acquisition, cognitive development, and social-emotional learning. This can be achieved through personalized learning journeys that adapt content and difficulty based on individual progress and interests (Grant & Basye, 2014). Additionally, integrating playful elements like rewards, challenges, and points through gamification fosters motivation and sustains engagement (Jordan, 2009). Finally, providing positive reinforcement and constructive feedback guides learning progress, further enhancing the perceived value for young users. In addition, "ease of use" for preschoolers translates to intuitive design and simple navigation. This means utilizing large, colorful buttons and icons that are easily manipulated by small hands and limited motor skills (Montessori, 1967). Furthermore, age-appropriate language and visuals in minimal text and clear instructions ensure comprehension for young learners (Montessori, 1967). Lastly, presenting a focused learning environment with limited options and choices prevents overwhelming young minds, ultimately contributing to a positive user experience.

It is also important to take into account parental acceptance of preschoolers' mobile learning. As gatekeepers, parents ultimately decide whether and how their children engage with technology. For parents, perceived usefulness translates to mobile learning demonstrably supporting their child's cognitive, social, and emotional development. This can be achieved through clear learning objectives and age-appropriate content aligned with established developmental milestones and early childhood education frameworks (Grant & Basye, 2014). Additionally, integrating mobile learning with existing learning methods, rather than replacing them entirely, and providing tangible evidence of progress and skill development through the app, further enhance parental acceptance (Kettler et al., 2019). Perceived ease of use for parents focuses on features like usage time limits, content filtering, and progress reports, empowering them to feel in control (National Scientific Council on the Developing Child, 2007). Furthermore, providing resources and tutorials for parents to understand the app and guide their child's learning journey, alongside seamless integration with existing devices, offline functionality, and promoting shared learning experiences, fosters a more positive and supportive environment for mobile learning adoption (Jordan, 2009). By addressing these specific aspects of perceived usefulness and ease of use for parents, mobile learning apps can gain wider acceptance and support from the crucial gatekeepers in a preschooler's life.

As has been discussed, in order to guarantee the longevity of the *Enspire Online app*, it is imperative that the developers comprehend the principles of language learning activity design and development, as well as the implementation of the TAM model for children and parents. By incorporating the principles of Piaget and Montessori into the creation and use of technology-based learning environments, preschoolers and parents are encouraged to actively participate, interact, and embrace technology in language learning. Such approach has the potential to improve students' learning experiences and results, while also encouraging the embrace of technology in educational environments.

8. ENSPIRE ONLINE DEVELOPMENT PROCESS

Crafting a compelling language learning app for preschoolers requires meticulous attention to detail across various stages of development. These are the steps that have been taken for developing the *Enspire Online* – a language learning app for preschoolers in Vietnam.

1. Analysing target users

   Vietnamese Preschool Education Context: it is imperative to conduct a comprehensive examination of the unique learning patterns and requirements of Vietnamese preschoolers within their educational environment. This is beneficial for comprehending their current language abilities, preferable learning methods, and any cultural subtleties that may affect their interaction with the application. It also provides information on the English language teachers, their expectations, the study curriculum, and the frequency of language lessons, as well as their advantages and difficulties. Additionally, it furnishes data regarding parents' expectations and their readiness to permit their children to utilize a language learning application.

Developmental Milestones: ensuring that the app's content and features are in accordance with the established developmental milestones for preschoolers to ensure that it effectively supports their cognitive, social, and emotional development. This also entails the integration of age-appropriate vocabulary, grammar structures, and social-emotional learning elements that are pertinent to the Vietnamese early childhood education framework introduced by the Ministry of Education and Training.

2. Creating Content

Select engaging and culturally relevant content: the app's heart lies in its content. Instead of dry grammar drills, the app uses a vibrant playground filled with interactive games, where children can playfully learn new vocabulary through matching exercises, memory challenges, and role-playing scenarios. Catchy songs and interactive stories further immerse them in the language, fostering natural language acquisition through repetition and association. The selected content is carefully curated to align with established developmental milestones and early childhood education frameworks, ensuring it demonstrably supports the child's cognitive, social, and emotional development.

Personalized learning pathways: To keep young learners engaged, the app should offer personalized learning experiences. This can be achieved by providing a wide range of topics that attract different interests of students.

3. Providing Intuitive User Interface and User Experience:

Vietnamese language interface: a user interface is created entirely in Vietnamese for accessibility and comprehension.

Playful design elements: utilizing vibrant colors, playful animations, and familiar characters creates a visually appealing and engaging interface that attract young learners.

Voice recognition and pronunciation practice: integrating voice recognition technology that allows for interactive pronunciation practice, further enhancing language acquisition.

4. Selecting Platform and Accessibility:

Mobile-first approach: given the high mobile phone penetration in Vietnam, prioritizing a mobile-first approach ensures accessibility and convenience for both children and parents.

Offline functionality: considering potential internet connectivity limitations in some regions of Vietnam, offering offline functionality allows for continued learning even without an internet connection.

5. Providing User testing and feedback:

    Engaging various stakeholders: conducting rigorous user testing with preschoolers, language teachers, parent, education officials to gain invaluable insights into their preferences, challenges, and areas for improvement. This iterative process allows for continuous refinement of the content, UI, and overall learning experience to ensure it effectively caters to the specific needs of young Vietnamese language learners.

6. Distributing and training

    Collaborations with public nurseries and kindergarten to reach wider circles of users

    Parental Engagement and Support: providing resources and guidance for parents on how to effectively utilize the app and support their child's language learning journey fosters a collaborative learning environment.

Meticulously addressing these key stages of development helps *Enspire Online* evolve into a compelling and culturally relevant language learning app that effectively supports the linguistic and developmental needs of young Vietnamese preschoolers.

9. ENSPIRE ONLINE FINAL PRODUCT

Figure 1. Application interface

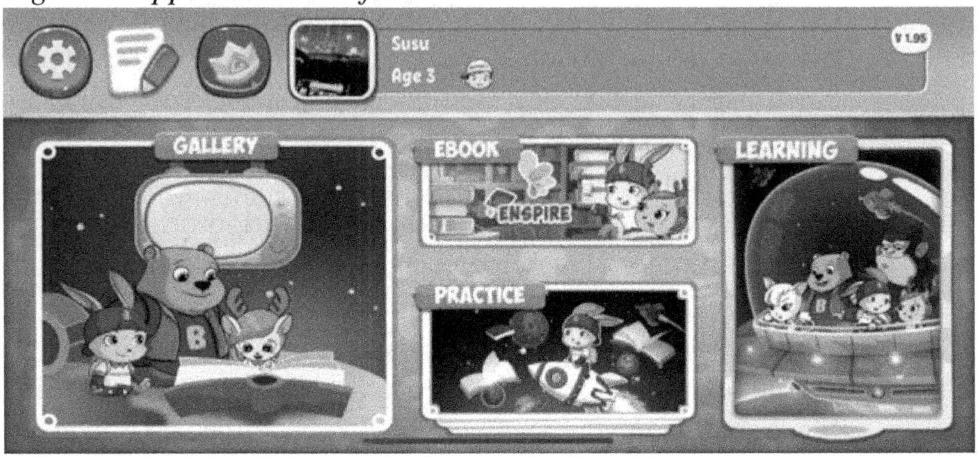

The application boasts a user interface specifically designed to be welcoming and engaging for young learners. The interface utilizes colorful cartoon characters that create a playful and stimulating atmosphere, effectively capturing children's interest and encouraging interaction. Recognizing the importance of parental involvement, the interface offers seamless switching between Vietnamese and English. This caters to parents who may not be proficient in English, ensuring they can still actively participate in their child's learning journey at home. Furthermore, news is delivered in Vietnamese, informing parents about their child's classroom activities, suggesting engaging home practices, and outlining ways parents can provide support.

To personalize the experience, the interface allows for uploading a child's picture, nickname, and age. Beyond basic communication, the interface provides a rich learning ecosystem. A gallery showcases children's participation in various classroom activities, fostering a sense of pride and accomplishment. An accompanying e-book reinforces in-class learning content, providing a valuable resource for home review. Additionally, a dedicated "Practice" section offers interactive exercises to solidify learning, while the "Learning" section caters to children's curiosity, offering age-appropriate content that stimulates their desire to explore the world around them. This comprehensive interface fosters a welcoming and engaging learning environment, promoting active participation from both children and parents.

Figure 2. Learning content

The application's learning content is structured across three levels, catering to a child's progressive development. Level 1 lays the foundation for language acquisition by introducing children to familiar sounds and images. Through engaging activities, children begin to associate sounds with their corresponding visuals, establishing a strong base for further learning. Level 2 builds upon these foundational skills, introducing basic vocabulary and short phrases. Children engage with interactive exercises to develop their comprehension and build confidence in using newly learned words. By the completion of this level, children can begin to follow simple stories, songs, and short texts, fostering a sense of accomplishment and a growing love for language. Level 3 caters to children who possess a foundational understanding of language. This level focuses on expanding vocabulary and sentence structures related to common topics and situations encountered in everyday life. Activities within this level encourage children to develop their concentration and memory, equipping them to follow more complex stories and texts.

The content within each level is meticulously organized, adhering to a child's natural developmental needs. Early lessons prioritize topics related to the child themselves, such as body parts and personal belongings. This fosters self-awareness and provides a comfortable foundation for learning. Following this, lessons transition to topics related to the child's physical surroundings and primary caregivers. This strengthens a child's understanding of their immediate environment and the important relationships within it. As children progress through the levels, more abstract concepts, such as expressing emotions, are introduced. This gradual progression ensures that children are challenged appropriately at each stage, promoting a successful and engaging learning experience.

9.2. Learning Sequence

Each lesson within the application is designed to create an engaging and interactive learning experience.

Following a developmentally appropriate approach, lessons begin with a naming activity. Children have the opportunity to touch objects on the screen, triggering the pronunciation of the corresponding word in English. This interactive process allows children to actively engage with the learning content, associating the spoken word with the visual representation. Furthermore, to facilitate the transition towards pre-reading skills, the corresponding letter may appear on the screen alongside the spoken word. This subtle introduction of letters lays the groundwork for future literacy development.

Figure 3. Engaging learning experience.

To solidify word memorization and enhance learning, each lesson incorporates a fun and interactive activity called "Trace and Color." Children are encouraged to trace the outline of the object on the screen, fostering the development of fine motor skills and hand-eye coordination. These refined motor skills provide a crucial foundation for future writing abilities. The act of coloring the object further reinforces the association between the object and its corresponding English word, solidifying learning in a playful and engaging manner.

Figure 4. Trace and color.

Following the engaging introduction of vocabulary, each lesson seamlessly transitions to an activity designed to develop children's observation and fine motor skills. This activity incorporates auditory learning to further enhance the learning experience. Children are presented with a sound, prompting them to create a mental image of the corresponding object based on their previously learned vocabulary. Leveraging their newly acquired knowledge of sounds and images, children then engage in a puzzle-solving activity. This activity typically involves rearranging scattered pieces to form a complete picture. Successfully completing the puzzle reinforces their understanding of the target vocabulary while providing a sense of accomplishment.

Figure 5. Puzzle for target vocabulary

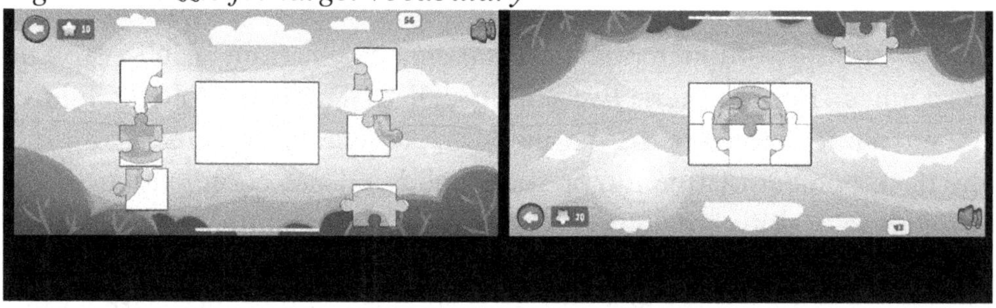

Throughout this process, the application offers positive reinforcement. Children hear encouraging comments such as "you are doing a great job" upon successful completion of the puzzle. Alternatively, for incorrect placements, gentle prompts like "oh no, let's try again" are provided, fostering a growth mindset and encouraging persistence. These interactive elements contribute to the development of basic communication skills by exposing children to positive affirmations and constructive feedback. Overall, this activity provides a valuable opportunity for children to refine their observation skills, strengthen fine motor control, and gain confidence in their abilities.

Once children have completed the engaging activities focused on naming and memorization, they transition to a dynamic activity designed to nurture their oral communication skills during this critical developmental period. This activity takes the form of a simulated phone call conversation, offering a unique and interactive learning experience.

Figure 6. Receiving a call from an English speaker.

Children receive a “call” from their teacher, a native English speaker. The conversation begins with the teacher asking the child questions related to their personal information, such as their name or age. This familiar context eases children into the conversation, fostering a sense of comfort and confidence. Following the initial exchange, the teacher transitions into a discussion about the topic covered in the previous activities. This carefully designed activity serves a dual purpose. Firstly, it provides valuable opportunities for revision. By integrating vocabulary and sentence structures learned in earlier lessons, the conversation reinforces understanding and strengthens memory retention. Secondly, and more importantly, this activity introduces children to the basic rules of social interaction. Through the simulated phone call, children learn the importance of active listening, taking turns to speak, and conducting a conversation in a polite and respectful manner. These essential communication skills are crucial for successful social interaction in both English and their native language. Overall, the phone call activity provides a dynamic and engaging platform for children to develop their oral communication skills in a safe and supportive environment. By interacting with a native English speaker, children gain valuable exposure to correct pronunciation and sentence structure, setting the foundation for future language acquisition.

Upon successful completion of their core learning tasks, children are invited to explore the Learning Zone. This exciting section empowers them with the freedom to choose any topic that sparks their curiosity from six engaging areas: Math, Food, Amazing Me, My Kindergarten, My Town, Festivals, and Animals. These diverse topics cater to a variety of interests, nurturing children's imagination and creativity as they embark on a journey of discovery.

Figure 7. Learning Zone

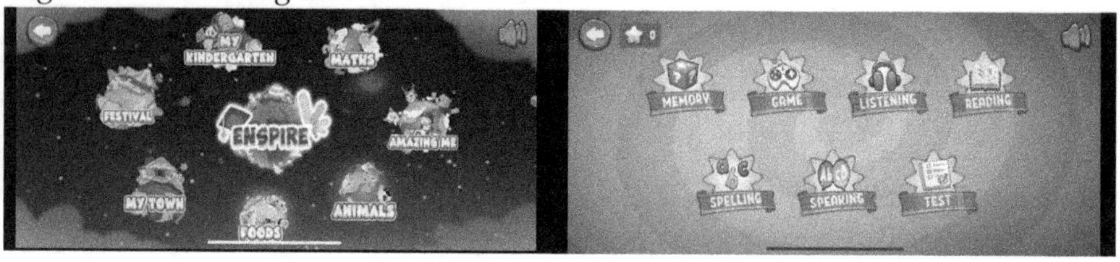

The Learning Zone caters to children at various developmental stages by offering content that can be explored through different language learning perspectives. Younger children, still developing their foundational skills, can focus on listening activities, enhancing their sound recognition abilities and building a strong foundation for future language acquisition. Preschool children, with a more developed grasp of language, can delve deeper into reading and spelling activities, solidifying their growing literacy skills. Additionally, for those seeking a more playful approach, the Learning Zone offers engaging games designed to reinforce understanding of concrete and abstract concepts in a fun and interactive manner. Overall, the Learning Zone serves as a springboard for children's curiosity. By providing a safe and stimulating environment for self-directed exploration, this section fosters a lifelong love of learning and empowers children to become independent thinkers and confident discoverers of the world around them.

9.3. Fostering Parental Involvement

As previously discussed, parental involvement plays a critical role in a child's digital learning journey. This mobile application recognizes this essential element and incorporates several features to facilitate a collaborative learning environment between parents and children.

Figure 8. Facilitating collaborative learning between parents and children.

Beyond the bilingual interface and the news section serving as a communication channel between teachers and parents, the application boasts an achievement window. This dedicated section empowers parents to track their child's progress. They can gain valuable insights into the topics their child has mastered and their overall level of proficiency. Access to this information allows parents to provide targeted support and guidance at home, directly aligning their efforts with the child's learning experience in the application. Furthermore, the gallery showcasing pictures of children participating in classroom activities fosters a sense of connection between parents and the learning process. Parents can witness their child's engagement and celebrate their achievements firsthand. This connection can serve as a powerful motivator, encouraging children to continue their learning journey with enthusiasm. By integrating these features, the application fosters a collaborative learning environment where parents and teachers work together to support a child's development. This collaborative approach is crucial for fostering a love of learning and setting children on the path to future success.

10. REFLECTION AND CONCLUSION

The process of designing and developing *Enspire Online*, an English learning app for young children aged 3-6, has been a revelation in the dynamic nature of curriculum design within a digital environment. It has underscored the critical importance of understanding young children's learning needs in both physical and digital settings. This project highlighted the roles of various stakeholders and the need to cater to each party's interests.

The learning journey for young children is not just their initial step towards understanding the world; it serves as the foundation for lifelong learning habits. *Enspire Online's* development emphasized the importance of considering the "absorbent mind" of a child. Selecting and developing appropriate learning activities and materials necessitated the developers to truly see things from both the child's and parent's perspectives. By adopting this empathetic approach, the final product not only meets a child's learning needs but also resonates with parents, encouraging their active involvement in the learning process.

Enspire Online stands as a testament to the power of collaboration. By acknowledging the diverse needs of stakeholders, from children and parents to teachers and learning specialists, the curriculum designers were able to craft a comprehensive learning experience that is both engaging and effective. This collaborative spirit, coupled with a deep understanding of child development and the digital learning landscape, has paved the way for *Enspire Online* to become a valuable tool in fostering a love for learning in young children.

REFERENCES

Bergert, C., Köster, A., Krasnova, H., & Turel, O. (2020). Missing Out on Life: Parental Perceptions of Children's Mobile Technology Use. [Zentrale Tracks]. *Wirtschaftsinformatik*, •••, 568–583.

Bibizadeh, R. E., Procter, R., Girvan, C., Webb, H., & Jirotka, M. (2023). Digitally un/free: The everyday impact of social media on the lives of young people. *Learning, Media and Technology*, 1–14. Advance online publication. DOI: 10.1080/17439884.2023.2237883

Dang, T. P., & Boyd, W. A. (2014). Renovating early childhood education pedagogy: A case study in Vietnam. *International Journal of Early Years Education, 22*(2), 184–196. DOI: 10.1080/09669760.2014.909306

Davis, F. D. (1989). Perceived usefulness, perceived ease of use, and user acceptance of information technology. *Management Information Systems Quarterly, 13*(3), 319–340. DOI: 10.2307/249008

Democratic Republic of Vietnam. (1946). S c l nh v đ t nh ng nguyên t c cơ b n c a n n giáo d c m i (The decree sets up the basic principles of the new education). Hanoi, Vietnam. Retrieved from https://thuvienphapluat.vn/van-ban/Giaoduc/Sac-lenh-146-dat-nguyen-tac-can-ban-nen-giao-duc-moi/36075/noi-dung.aspx

Gelman, R. (2002). Cognitive development. In Kail, R. V. (Ed.), *Major reference works*. Wiley. DOI: 10.1002/0471214426.pas0212

Golinkoff, R. M., & Hirsh-Pasek, K. (1999). *How babies talk: The magic and mystery of language in the first three years of life*. Dutton.

Grant, P., & Basye, D. (2014). *Personalized learning: a guide for engaging students with technology*. International Society for Technology in Education.

Hall, C., & Bierman, K. (2015). Technology-assisted interventions for parents of young children: Emerging practices, current research, and future directions. *Early Childhood Research Quarterly, 33*, 21–32. DOI: 10.1016/j.ecresq.2015.05.003 PMID: 27773964

Jordan, T. (2009). The ecology of games: Connecting youth, games and learning. *Information Communication and Society, 12*(2), 291–293. DOI: 10.1080/13691180802552890

Kapella, O., Schmidt, E., & Vogl, S. (2022). Integration of digital technologies in families with children aged 5-10 years: A synthesis report of four European country case studies. DigiGen Working Paper Series, No. 8. https://doi.org/DOI: 10.5281/zenodo.6411126

Kettler, T., Lamb, K., & Dekelaita-Mullet, D. (2019). *Developing creativity in the classroom: learning and innovation for 21st-century schools.* Routledge., DOI: 10.4324/9781003234104

Lillard, P. P. (1972). *Montessori, a modern approach.* Schocken Books.

Liu, S., & Tian, A. (2023). The influence of Montessori education on children's personality development and the way of thinking. *Lecture Notes in Education Psychology and Public Media, 16*(1), 173–180. Advance online publication. DOI: 10.54254/2753-7048/16/20231141

Livingstone, S., Mascheroni, G., Dreier, M., Chaudron, S., & Lagae, K. (2015). *How parents of young children manage digital devices at home: The role of income, education and parental style.* EUKids Online, LSE

Marsh, J., Plowman, L., Yamada-Rice, D., Bishop, J., Lahmar, J., & Scott, F. (2018). Play and creativity in young children's use of apps. *British Journal of Educational Technology, 49*(5), 870–882. DOI: 10.1111/bjet.12622

Ministry of Education and Training Vietnam. (2009). Thông tư c a B Giáo d c và Đào t o s 17/2009 ngày 25 tháng 7 năm 2009: Ban hành chương trình giáo d c m m non (Circular number 17/2009 dated 25th July 2009 on Issuing the Preschool curriculum). Retrieved from https://luatvietnam.vn/giao-duc/thong-tu-17-2009-tt-bgddt-bo-giao-duc-va-dao-tao-44312-d1.html

Ministry of Education and Training Vietnam. (2020). Thông tư 50/2020/TT-BGDĐT ban hành Chương trình làm quen v i ti ng Anh cho tr em m u giáo (Circular number 50/2020/TT/BGDDT on Issuing the English Familirisation Program). Retrieved from https://thuvienphapluat.vn/van-ban/Giao-duc/Thong-tu-50-2020-TT-BGDDT-Chuong-trinh-lam-quen-voi-tieng-Anh-danh-cho-tre-em-mau-giao-468715.aspx

Ministry of Education and Training Vietnam. (2022). *S li u th ng kê giáo d c m m non năm h c 2021 - 2022.* [Statistics on preschool education for the 2021-2022 academic year]. https://moet.gov.vn/thong-ke/Pages/thong-ke-giao-duc-mam-non.aspx?ItemID=8822

Montessori, M. (1967). *The discovery of the child.* Ballantine. (Work originally published 1948.)

National Scientific Council on the Developing Child. (2007). The science of early childhood development. Retrieved from http://www.developingchild.net

Nikken, P., & Jansz, J. (2014). Developing scales to measure parental mediation of young children's internet use. *Learning, Media and Technology, 39*(2), 250–266. DOI: 10.1080/17439884.2013.782038

OECD. (2019). *Providing quality early childhood education and care: Results from the Starting Strong Survey 2018. TALIS*. OECD Publishing., DOI: 10.1787/301005d1-

Pham, S. T., Le, T. A., Nguyen, T. A., Dinh, T. H., & Ho, M. T. (2006). *60 năm Giáo d c M m non Vi t Nam* [60 years of Vietnamese Preschool Education]. Hanoi, Vietnam: Nhà xu t b n Giáo d c (Education Publisher).

Phan, H. T. T. (2012). Current curriculum and pedagogy reform in Vietnamese Early Childhood Education: A socio-historic interpretation. In Chan, P. W. K. (Ed.), *Asia Pacific education, diversity, challenges and changes*. Monash University Publishing.

Piaget, J. (1952). *The origins of intelligence in children.* International Universities Press. DOI: 10.1037/11494-000

Piaget, J. (1970). *The psychology of the child.* Basic Books.

Plowman, L., & McPake, J. (2013). Seven myths about young children and technology. *Childhood Education*, *89*(1), 27–33. DOI: 10.1080/00094056.2013.757490

Prior, D. D., Mazanov, J., Meacheam, D., Heaslip, G., & Hanson, J. (2016). Attitude, digital literacy and self- efficacy: Flown effects for online learning behavior. *The Internet and Higher Education*, *29*, 91–97. DOI: 10.1016/j.iheduc.2016.01.001

Şad, S. N., Konca, A. S., Özer, N., & Acar, F. (2016). Parental e-nvolvement: A phenomenological research on electronic parental involvement. International. *Journal of Pedagogies and Learning*, *11*(2), 163–186.

Sarker, M. N. I., Wu, M., Cao, Q., Alam, G. M. M., & Li, D. (2019). Leveraging digital technology for better learning and education: A systematic literature review. *International Journal of Information and Education Technology (IJIET)*, *9*(7), 453–461. DOI: 10.18178/ijiet.2019.9.7.1246

Sylva, K., Melhuish, E., Sammons, P., Siraj-Blatchford, I., & Taggart, B. (2004). The Effective Provision of Pre-School Education (EPPE) Project: Technical Paper 12 – The Final Report: Effective Pre-School Education. Institute of Education, University of London.

Vasavakul, T. (2000). Managing the young anarchists: kindergartens and national culture in postcolonial Vietnam. In Wollons, R. W. R. (Ed.), *Kindergartens and cultures: The global diffusion of an idea* (pp. 214–250). Yale University Press.

Vu, T. T. (2021). Early childhood education in Vietnam, history, and development. *International Journal of Child Care and Education Policy*, *15*(3), 3. Advance online publication. DOI: 10.1186/s40723-020-00080-4

Chapter 2
Levelling Up Language Skills:
Gamified Elements for Language Learning

Richa Srishti
https://orcid.org/0000-0002-2551-9613
Christ University, India

ABSTRACT

This chapter explores the interesting and challenging world of gamified language learning. It focuses on how game mechanics and design principles can be utilised to transform language acquisition into an engaging and effective experience. It examines the benefits of gamification and specific game elements suitable for language learning. After exploring leading language learning platforms and applications, it provides practical strategies for educators and language learning platforms to effectively implement these elements to create immersive and motivating experiences for learners. Finally, it addresses the challenges in gamifying language learning and discusses the prospects of language learning, including the potential integration of AI-enhanced gamification to further enhance the learning experience.

DOI: 10.4018/979-8-3693-5477-3.ch002

INTRODUCTION

Play and games have been essential elements in the construction of societies and cultures throughout human history. Their incorporation into our daily routine makes us feel alive, i.e., it fulfils our inherent need for engagement. Games include competitions (physical or mental) with a set of rules, their final goal being entertainment or amusement. Throughout history, humans have always strived for merrymaking in daily activities/tasks. According to Chou (2014):

When a small group of people casually decide to compete against each other in hunting and gathering or simply start keeping the score of their activities and comparing it to their past records, they are adopting principles that are prevalent in modern games to make tasks more engaging. (p. 6)

In this way, games teach us that mistakes are an inevitable part of the process. Success often requires adaptability and persistence to overcome challenges and reach a specific goal. This is an essential life skill that can be developed through both game-based learning (GBL) and gamification. GBL involves the use of games to enhance educational experiences by promoting active learning, critical thinking, and problem-solving. Gamification, on the other hand, is "the process of adding games or game-like elements to something (such as a task) so as to encourage participation" (Merriam-Webster, 2019). Therefore, gamification "can be used to encourage desired behaviours in individuals, whether they be customers, employees, or students" (Christians, 2018). This feature of gamification makes it one of the best strategies in the education sector, as it can motivate students and enhance the learning experience. GBL and gamified education have been researched and have shown favourable results in improving learning outcomes.

The present chapter will begin by outlining the theoretical foundations of gamification, focusing on its capacity to make learning more interactive and enjoyable. It will review prominent research related to gamification and discuss the essential elements of language learning. The integration of AI in gamification has been examined too. The chapter will also address the challenges faced in traditional language learning methods and examine the use of gamification to overcome those. Some practical examples of gamification for different language learning objectives will be investigated and discussed. The chapter will posit that through the strategic use of gamification, language learning can become a more effective and deeply engaging journey for learners of all ages and backgrounds.

Background

Dreimane (2021) argues that due to technological advancements in contemporary society, new methods are being developed to engage learners, including gamification. He credits computer programmer Nick Pelling with coining the term "gamification" and emphasising the potential to apply game elements in various areas of learning, including education. One of the earliest gamification applications was explored by Charles Coonradt, President and CEO of Game of Work consultancy founded in 1973. Forbes provided him with the title 'The Grandfather of Gamification.' He is also considered the original creator of gamification theory. He adapted the gameplay practices within the workplace to increase employee involvement and engagement to boost company productivity (Thompson & Rains, 2022). His principles 'Motivation of Recreation,' though originally designed for workplace settings, do offer valuable insights for educational contexts. The principles are:

a) Clearly defined goals
b) Better scorekeeping and scorecards
c) More frequent feedback

'Clearly defined goals' help learners understand what is expected of them, instilling focus and commitment. 'Better scorekeeping and scorecards' provide a way to track progress, which can help both learners and educators identify areas for improvement. 'More frequent feedback' encourages continuous improvement and helps learners adjust their strategies in real-time, enhancing engagement. However, while these principles contribute to increasing motivation and accountability, they focus more on extrinsic motivation, which may not fully capture the internal cognitive processes critical to education.

The groundwork for the theory of gamification was laid down by Thomas W. Malone, an American organisational theorist. Malone (1981) built a theory of intrinsically motivating instruction by analysing existing theories of motivation and studying engaging computer games. He proposed three pillars for captivating learning: challenge (goals with uncertain outcomes), fantasy (mental engagement with the learning content), and curiosity (aroused by presenting knowledge gaps). Though the focus was on fun and not education, it paved the way for further research that integrated educational aspects and a deeper understanding of motivation. Building on these foundations, Kapp, Blair, & Mesch (2013) distinguish two types of gamification - structural and content. Structural gamification involves applying game design elements to the overall structure of the learning experience. It focuses on organising the learning content in such a way that resembles a game. Content gamification, on the other hand, involves altering the content itself to make it more game-like. In other words, the learning material is curated to be more appealing and interactive, so that there is an increased learner engagement and improved retention. Kapp, Blair, & Mesch (2013) also suggest that intrinsic and extrinsic motivation should not be seen as mutually exclusive, but rather as complementary aspects that, when combined, create optimal gamification.

Extending this framework, Landers (2014) proposes a theory of gamified learning, comprising two components - framework and model. The framework includes those game elements that potentially improve learning (e.g., game fiction, control, immersion), and the model links gamification efforts to learning outcomes through attitudinal and behavioural changes. He mentions the following game elements categories - action language, assessment, conflict/challenge, control, environment, game fiction, human interaction, immersion, and rules/goals. Landers and Landers (2014) focus on leaderboards (a common gamification element) and their impact on learning outcomes. The results suggest that leaderboards increased engagement, measured by time spent on the learning task. However, as this study only explores leaderboards in one specific learning context and does not address learner motivation, it is considered limiting in nature. Landers et al. (2017) provide specific psychological theories that support particular game elements and mentioned that more empirical studies should be conducted to evaluate the effectiveness of the interventions used in different learning environments.

Liu et al. (2017) highlight the need for a standardised way to categorise gamification elements as they identified inconsistencies in how these terms were used across different fields. Reviewing existing literature and building on previous taxonomies, they propose a framework based on user engagement with both practical goals and a positive experience. This system has two main categories: gamification objects and mechanics. Gamification objects, i.e. the fundamental building blocks of a gamified system, can be visual, auditory, interactive or a combination. They can serve various purposes: creating a visually appealing experience (aesthetics), engaging the user's mind (narratives), or having a functional use within the gamified system. Liu et al. (2017) also suggest theoretically derived design principles for gamification. The first principle they propose is the 'general principle' that sets the overall framework - "Game design elements incorporated in a target system must match the intended purpose of the system" (p. 1018). In other words, the fun elements, like points or badges, should be designed to motivate users towards the main goal (e.g. learning a language or improving fitness). This makes the system both enjoyable and effective. According to Liu et al. (2017), six other gamification principles follow the general principle.

Principle A. Congruence with Target Task: Gamification design elements must align with the target task.
Principle B. User Characteristic Matching: Gamification design elements must match user characteristics.
Principle C. Technological Compatibility: Gamification design elements must fit with target system technologies.
Principle D. User-System Interaction Matching: Gamification design elements must match desired user-system interactions.
Principle E. Recurrence of System Use Matching: Gamification design elements must match the expected recurrence of system use.
Principle F. Meaningful Engagement: Enhanced experiential outcomes should be associated with higher levels of instrumental outcomes to create meaningful engagement in gamified systems.

These principles highlight the importance of alignment, balance, consistency, diversity, immersion, and connecting fun with a purpose. If we follow these principles, we can utilise gamification as an effective tool for boosting engagement and achieving the required results. Principles A, B, C, D and E underscore the need to align the gamification elements. This alignment ensures that the gamification remains natural and relevant, not forced. Taking this a step further, Principle F states that meaningful engagement comes from connecting the fun, 'experiential outcomes' of gamification with the desired 'instrumental outcomes' (like completing tasks or learning new skills). This creates a positive reinforcement loop and motivates users to keep returning. This can be helpful in acquiring new skills, completing tasks, or making positive behavioural changes. In other words, these principles provide a framework for designing gamification experiences in such a way that they are enjoyable and produce meaningful results.

Gamification in Education

According to (Sanchez, 2017), games can inculcate collaboration and healthy competition among students, promoting the development of collaboration and communication skills. While the concept of learning styles has been debated, gamification can still help educators create personalised learning experiences tailored to individual student needs and preferences. This personalisation can lead to a more effective learning environment for all students. Because gamification elements make learning fun and interactive, there can be an increase in student engagement with the study material. Increased engagement can lead to improved knowledge retention while students actively participate in gamified learning activities compared to traditional methods (Hamari et al., 2014). According to Dicheva et al. (2015), incorporating gamification into education can be advantageous for both students and teachers. Students can feel energetic when participating and interacting with their peers. Teachers can gain deeper insights into student performance and progress. Therefore, they can use gamified elements to encourage collaboration and nurture healthy competition. Toda et al. (2019) further contribute to this field by presenting a taxonomy of game elements in gamified learning environments. They identify the lack of formal definitions and naming conventions as a major obstacle to gamification adoption. The authors propose an extension of their previously developed taxonomy, adding five dimensions related to the learner and the learning environment. These dimensions include Performance/ Measurement, Ecological, Social, Personal, and Fictional.

Figure 1. Gamification Taxonomy by Toda et al. (2019)

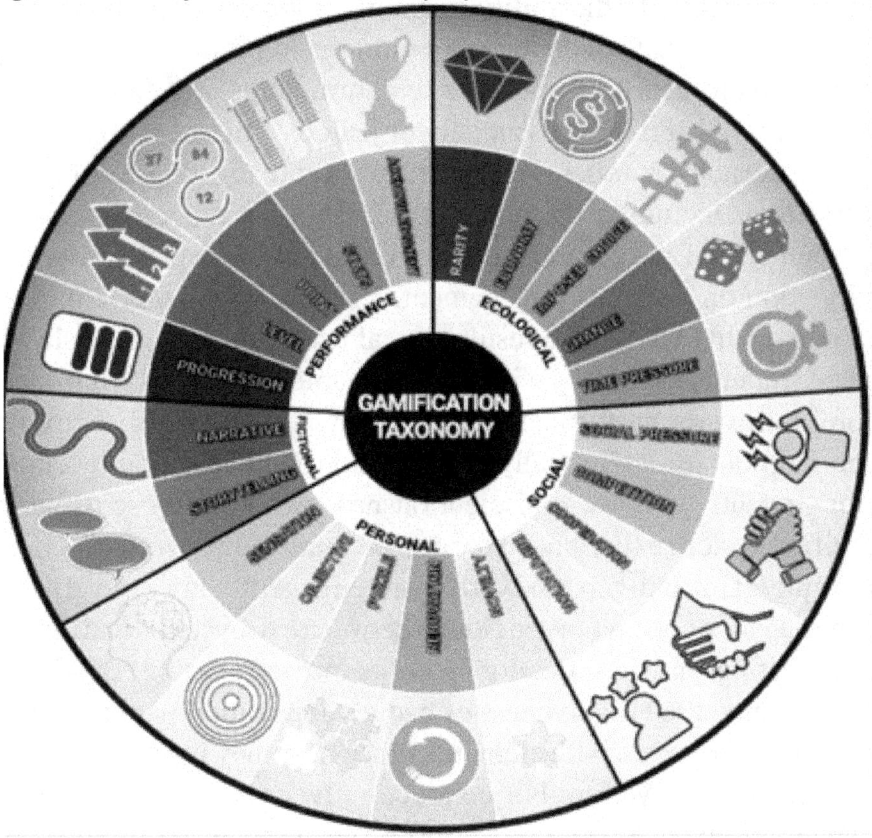

The authors also provide examples of how these elements can be applied in educational environments, using Duolingo and MeuTutor as case studies. They analyse the game elements in these platforms and discuss their advantages and disadvantages. They also propose a hierarchy for classifying the game elements, suggesting that certain elements are more relevant than others.

Addressing the buzz and controversy surrounding the effectiveness of gamification in education, Bai et al. (2020) present a meta-analysis of the effects of gamification on student learning achievements. Their results reveal a significant medium effect size in favour of gamification, However, the authors highlight the need to examine the reasons behind learners' enjoyment and dislike of gamification. They argue that these insights can inform the design of future gamified interventions. They identify four reasons for learners' enjoyment - the ability of gamification to foster enthusiasm, provide feedback, fulfil needs for recognition, and promote goal setting. On the other hand, learners may dislike gamification if it fails to bring additional utility or if it induces anxiety or jealousy. In line with previous researchers, the authors reiterate the need to explore the long-term effects of gamification, including the potential for negative outcomes, such as inflated competition and cheating. Smiderle et al. (2020) explore the impact of gamification on students' engagement, learning, and behaviour based on their personality traits. The results reveal that gamification positively influenced students' accuracy with low agreeableness and low openness. Therefore, introverts performed better in the second half of the online programming course. Additionally, gamification helped maintain accuracy levels for students with low conscientiousness, whereas those using the non-gamified system experienced reduced accuracy. Introverted students who used the gamified version were more engaged than extroverts. An interesting negative correlation was found between extroversion and ranking views, suggesting that gamification benefits introverts more. Balci et al. (2022) investigate the effectiveness of badges and leaderboards in online education. They compare both elements to see how they influence student performance and motivation. For conducting two experiments with two online undergraduate physics courses, they put students into groups with either badges only, leaderboards only, both, or neither. Although the results indicated that neither badges nor leaderboards had a significant effect on academic performance (quiz and assignment scores), students expressed a positive affective response to both elements. This affirmative attitude motivated them to advocate for the incorporation of these elements in future courses. This finding suggests that while gamification elements may not always directly improve academic performance, they can enhance the overall learning experience, promoting a more interactive and inspiring learning atmosphere. Khaldi et al. (2023) argue that besides Points, Badges, and Leaderboards (PBL) elements, there is an increasing trend towards using 'deeper' elements like challenges and storytelling. They point out that only a few studies revolve around motivational theories, gamification frameworks, and content gamification (i.e. integrating game elements directly into the educational content) compared to structural gamification (i.e. applying game-like elements to the structure or interface of the learning environment).

According to Fernando & Premadasa (2024), gamification and game-based learning are effective teaching-learning approaches to engage Generation Alpha (those born after 2010) as this generation is deeply rooted in technology. Fernando and Premadasa, H. K. Salinda (2024) explore adaptive or personalised gamification in Gen Alpha students, highlighting its potential to enhance motivation, attention, and performance. They conclude that adaptive gamification strategies are well-suited to Gen Alpha's behavioural characteristics. They also emphasise the importance of integrating technology-enhanced learning into educational curricula and highlight the need for educators to develop technical and pedagogical skills to implement digitally gamified learning environments effectively.

Why Gamify Language Learning?

The theoretical foundations in gamification show that gamification can be applied to any learning area. Language learning is one of the relevant domains in education, and gamification has started to be used for better results. But the question arises - why do we require gamification in language learning? As educators, we know that the main purpose of any language learning is to enable learners to understand, speak, read, and write in that specific language. Language learning also requires understanding cultural competence and expressing ideas in that context. The mental processes involved in learning and using language are memory, attention, and problem-solving skills. Besides this, the learner's motivation, attitude, and psychological factors also influence the language learning process. Hence, due to the complex cognitive and affective processes involved in language learning, the need of the hour is to engage learners and enhance their motivation.

A Duolingo survey (FE Education, 2022) supports this idea, revealing that 95% of respondents believe that combining fun with education improves learning outcomes. Moreover, 85% of respondents prefer gamified apps over traditional classrooms for language learning as they make language learning easier by engaging the learners. Traditional language learning methods are known to have a fixed curriculum with a selection of lessons and exercises. This structured curriculum may not suit every learner due to diverse individual needs and learning preferences. Traditional methods are also instructor-led, which may limit the flexibility and adaptability of the learning experience. Furthermore, in traditional classrooms, instructors may fail to provide immediate or detailed feedback due to the large number of students in a single class. In many cases, even if feedback is provided, it may be possible only at set intervals, such as during quizzes or exams, rather than after each lesson or activity. Traditional language learning approaches often require learners to adhere to fixed schedules and locations, which may not always align with their preferences or needs. In contrast, gamification in language learning can offer a more flexible and engaging experience. This can be achieved through various means, including interactive lessons, games, and activities that create a sense of progression and achievement. Gamified elements like levels, points, leaderboards, and badges can be incorporated into different learning environments, allowing learners to learn at their own pace and adapt to their individual skill levels and preferences. Learners can select their focus areas based on interests and receive personalised comments and suggestions. The gamified tools, such as Duolingo, HelloTalk, Busuu etc. provide immediate feedback and sometimes rewards, too. This instant feedback loop motivates learners to continue learning and improving. Learners can also access the materials anytime, anywhere, which makes language learning more convenient and adaptable. A number of gamified language learning tools also incorporate social features through which learners can connect, interact, and compete with others. This promotes a sense of community and friendly competition. Hence, learners are encouraged to stay engaged constantly. Even introverted learners do not hesitate to explore their potential, as they don't experience the in-person pressures as they feel shy in traditional classroom environments.

Francisco et al. (2015) highlight the positive impact of gamification on the L2 learning experience and acknowledge the importance of aligning gamification objectives with learning goals. They suggest that gamification in language learning helps L2 learners with various personality factors and enhances their motivation through positive feedback and game elements.

Tao et al. (2020) conducted an exploratory, cross-sectional study to find the success factors in the design of a Gamified Language Learning Platform (GLLP). Their participants's average responses regarding their experience with gamified apps indicated a positive sentiment (exceeding the neutral point). This suggests that the apps stimulate enjoyment, a sense of time flying by, a perception of being understood, and a belief that the learning time was well-spent. There also emerged the following eight primary factors responsible for the success of the apps: specific and clear objectives; concrete challenges and missions; useful learning tasks with increasing complexity; personalisation; visible progress indicator; immediate feedback with rewards; freedom to choose study paths; possibility of failure; and easy access to learning. Al-Dosakee & Ozdamli (2021) conducted a systematic literature review to investigate the effectiveness of gamification in language learning. The review, which included 103 studies published between 2010- 2020, was carried out across three databases: Web of Science, Science Direct, and Scopus. The authors' findings suggest that gamification can be a valuable tool for educators. 74.1 per cent of the participating students in their study felt highly engaged and motivated to learn the language. Safatian (2023) utilises mixed methods to explore the effectiveness of gamification in mobile language learning applications. The findings underscore the positive effects of integrating gamification elements in these apps. The researcher reports "positive correlations between app usage frequency, app usage duration, gamification elements, language learning outcomes, motivation, and engagement" (p. 37). Her findings align with previous studies and suggest that greater engagement with gamification features and more frequent use of apps are linked to better language learning outcomes, including improved performance, increased motivation, and more active participation.

Therefore, gamified language learning apps/platforms are considered to offer a more interactive, flexible, and personalised learning experience. They leverage game-like elements to make language learning more engaging, motivating, and accessible to users. Traditional language learning methods, while structured, may not always cater to individual needs and preferences, and they often lack the social and competitive features that gamified apps/platforms provide. Hence, there is no doubt that gamified learning apps and platforms make language learning more enjoyable and interactive than traditional classroom learning.

Gamification Strategies for Language Learning Objectives

According to Brown (2007), learning is the retention of information or skills. Learning also involves a conscious focus on the part of the learner and involves 'reinforced practice.' There are some additional factors that also influence learning, such as learners' age, level of education, and learning preferences. Therefore, language learning lessons need to be designed, taking all those factors into consideration. A language learning lesson is successful and effective only when it helps learners develop an ability to understand, speak, read, and write in the target language. It also requires focused activities and repeated practice. There are three main areas that need to be addressed by the language educator/facilitator: receptive skills, productive skills, and cultural awareness. Receptive skills include listening and reading comprehension. Listening comprehension comprises understanding lectures, conversations, podcasts, videos, etc. The learner should develop the ability to identify main points, follow different kinds of conversations, and recognize intonations that convey the speaker's intention and implied meaning.. On the other hand, reading comprehension is the ability to understand written language, from simple instructions to complex texts such as novels or academic articles. To be skilled at reading, learners should be able to identify core ideas, follow arguments, and understand the domain-specific lexicon. They must have the ability to draw conclusions. Hence, receptive skills focus on the 'competence' of the learner. On the contrary, productive skills, i.e. speaking and writing focus on the 'performance' of the learner. The learner should be able to communicate effectively in the target language. They should be fluent and accurate in grammar and pronunciation. They should use appropriate vocabulary and be able to express themselves clearly and confidently in different situations. The same goes for their communication ability in written language. Learners should write clear and grammatically correct sentences and paragraph structure, use appropriate vocabulary, and have the ability to write for different purposes (e.g. emails, essays, reports). Both receptive and productive skills come under linguistic knowledge. The task of the language educator does not end here. They have to make the learners aware of the cultural aspects of the target language. The learner must know the traditions, customs, social norms, etiquette, and different cultural values associated with the speakers of that language. It helps the learners choose appropriate language suitable for different contexts. Thus, the learners can avoid miscommunication and misunderstandings due to cultural differences.

Based on the factors discussed above, we will frame some gamification strategies. For young learners, we can focus more on visual elements, points, and badges. Youngsters have a shorter attention span than adults, so longer activity-based games won't suit them. Shorter games will keep them motivated and focus on learning. For adult learners, we can leverage existing games and tools with more strategic challenges and leaderboards. For both young and adult learners, we can incorporate real-world scenarios into related language activities. As far as the language proficiency level is concerned, beginners require simple and engaging games focusing on vocabulary and grammar because these are the building blocks of language learning. For advanced learners, complexity can be incorporated along with problem-solving elements. Learners learn or understand new information differently. Gamification can be implemented based on learners' specific preferences. Language activities for those who prefer learning with visuals can include diagrams, flowcharts, images, videos, and infographics. Listening and pronunciation exercises cater to individuals with a preference for auditory processing, helping them retain information more effectively. For those with a preference for hands-on experiences, we can design gamified activities that incorporate movement, role-playing, and interaction with virtual environments, catering to their kinaesthetic preferences. The following table sums up the strategies for better understanding.

Table 1. Gamification language learning strategies & different factors

Factor	Young Learners	Adult Learners
Attention Span	Shorter bursts of activity	Longer activities possible
Motivation	Visual elements, points, badges, immediate feedback	Strategic challenges, leaderboards
Learning Preferences	Visual: Diagrams, images, videos, infographics	Visual: As above
	Auditory: Listening exercises, pronunciation challenges	Auditory: As above
	Kinesthetic: Movement, role-playing, virtual environments	Kinesthetic: As above (maybe less emphasis)
Language Proficiency Level	Beginners: Foundational (engaging, interactive) games	Advanced: Pragmatic and discursive games
Focus	Vocabulary, grammar	More complex language use
Examples	Matching games, short quizzes with visuals	Simulations, debates, collaborative writing

We can extend this to frame gamification strategies that target LSRW (listening, speaking, reading, writing) skills. We can create activities based on the requirements of the learners. To develop listening skills in young learners, we can create activities incorporating short audio/video clips, followed by interactive quizzes. These activities can focus on recognising diverse pronunciations of words (e.g., regional accents, individual variations), identifying and interpreting different intonations (e.g., rising, falling, neutral), and understanding language use in context (e.g., idiomatic expressions, colloquialisms). This will help learners improve their listening skills and better comprehend language nuances in real-world situations, applicable to both ESL (English as a Second Language) and EFL (English as a Foreign Language) contexts. Points can be awarded for the identification of main points or for correctly following conversations. For adult learners, gamified audio dialogues can be incorporated where they can participate in dictation games or answer comprehension questions, earning points for accurate and speedy responses. They can also earn badges by overcoming challenges and progressing through different difficulty levels, demonstrating their mastery of core listening skills such as comprehension, vocabulary, and pronunciation.

The games targeting speaking can include role-playing scenarios where educators can set goals, and points can be awarded to the learners for using correct grammar, pronunciation, and clear communication. Different situations can be created for different learners based on their levels and preferences. Learners can compete in 'dialogue duels' where they can deliver convincing arguments or complete conversations. Additionally, they can earn badges for fluency and accuracy. To improve reading comprehension skills, learners can be provided with interesting stories where they can get options to create branching narratives based on comprehension choices. As they progress through the story, points and badges can be awarded for making correct choices and reaching the next level accordingly. To enhance vocabulary, learners can be engaged in gamified crosswords or 'meaningful duels' where they can match words to meanings and earn points as well as badges to go to the next level. Writing skills can be improved both individually and collaboratively. There can be writing games for individuals and teams to create grammatically correct and engaging stories/essays, with points awarded for vocabulary usage, sentence structure, and teamwork (in the case of games specific for groups). Moreover, timed writing challenges can be introduced, focusing on specific prompts and themes with deadlines. Learners can earn points for creativity in their writing, such as fresh perspectives, innovative ideas, and effective use of language devices, as well as accuracy in grammar, spelling, and punctuation, and meeting deadlines. The following table clearly highlights the strategies for LSRW skills.

Table 2. Gamification language learning strategies for LSRW skills

Skill	Development	Strategies
Listening	Grasp key points, intonations, and follow conversations	Young Learners: Short audio clips & quizzes with visuals (award points for key points & intonations)
		Adult Learners: Audio dialogues & games (dictation games, comprehension questions) (award points for accuracy & speed
Speaking	Practice grammar, pronunciation, and fluency in various situations	Young & Adult: Role-playing scenarios with goals & points (award points for appropriate language, pronunciation, clear communication)
		Adult Learners: Dialogue duels (compete in pairs, deliver arguments/complete conversations) (earn badges for fluency & accuracy)

continued on following page

Table 2. Continued

Reading	Grasp ideas, follow arguments, build vocabulary	Young & Adult: Interactive stories with choices (branching narratives based on choices, award points for correct choices & progress); Gamified crosswords & definition duels (match words to meanings) (award points & badges for successful completion)
Writing	Express clearly & grammatically, improve vocabulary usage, sentence structure, and communication	Young Learners: Short prompts with timed challenges (encourage concise writing, award points for meeting deadlines)
		Young & Adult: Collaborative writing games (compete in teams to create grammatically correct stories/essays) (award points for vocabulary, sentence structure, teamwork)

The next table shows some interesting games targeting specific LSRW skills:

Table 3. Bonus activities based on LSRW skills

Skill	Activity	Task	Learner Age	Points/badges
Listening	Guess the Intonation	Listen to short audio clips and identify different intonations.	Adult	Correct guesses
Speaking	Dub the Ad	Watch short videos with muted audio and create dialogues to match the visuals.	Young & Adult	Creativity Humour Grammar
Reading	Vocabulary Bingo	Read passages and identify specific vocabulary words.	Young & Adult	Form a row/bingo
Writing	Microblog Challenge	Write short stories or poems based on specific prompts.	Young & Adult	Creativity Vocabulary Theme

Moving on to cultural understanding as an essential part of language learning, we now explore some of the ways to incorporate this aspect. Lev Vygotsky, the seminal Russian psychologist, propounded the cognitive development theory. He considered culture important in an individual's learning and development. Hence, while gamifying, educators must address cultural awareness and re-explain cultural nuances before the lessons. Cultural quizzes and challenges are a few good options to test learners' knowledge of different traditions, customs, and social norms associated with the target language. Similar to other skills, points and badges can also be awarded to the learners wherever they indicate cultural understanding. Vygotsky (1978) also suggested that learning happens while an individual interacts with others around them within the community. Learning, in this sense, is a continuous process. This can inspire virtual simulations to be created to design language games where learners can immerse themselves and navigate the target culture. The learners can be given choices where they can utilise their knowledge and earn rewards for successful interactions.

Table 4. Gamified activities for cultural understanding

Learner Age	Learning Preference	Activity	Gamification	Focus
All ages	All preferences	Cultural Quiz	Points, Leaderboards	Knowledge of traditions, customs
Young Learners	Visual, Kinesthetic	Virtual Marketplace	Points, Unlocking Features, Virtual Currency, Avatars	Applying cultural knowledge in scenarios
Adult Learners	Auditory, Kinesthetic	Role-Playing	Points, Badges	Fluency & Culturally Appropriate Communication
Young Learners	Auditory, Social	Collaborative Storytelling	Points, Badges	Collaboration, Cultural Awareness, Storytelling
Adult Learners	Visual, Social	Cultural Hashtag	Points, Badges	Cultural understanding in modern communication

Finally, we overview relevant language learning models that can provide insights for developing gamification strategies for language learning. Language learning models can be categorised into cognitive, psycholinguistic, statistical, and neural network models. Cognitive and psycholinguistic models explain how humans learn languages. Statistical models statistically analyse large amounts of text data to identify language patterns and predict the next word (helpful in translation). Neural network models are based on the structure and function of the human brain. These models utilise artificial neural networks to process language data and can understand the complex relationships between words. On the other hand, statistical and neural network models are computational models that help process and understand language data. Significant psychological models include the Processing Continuum Model (PCM) by Bialystok (1978), the Monitor Model by Krashen (1982), the Interaction Hypothesis by Long

(1981), and the Natural Approach by Krashen & Terrell (1983). N-gram models, Hidden Markov Models (HMMs), Recurrent Neural Networks (RNNs), Long Short-Term Memory (LSTM) networks, and Transformers are categorised under statistical and neural network models (Jurafsky & Martin, 2009).

According to Bialystok (1978)'s Processing Continuum Model (PCM), language learners operate on a continuum between controlled processing (conscious effort) and automated processing (effortless use). When the learner is a novice, the educator should focus on a conscious effort where providing immediate feedback and clear-cut goals can help 'controlled processing,'e.g. points for identifying grammar mistakes. As learners progress, educators can emphasise 'automated processing', focusing on fluency and communication, e.g. points for delivering an effective speech. For beginner learners, interactive sentence completion games where immediate feedback is given for grammar mistakes can be extremely effective. As they progress, more complex challenges such as timed debates or improvised speeches can be introduced. The game mechanics (points for accuracy or fluency) keep learners motivated as they transition from controlled to automated processing.

Krashen (1982)'s Monitor Model suggests that language acquisition happens subconsciously through comprehensible input, while the monitor (a conscious process) edits and filters output according to the learner's confidence. This insight allows educators to provide more comprehensible input, e.g., listening to dialogues and interactive stories. It helps them provide more output for the monitor. Educators can create interactive dialogues or virtual language labs where learners practise speaking with an AI-driven chatbot. The chatbot provides comprehensible input (e.g., through everyday conversational practice), and learners use their internal 'monitor' to correct and refine their responses. Points and badges can be awarded for fluent conversation, maintaining learners' engagement and providing measurable progress.

Long (1981)'s Interaction Hypothesis foregrounds meaningful interaction for language acquisition. Educators can create collaborative games for both young and adult learners. This can facilitate interaction and negotiation over language use. Learners can receive points for their teamwork skills in addition to their vocabulary usage and grammatical accuracy.

This encourages collaboration and language learning. Collaborative games that mimic real-world language interactions are particularly effective. For instance, learners might participate in a simulated negotiation in a virtual marketplace, where they must haggle prices using the target language. Points could be awarded for correct language use, while teamwork and strategy add an additional layer of gamification. This encourages active language use in authentic contexts, in line with the Interaction Hypothesis.

Statistical Models, on the other hand, can analyse text data to identify patterns and predict word sequences. This could enable educators to create games that incorporate context-appropriate language. One effective example could be interactive narratives with choices, which may provide learners with branching storylines and the ability to influence the narrative's direction. This feature may empower learners, making them feel more invested in the story and their language learning journey. N-gram models can be used to generate grammatically correct responses based on the learner's selections, creating a more immersive and natural language learning experience. Interactive 'choose-your-own-adventure' narratives allow learners to shape the story through their language choices. This kind of game engages learners by rewarding them for making contextually appropriate decisions, thus improving their understanding of sentence structure and vocabulary. The interactive 'choose-your-own-adventure' type narratives in gamified language learning platforms align with the general characteristic of being in control, as learners are empowered to shape the story through their language choices. This feature taps into the human desire for agency and autonomy, allowing learners to take ownership of their learning experience and make decisions that impact the narrative. By being in control of their learning journey, learners are more likely to be engaged, motivated, and invested in the learning process. These models can also support adaptive feedback systems, which recommend new learning challenges based on the learner's current skill level. For instance, if a learner struggles with verb tenses, the system can suggest targeted practice games that focus on this area.

Neural Network Models can inspire educators to include elements of personalisation and feedback. This will help them identify areas where learners need improvement. Immediate suggestions in the form of activities to address specific issues can be created, too. Each learner can have their own customised learning paths, with increasing difficulty levels. The feedback loop can be gamified by awarding points or badges as the learners show improvements in fluency, pronunciation, or sentence structure over time. This will motivate learners to refine their communication skills continuously. Additionally, educators can employ interactive chatbots or virtual tutors designed by game developers. These tutors can keep the learner engaged in the conversations and adapt their responses based on their level and progress. Educators can gamify bot/tutor interactions by awarding points and badges for correct answers, completing conversations on specific topics, or achieving specific goals (e.g., using a certain number of new vocabulary words). The following table summarises the activities as per learners' type and their learning preferences:

Table 5. Gamification activities: Based on language models

Model	Learner Age	Learning Preference	Activity	Gamification	Focus
Cognitive (PCM)	All Ages	All Preferences	Interactive Quizzes, Sentence Completion Games	Points, Badges	Grammar Accuracy
	Young & Adult Learners	All Preferences	Debates, Role-Playing	Points, Badges	Fluency in Communication
Monitor Model	All Ages	All Preferences	Interactive Dialogues, Collaborative Storytelling	Points, Badges, Leaderboards	Comprehension & Communication
Statistical (N-gram models)	All Ages	Visual & Kinesthetic	Interactive Narratives, Vocabulary Games	Points, Badges, Virtual Rewards	Contextual Language Use & Vocabulary
Neural Network (RNNs)	All Ages	All Preferences	Adaptive Learning Challenges, Personalised Pronunciation	Points, Badges, Customisation	Personalised learning & Fluency improvement

Apart from the above-mentioned models, Large Language Models (LLMs) can be used for learners of all ages and learning preferences. Educators can conduct 'Interactive Grammar Practice' and 'Group Storytelling' sessions with learners and provide them with appropriate LLM prompts. Learners can focus on grammar practice & collaborative storytelling with LLMs. Kinesthetic and competitive learners can be given time-based tasks or related challenges. A 'risk and reward' element can also be added by introducing a limited number of 'lives' per activity. It can sharpen strategic thinking skills as learners have to be more cautious and focus on avoiding mistakes. Learners could work in teams to co-author a story, with LLMs assisting by providing suggestions for grammar improvements or expanding vocabulary choices.

The key to successful gamification lies in striking the right balance between fun and learning. While the mechanics of points, badges, and leaderboards motivate learners, the primary focus should always be on reinforcing language skills. Through well-designed activities that align with cognitive and statistical models, learners are not only entertained but also equipped with the skills necessary to progress in their language learning journey. Educators can also leverage the flexibility of these models to personalise the learning experience. For instance, they can adjust the weightage of different gamification elements (e.g., more points for fluency than for vocabulary recall) based on the learners' needs and progress. This adaptability ensures that the gamified learning environment remains effective, engaging, and suited to learners of all ages and proficiencies. By incorporating these language learning models into their gamification strategies, educators can ensure that learners remain motivated, engaged, and challenged at every stage of their language acquisition journey.

Gamified Language Learning Platforms and Apps

In this section, we will explore how various gamification strategies are effectively implemented in popular gamified language-learning apps (see figure 2 below).

Figure 2. Leading language learning apps (Ceci, 2023)

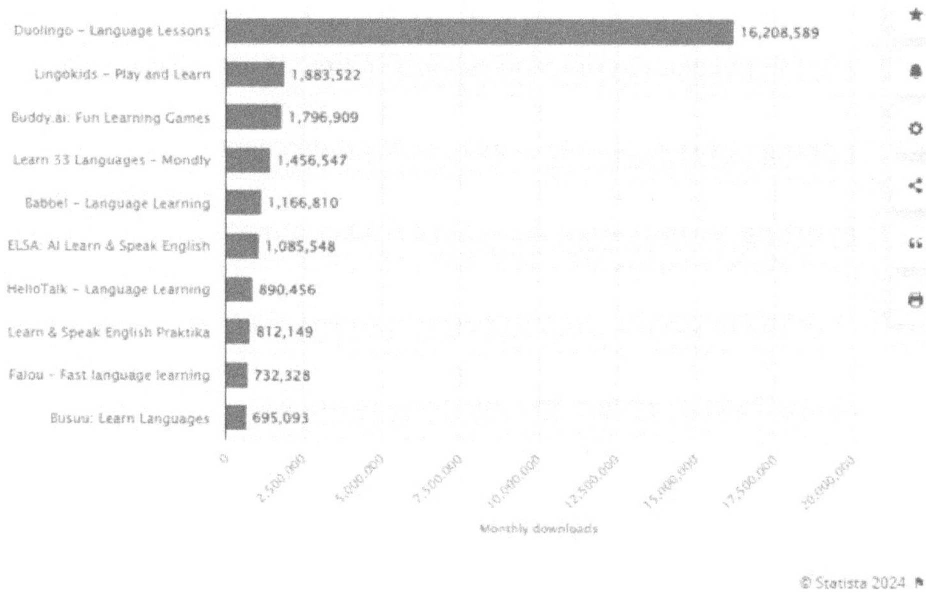

According to a report by Statistica in the year 2024, Duolingo is the most popular language-learning app. It's interactive grammar exercises align with the Processing Continuum Model, as they require learners to actively process and practice language rules, moving from controlled to automatic processing. This app is appropriately designed to balance fun and structured learning. For beginners, the focus is on basic vocabulary, grammar rules, and pronunciation. Gamification elements such as streaks, experience points (XP), and leaderboards are introduced to motivate beginners and to establish consistent learning habits. For intermediate learners, Duolingo introduces complex language structures, idiomatic expressions, and cultural nuances. The learners have to solve timed quizzes and skill tests that encourage intermediate learners to push their language skills further. As advanced learners aim for fluency and proficiency, the app offers immersion exercises as well as story-based lessons.

The second most popular app is Lingokids. Specially designed for children, this app has interactive games, colourful visuals, and engaging activities. This aligns with the Cognitive Model's emphasis on mental processes and cognitive skills. Its gamification elements focus on playful interactions, rewards for progress, and age-appropriate content. Lingokids also involve parents so that they are aware of the child's progress and can suggest appropriate activities for their child. The next popular app is Buddy, an AI-powered language learning app. The app leverages AI algorithms to recommend lessons, exercises, and activities. Its gamification elements focus on adaptive learning, real-time feedback, and personalised content. Mondly app also involves AI-driven personalisation and speech recognition. It focuses on a comprehensive language learning experience with a wide range of languages as well as immersive simulations. Babbel is an app that emphasises practical language skills and real-world application. Hence, it is ideal for learners who prioritise conversational proficiency. Its interactive lessons and dialogues focus on everyday conversations, workplace scenarios, and social interactions. Learners can also customise their vocabulary lists, track their progress, and earn rewards.

The ELSA (English Language Speech Assistant) app and HelloTalk are other popular language-learning apps. They offer unique features that set them apart from other apps in the market. ELSA stands out with its advanced speech recognition technology and AI-driven pronunciation evaluation, based on a Neural Network Model to analyse and evaluate users' speech patterns and pronunciation. On the other hand, HelloTalk facilitates language exchange and cultural interactions among users worldwide through text, voice, and video chats. Based on the Processing Continuum Model, it creates a conducive environment for language practice and learning. LearnEnglish Praktika has been developed by the British Council. Therefore, this app's content reflects the expertise of the British Council in English language education, ensuring high-quality materials and reliable language resources. Based on Statistical and Neural Network Model, Falou is a fast language learning app that employs accelerated learning techniques, immersive experiences, and personalised learning paths. It has audiovisual resources to facilitate efficient language acquisition. Busuu is an app that focuses on social interaction and collaborative learning (cf. Interaction Hypothesis). It facilitates peer feedback and cultural immersion. It has a language exchange feature that allows learners to interact with native speakers, receive feedback on their writing and speaking exercises, and also engage in real-time language exchanges. It provides lessons, audio recordings, and multimedia resources pertaining to that specific culture so that the learners can understand cultural aspects, traditions, and customs. In addition to the above-mentioned apps, Extended Reality (XR) apps have emerged as one of the most powerful tools for language learning. They are based on Statistical and Neural Network Models. XR includes Artificial Intelligence (AI), Virtual Reality (VR), and Augmented Reality (AR). While AR can overlay digital content in the real world, creating interactive scenarios, MR blends elements of virtual and real, opening up more possibilities for engaging and realistic language learning experiences. Language learning with XR creates immersive and interactive environments that can take the language learning experience to a new height.

Trancy AI Talk is an immersive language learning app based on ChatGPT. It claims to eliminate nervousness and embarrassment and instil confidence in 30 days. It seamlessly integrates popular streaming services like YouTube and Netflix and transforms them into personalised study materials. Currently, Trancy only has an extension and a web-based learning centre. The developers are working on its mobile version in the future so that users can learn anytime and anywhere. In addition, they are also working on integrating more streaming and music websites and trying to convert popular podcast content into language-learning materials. Similarly, VirtualSpeech addresses the fear of public speaking by offering realistic practice. Recognising that traditional methods like rehearsing in front of a mirror were insufficient, VirtualSpeech developed VR simulations of various audience sizes and distractions to build real-world confidence and skills. The platform has collaborated with Fortune 500 companies to focus on essential communication skills like public speaking, sales, and leadership. Its website claims to have helped over 550,000 users in more than 125 countries and has been featured in major publications, including The New York Times, Forbes, BBC, Wall Street Journal, and Huffington Post (VirtualSpeech - Soft Skills Training with VR, 2019). With over 30 languages available, Mondly is another language-learning app that integrates AR and VR. It integrated both Statistical and Neural Network Models as well as Processing Continuum Model (PCM). Its latest speech recognition technology helps learners practise pronunciation, and chatbots simulate real-world conversations. Enabling learners to interact with virtual objects and characters, Mondly "offers a complete language learning experience that is easy to use and access anytime, anywhere"

(Mondly, 2017). Memrise is a platform founded by Memrise, Ed Cooke (Grand Master of Memory), Ben Whately (an experimental psychologist & entrepreneur), and Greg Detre (a neuroscientist). It utilises memory techniques, neuroscience insights, and innovative language acquisition methods to simplify and accelerate language learning. It has an AI language tutor and claims to have "48,000+ conversations between real natives" (Memrise, 2017). Noun Town is a VR language-learning game featuring exclusive minigames. As its name suggests, it is set in a virtual town where the users interact with characters and complete specific quests to learn new words and phrases. Learners can click on objects, buildings, and people to reveal associated nouns, presented with translations, pronunciations, and contextual sentences. Thirteen languages can be learnt through Noun Town, and ten languages can be used for the menus/user interface.

With the rise of AI, XR, and personalised learning, educators can create more immersive, interactive, and effective language learning experiences for the learners. AI can build a detailed learner profile collecting data over time and help educators understand the learners' progress and tailor the pace of learning. However, it is essential to prioritise accessibility, cultural sensitivity, and learner-centric design to ensure these advancements benefit all language learners. These technologies open new possibilities, enabling learners to connect with languages and cultures from around the world in more meaningful ways.

Challenges in Gamifying Learning

While gamified language learning apps are gaining exponential popularity due to their creative and engaging methods, they have their share of challenges, too. Addressing these challenges is crucial for maximising the potential benefits of gamified learning platforms. The first and foremost challenge in language learning is maintaining consistency and (extrinsic) motivation over the long term. As gamified apps rely heavily on keeping learners engaged, the novelty of games may wear off in many instances, leading to decreased motivation. Some apps introduce varied content and new challenges regularly, which can help retain learners' motivation to a great extent. It is also essential to integrate strategies that promote a balance of external and internal motivators The second challenge is to ensure comprehensive language proficiency, particularly in writing, complex grammar, and conversation skills. To overcome this, some apps include real-time interaction for holistic skill development. Gamified learning systems require considerable resources and expertise. The main challenge is encountered in less developed countries, where access to reliable internet and compatible devices can be a barrier. It limits the learner's ability to utilise these language learning apps fully. To mitigate this, some apps have included partial offline modes. It allows learners to download lessons and practice exercises. Moreover, providing lightweight versions of the apps that require less bandwidth and storage can also make them more accessible to users with limited technological resources. Thurairasu (2022) suggests that mobile language learning can be explored "owing to the accessibility and omnipresence of smartphones" (p. 67). By improving accessibility, developers can create more effective and enjoyable learning experiences. This will guarantee that learners not only remain engaged but also achieve their language learning goals with greater efficiency. By mitigating the challenges and issues, gamified language learning apps can facilitate a more immersive, enjoyable, and effective learning experience for language learners globally.

The Future of Gamification in Language Learning

According to Thurairasu (2022), 'gamification-based learning' is the 'current trend in education' and is the future of language learning. Additionally, he recommends language education at primary levels and for learners with special needs. Language learning is most effective when learners can practise in realistic contexts, and gamification includes role-playing scenarios where learners adopt new identities and interact in simulated environments. Gamification provides practical experience by using the language in various contexts, which is crucial for both FLL (Foreign Language Learning) and SLL (Second Language Learning).

Oxford Analytica's report on Gamification (*Gamification and the Future of Education*, 2016) explores the application of game mechanics in education to enhance performance outcomes. It provides initial evidence from case studies and expert interviews highlighting gamification's potential in education. It explains how entertainment's primary role of escapism (i.e., temporarily allowing one to experience a different life) is central to children's play and a powerful educational tool. Gamified language learning leverages this concept by incorporating role-playing elements where students adopt new identities. This method encourages them to see the world through different perspectives, deepening their understanding and knowledge. By communicating how their new identity would act in various situations, learners enhance their language skills while fostering empathy, making the learning process both immersive and effective.

Exploring the potential of Virtual reality-assisted language learning (VRALL), Parmaxi (2020) demonstrates that the performance and motivation of language learners can be improved through immersive VR. Panagiotidis (2021) states that global demand for XR (Extended Reality) technologies is projected to grow by 45.0%, reaching $346.39 billion by 2026, driven by innovations and advancements in network technologies like Wi-Fi 6 and 5G. XR also helps reduce anxiety and increase cultural awareness in learners. Besides enhancing creativity, collaboration, and communication, it improves problem-solving and critical-thinking skills. It can revolutionise language learning for the elderly and learners with special needs.

Huang & Liu (2021) argue that the integration of artificial intelligence (AI) in education has transformed teaching and learning methods, with applications such as adaptive learning, teaching evaluation, and virtual classrooms, enhancing teachers' effectiveness and students' learning outcomes. Tan & Cheah (2021) created a prototype AI-enabled gamification platform for university introductory physics courses. They also conducted a small-scale evaluation study to gather feedback from students on that prototype. The results showed that students generally have a positive perception of the application and its features. Notably, 83% of respondents agreed that they would use the application to support their physics learning, and 75% believed that the application would encourage students to remain engaged in the physics course. Bezzina & Pfeiffer (2022) argue that gamification's static approach can fail to keep learners engaged and AI can be combined to overcome this shortcoming. By leveraging AI's adaptive affordances, their study proposes to move beyond static gamified interventions and enable dynamic user interactions in digital assessment and learning. Yang et al. (2023) investigate a gamified Artificially Intelligent Educational Robot

(AIER) system's effectiveness in improving students' learning outcomes and motivation. They also introduce a GAFCC (Gamification, Access, Feedback, Challenge, Collaboration) model-based design. Their results show significant improvements in learning achievement, motivation, and flow experience, with reduced cognitive load. Moreover, their GAIER (Gamified Artificially Intelligent Educational Robot) system improves learning outcomes, and Augmented Reality (AR) enhances engagement. Kherazi & Bourray (2024) conducted a study on the popular app Duolingo to investigate the role of AI-assisted gamification in enhancing user engagement in mobile language learning apps. They gathered user feedback through surveys and interviews to understand the impact on learner motivation and satisfaction. The study highlights AI's role in personalising the learning experience through tailored challenges and rewards, leading to increased engagement and enjoyment. Their preliminary findings show that gamification creates an effective and motivating learning environment, with users reporting increased appeal and engagement.

As far as language learning is concerned, AI can analyse learner data and accordingly optimise language lessons (increasing or decreasing difficulty) and provide tailored feedback. This adaptive approach can enable learners to progress at their own pace, boost engagement and motivation. Additionally, AI-enhanced language learning can include immersive conversational simulations that allow learners to hone their speaking and listening skills in realistic contexts. Personalised language learning pathways, intelligent tutoring systems, and adaptive assessments further improve the learning experience. As a result, language learners can develop a more authentic and effective command of the language, preparing them for practical communication in everyday situations.

However, with the integration of AI into language learning, several ethical considerations need to be addressed to ensure responsible implementation. As AI systems collect vast amounts of sensitive data (e.g. speech patterns and learning preferences), privacy concerns may arise. This data has to be securely managed and not misused so that language learners maintain trust in these technologies. Furthermore, AI systems may exhibit biases, especially if they are trained on limited or skewed linguistic and cultural datasets. It can potentially lead to inaccurate assessments or incomplete learning experiences for those who speak with regional accents or dialects. These issues can be mitigated only when more inclusive, culturally diverse datasets are created. Additionally, ensuring equitable access to AI-enhanced learning tools is vital to prevent the digital divide from widening, particularly in regions with limited access to technology. Addressing ethical challenges is deemed necessary in order to maximise AI's benefits in education and hence, to protect learners' rights. Al-Zahrani & Alasmari (2024)'s study provides insights for various stakeholders, informing decision-making on AI's ethical and educational implications in higher education. They emphasise the need for comprehensive implementation strategies, addressing technical, ethical, social, and educational considerations. Their recommendations include developing ethical guidelines, investing in professional development, and addressing data ethics and privacy concerns.

Though AI-enhanced gamification alone is not the panacea to all language learning challenges, its strategic incorporation into different educational systems and private sectors can indeed bring significant change in language learning. Successful implementation requires aligning objectives, assessment criteria, and selection of tasks/tools. Educators must remember that the aim of gamification is to provide learners with meaningful learning experiences and not just the incorporation of game elements for fun. The language teacher's role is not only as a facilitator but also as a guide who encourages critical thinking, creativity, and contemplation. As technology advancements continue to evolve and AI seamlessly integrates with education, the future of gamified language learning appears promising. However, privacy concerns regarding data collection and usage must be addressed through transparent policies and secure platforms. Vigilance against biases and stereotypes in game content is vital. Game developers must ethically deploy AI and machine learning algorithms and conduct regular audits to check potential biases. Continuous monitoring and evaluation are crucial to ensure effectiveness and impact. Educators need ongoing training and support to effectively integrate AI-enhanced gamification. AI-enhanced gamification has the potential to cater to individual learning preferences more effectively. Accessibility and inclusivity must be prioritised to ensure equal opportunities. By ensuring transparent policies, secure platforms, and continuous improvement, gamified language learning can lead the

REFERENCES

Al-Dosakee, K., & Ozdamli, F. (2021). Gamification in teaching and learning languages: A systematic literature review. *Revista Românească Pentru Educaţie Multidimensională, 13*(2), 559–577. Researchgate. https://doi.org/DOI: 10.18662/rrem/13.2/436

Al-Zahrani, A. M., & Alasmari, T. M. (2024). Exploring the impact of artificial intelligence on higher education: The dynamics of ethical, social, and educational implications. *Humanities & Social Sciences Communications, 11*(1), 1–12. DOI: 10.1057/s41599-024-03432-4

Bai, S., Hew, K. F., & Huang, B. (2020). Does gamification improve student learning outcome? Evidence from a meta-analysis and synthesis of qualitative data in educational contexts. *Educational Research Review, 30*, 100322. DOI: 10.1016/j.edurev.2020.100322

Balci, S., Secaur, J. M., & Morris, B. J. (2022). Comparing the effectiveness of badges and leaderboards on academic performance and motivation of students in fully versus partially gamified online physics classes. *Education and Information Technologies, 27*(6), 8669–8704. DOI: 10.1007/s10639-022-10983-z PMID: 35308640

Bezzina, S., Dingli, A., & Pfeiffer, A. (2022). Leveraging gamification in education through artificial intelligence. In *Proceedings of the 16th International Technology, Education and Development Conference (INTED2022)*, DOI:DOI: 10.21125/inted.2022.2206

Bialystok, E. (1978). A Theoretical Model of Second Language Learning. *Modern Language Journal, 28*, 69–83.

Brown, H. D. (2007). *Principles of language learning and teaching* (5th ed.). Pearson Longman.

Ceci, L. (2023, May 3). *Top language learning apps by downloads 2021*. Statista. https://www.statista.com/statistics/1239522/top-language-learning-apps-downloads/

Chou, Y.-K. (2014). *Actionable Gamification: Beyond Points, Badges, and Leaderboards*. Octalysis Group.

Christians, G. (2018). The Origins and Future of Gamification. *Senior Theses*, 1–65. https://scholarcommons.sc.edu/senior_theses/254

Dicheva, D., Dichev, C., Agre, G., & Angelova, G. (2015). Gamification in education: A systematic mapping study. *Journal of Educational Technology & Society*, *18*(3), 75–88. https://www.jstor.org/stable/jeductechsoci.18.3.75

Dreimane, S. (2021). Gamification before its definitions – An overview of its historical development. *INTED2021 Proceedings*, 7187–7193. DOI: 10.21125/inted.2021.1434

Education, F. E. (2022, May 24). 85% Indians consider gamified apps as better language learning tool: Duolingo survey. Financial Express. https://www.financialexpress.com/jobs-career/education-85-indians-consider-gamified-apps-as-better-language-learning-tool-reveals-duolingo-survey-2536383/

Fernando, P. A., & Premadasa, H. K. Salinda. (2024). A systematic literature review. Educational Technology & Society, 27(2), 114–132. JSTOR. https://doi.org/DOI: 10.2307/48766166

Francisco, J., Flores, F., Del Este, U., & Rico, P. (2015). Using Gamification to Enhance Second Language Learning. https://files.eric.ed.gov/fulltext/EJ1065005.pdf

Hamari, J., Koivisto, J., & Sarsa, H. (2014). Does gamification work?—A literature review of empirical studies on gamification. *Proceedings of the 47th Hawaii International Conference on System Sciences*, 3025–3034. https://doi.org/DOI: 10.1109/HICSS.2014.377

Huang, J., Saleh, S., & Liu, Y. (2021). A review on artificial intelligence in education. *Academic Journal of Interdisciplinary Studies*, *10*(3), 1–15. DOI: 10.36941/ajis-2021-0077

Jurafsky, D., & Martin, J. H. (2009). *Speech and language processing: An introduction to natural language processing, computational linguistics, and speech recognition*. Pearson Prentice Hall.

Kapp, K. M., Blair, L., & Mesch, R. (2013). *The gamification of learning and instruction fieldbook: Theory into practice*. John Wiley & Sons.

Khaldi, A., Bouzidi, R., & Nader, F. (2023). Gamification of e-learning in Higher Education: A Systematic Literature Review. *Smart Learning Environments*, *10*(1), 10. Advance online publication. DOI: 10.1186/s40561-023-00227-z PMID: 40478066

Kherazi, A., & Bourray, M. (2024). Gamification and m-learning: An innovative approach to sustainable language learning. E3S Web of Conferences, 477, 00066. .DOI: 10.1051/e3sconf/202447700066

Krashen, S. D. (1982). Principles and practice in second language acquisition. *Modern Language Journal*, *67*(2). https://www.sdkrashen.com/content/books/principles_and_practice.pdf

Krashen, S. D., & Terrell, T. D. (1983). *The natural approach: Language acquisition in the classroom*. Pergamon Press.

Landers, R. N. (2014). Developing a Theory of Gamified Learning. *Simulation & Gaming*, *45*(6), 752–768. DOI: 10.1177/1046878114563660

Landers, R. N., Armstrong, M. B., & Collmus, A. B. (2017). How to Use Game Elements to Enhance Learning: Applications of the Theory of Gamified Learning. *Serious Games and Edutainment Applications*, 457–483. DOI: 10.1007/978-3-319-51645-5_21

Landers, R. N., & Landers, A. K. (2014). An Empirical Test of the Theory of Gamified Learning. *Simulation & Gaming*, *45*(6), 769–785. DOI: 10.1177/1046878114563662

Liu, D., Santhanam, R., & Webster, J. (2017). Toward Meaningful Engagement: A Framework for Design and Research of Gamified Information Systems. *Management Information Systems Quarterly*, *41*(4), 1011–1034. DOI: 10.25300/MISQ/2017/41.4.01

Long, M. H. (1981). Input, interaction, and second-language acquisition. *Annals of the New York Academy of Sciences*, *379*(1), 259–278. DOI: 10.1111/j.1749-6632.1981.tb42014.x

Malone, T. W. (1981). Toward a Theory of Intrinsically Motivating Instruction. *Cognitive Science*, *5*(4), 333–369. DOI: 10.1207/s15516709cog0504_2

Memrise. (2017). *Memrise - Learn a language. Meet the world.* Memrise. https://www.memrise.com/

Merriam-Webster. (2019). *Definition of GAMIFICATION.* Merriam-Webster.com. https://www.merriam-webster.com/dictionary/gamification

Mondly. (2017). *Learn Languages Online for Free with Mondly - Get Fluent Now!* Mondly.com; Mondly Languages. https://www.mondly.com/

Panagiotidis, P. (2021). Augmented and Mixed Reality in Language Learning. *European Journal of Education, 4*(2), 28. DOI: 10.26417/501ibq23c

Parmaxi, A. (2020). Virtual Reality in Language Learning: A Systematic Review and Implications for Research and Practice. *Interactive Learning Environments, 31*(1), 172–184. DOI: 10.1080/10494820.2020.1765392

Safatian, F. (2023). Exploring the Effectiveness of Gamification in Mobile Language Learning Applications: A Mixed-Methods Study. *Education and Linguistics Research, 9*(1), 29–42. Researchgate. https://doi.org/DOI: 10.5296/elr.v9i2.21425

Sanchez, E. (2017). Competition and collaboration for game-based learning: A case study. In *Instructional Techniques to Facilitate Learning and Motivation of Serious Games* (pp. 161–184). Springer Nature. DOI: 10.1007/978-3-319-39298-1_9

Smiderle, R., Rigo, S. J., Marques, L. B., Peçanha de Miranda Coelho, J. A., & Jaques, P. A. (2020). The impact of gamification on students' learning, engagement and behavior based on their personality traits. *Smart Learning Environments, 7*(1). https://slejournal.springeropen.com/articles/10.1186/s40561-019-0098-x

Tan, D. Y., & Cheah, C. W. (2021). Developing a gamified AI-enabled online learning application to improve students' perception of university physics. *Computers and Education: Artificial Intelligence*, 2, 100032, https://www.sciencedirect.com/science/article/pii/S2666920X21000266?via%3Dihub

Tao, J., Ferrão, S., Vitoria, F., & Silva, R. (2020). Gamification for Technology-Enhanced Language Learning (TELL) – Success factors of gamified language learning platform design. *Revista Iberoamericana de Informática Educativa, 31*, 54–69. Researchgate. https://www.researchgate.net/publication/342590083_Gamification_for_Technology-Enhanced_Language_Learning_TELL_-_Success_factors_of_gamified_language_learning_platform_design

Thompson, J., & Rains, S. (2022). *Chuck Coonradt: Data Creates a Culture of Growth - Blue Margin*. Www.bluemargin.com. https://www.bluemargin.com/ttd/forbes-grandfather-of-gamification-data-creates-a-culture-of-growth#:~:text=From%20this%20observation%2C%20Chuck%20started

Thurairasu, V. (2022). Gamification-Based Learning as The Future of Language Learning: An Overview. *European Journal of Humanities and Social Sciences*, *2*(6), 62–69. DOI: 10.24018/ejsocial.2022.2.6.353

Toda, A. M., Klock, A. C. T., Oliveira, W., Palomino, P. T., Rodrigues, L., Shi, L., Bittencourt, I., Gasparini, I., Isotani, S., & Cristea, A. I. (2019). Analysing gamification elements in educational environments using an existing Gamification taxonomy. *Smart Learning Environments*, *6*(1), 16. Advance online publication. DOI: 10.1186/s40561-019-0106-1

Vygotsky, L. (1978). *Mind in Society: The Development of Higher Psychological Processes*. Harvard University Press.

Yang, Q. F., Lian, L. W., & Zhao, J. H. (2023). Developing a gamified artificial intelligence educational robot to promote learning effectiveness and behavior in laboratory safety courses for undergraduate students. *International Journal of Educational Technology in Higher Education*, *20*(1), 18. DOI: 10.1186/s41239-023-00391-9

Chapter 3
Leveraging AI Tools to Enhance Writing Skills and Assessment in Language Education

Christina Kitson
https://orcid.org/0000-0002-3545-0955
University of Central Missouri, USA

Nabat Erdogan
University of Central Missouri, USA

ABSTRACT

This chapter examines the integration of artificial intelligence (AI) in education, particularly ChatGPT. It provides an overview of the historical use of computers in education and the recent advancements making AI tools more accessible. ChatGPT's applications in writing support, assessment, personalized learning, and language learning are explored, highlighting its potential to enhance educational experiences. The chapter addresses concerns regarding academic integrity, ethical use, and the need for clear policies on AI integration. It emphasizes the benefits for teachers, including lesson planning, grading assistance, and fostering student engagement. The chapter concludes that responsible AI use can significantly improve personalized learning, provide timely feedback, and support diverse ed-

DOI: 10.4018/979-8-3693-5477-3.ch003

ucational needs, suggesting a shift towards a process-oriented approach in education. The authors argue for a balanced approach that utilizes AI as a supportive tool while preserving the essential role of human teachers in fostering creativity, critical thinking, and ethical use of technology.

INTRODUCTION

Students have been utilizing computers for learning since the 1980s when individual computers became more widely available. Today, students have access to word processing software, electronic dictionaries, thesauruses, and the World Wide Web (WWW), which contains a wealth of information. Recently, Artificial Intelligence (AI) has become more approachable for users through the release of online applications that do not require coding or advanced AI knowledge. ChatGPT, an AI-powered conversational agent created by OpenAI, was made freely available online in the fall of 2022 and has since gained attention. It is important to understand what conversational agents, like ChatGPT, are and how they work. Noam Chomsky (Chomsky et al., 2023) provided an explanation of what these conversational agents are by stating that "Roughly speaking, they take huge amounts of data, search for patterns in it and become increasingly proficient at generating statistically probable outputs — such as seemingly humanlike language and thought" (p. 1). AI is capable of producing language that sounds like it was human created but was not. So, why do AI and ChatGPT exist? What are they supposed to do?

Here is a description of ChatGPT in its own words when asked: "What is ChatGPT?"

ChatGPT is a language model developed by OpenAI, based on the GPT (Generative Pre-trained Transformer) architecture. It is a variant of the GPT-3 model specifically fine-tuned for natural language understanding and generation in a conversational context. ChatGPT is designed to generate human-like responses in a chat or conversation format. It was trained using a diverse range of internet text and is capable of understanding and generating coherent and contextually relevant responses to user inputs. While it can be used for a variety of natural language processing tasks, its strength lies in generating human-like text and engaging in conversations. It has been used in various applications, including chatbots, virtual assistants, and other conversational interfaces. (OpenAI, 2024)

According to its description, ChatGPT is confident that it will have a significant impact on the world. Judging by the amount of attention it is receiving on social media (Wibowo et al., 2024), educational conferences and research papers (Lo, 2023), it seems likely that this prediction will come true. ChatGPT has been a major discussion topic in higher education. Many faculty members and instructors fear that students will use AI or AI assisted translators instead of doing their own homework and solving problems (Al-Jarf, 2024; Urlaub and Dessein, 2022; Zimotti et al., 2024), leading to a new kind of plagiarism that teachers will have to address (Guillén-Yparrea & Hernández-Rodríguez, 2024; Perkins, 2023). Perkins (2023) argues that to clarify students' use of AI-based tools and to determine whether doing so constitutes academic misconduct, careful policy development regarding academic integrity is required. It is essential to instruct students on how to use ChatGPT correctly and acknowledge their use of AI in their work.

Highlighting ChatGPT's countless creation possibilities compared to other AI platforms, Kasneci et al. (2023) state that it was "trained on a much larger dataset, i.e., texts from a very large web corpus, and have demonstrated state-of-the-art performance on a wide range of natural-language tasks ranging from translation to question answering, writing coherent essays, and computer programs" (p. 2). However, ChatGPT has also faced criticism. Chomsky (Chomsky et al., 2023) argues that ChatGPT's limited language ability is due to a lack of creativity and inability to differentiate between real possibilities and those that are not real, in other words real verifiable information is just as much a part of ChatGPTs training as false unverifiable information and ChatGPT can't tell the difference. This is a limitation of AI in regards to "critical thinking" but there are many other aspects of AI that are very useful. As reported by Kasneci et al. (2023), "[t]hrough the utilization of these models, opportunities for enhancement of learning and teaching experiences may be possible for individuals at all levels of education, including primary, secondary, tertiary, and professional development" (p. 2). This suggests that a less unique and more generic approach to language can be helpful for teaching fundamentals and consistency, even though it might lack creativity and critical thinking skills.

LITERATURE REVIEW

As Artificial Intelligence (AI) systems and machine learning algorithms continue to develop rapidly, there is growing interest in their potential applications for enhancing teaching and learning within education (Hartono et al., 2023; Kasneci et al., 2023; Pikhart, 2020). AI promises new modes of personalized and adaptive instruction powered by data analytics, automated assessment capabilities to ease instructor workload, and interactive virtual tutors that adapt to student needs (Tuomi, 2018). However, effectively leveraging these emerging technologies requires careful consideration of evidence-based best practices, ethical implications, and the optimal balancing of human teaching with AI support. There is also concern about the time investment required from teachers for integrating these technologies into their teaching and assessment practices, maintaining their proficiency with the tools, and adapting their instructional methods to work effectively with AI systems (Mohmed, & Elballat, 2024).

A prominent current application of AI in education involves using machine learning to develop intelligent tutoring systems (ITS) designed to provide customized learning support beyond the capacity of traditional stationary computer interfaces (Louly, 2024). This idea is not new, for example, as reported in 2014, AutoTutor helped teach physics concepts through conversational dialogue and responses to learner emotions (Nye et al., 2014). Alam (2023) focuses on AIs ability to adapt to learner needs, be personalized, and provide immediate feedback, making it an excellent tutor. Additionally, AI is increasingly used for automated analysis and scoring of written work. Tools such as writing mentors and e-graders provide instant formative feedback on drafts using criterion-based evaluations, helping students revise more effectively than peer reviews alone (Saeli et al., 2023). For instance, many companies, such as Educational Testing Service (ETS), have been using human and computer raters (e-raters) for years for tests such as the writing portion of the Test of English as a Foreign Language (TOEFL) (Condon, 2011; Ramineni & Williamson, 2013).

The advent of AI in education brings emerging benefits like offloading time-intensive tasks to optimize human teaching and increased personalization for self-directed learning outside the classroom, freeing teacher time for other activities and providing immediate tutoring many students need (Hartono et al., 2023). Researchers found that machine learning algorithms scored short written responses comparably to teachers while significantly faster, supporting more frequent feedback cycles (Saeli et al., 2023). Intelligent virtual teaching assistants helped students create deeper connections with content and facilitated the learning of concepts, fueling engagement compared to pre-recorded video lessons or simple chatbots (Essel et al., 2022). Virtual teaching assistants, such as ChatGPT, can personalize learning experiences, adjusting content to individual needs and facilitating natural interactions that increase student engagement (Correia, et al., 2024). AI also shows potential for enhancing accessibility and equity in education (United States Department of Education, Office of Educational Technology, 2023). AI can help automate the grading process, particularly in subjects like mathematics where speed of grading is important (Yang & Zhu, 2022). AI can also assist in providing students with personalized feedback (Sung et al., 2023).

AI does not have to work alone and can be a powerful tool to use in collaboration with a teacher or teaching assistant. This collaboration allows AI to provide support during the process as well as examples to improve their work (Pahi et al. 2024). When used alone, AI can help track student performance and adapt content allowing teachers more time to concentrate on other aspects of teaching (Kayali & Balat, 2024). All these points suggest that computers and AI can help ease the grading and feedback burden on teachers, thus saving time for other teaching tasks. A usage caveat, student data should not be directly entered into AI unless that student has consented, it is a controlled system where data stays local and it is not used to train the platform, and the school has approved this usage.

However, persistent challenges around ethical AI design, integration with learning sciences, and student privacy protection remain. Studies note concerns about over-automation in scoring complex competencies such as critical thinking or creativity, which require nuanced qualitative teacher insights (U.S. Department of Education, Office of Educational Technology, 2023). Educators also caution that technology platforms should supplement, not replace, human teachers' socio-emotional support capacities (Nye et al., 2014). Additionally, appropriate use policies must govern the constant collection of student learning data for power optimization algorithms (Kasneci et al., 2023). Further research on the ethical implementation of AI is necessary, along with conversations with students about ethical academic uses and appropriate attribution of AI assistance in their learning process.

As AI capabilities grow more sophisticated, emerging hybrid human-AI collaborations show immense promise in revolutionizing education (Hartono et al., 2023; Kasneci et al., 2023; Tuomi, 2018). Instead of competing with teachers, optimally designed intelligent assistants can enhance human expertise while managing repetitive tasks. Continued research synthesizing fields such as learning science, human-computer interaction, and ethics is essential to guide effective adoption (Xu et al., 2021). Overall, AI holds major disruptive potential in education, but thoughtfully directed through a student-centered lens, its classroom integration can enrich learning experiences. This chapter aims to explore different methods of using AI, and ChatGPT specifically, as the first publicly available and most common chatbot, for enhancing students' writing abilities, to discuss the revolutionary impact of AI on assessment practices, and to provide educators with insights and strategies for effective AI integration into their instruction and assessment.

Enhancing Writing Skills with AI

To promote writing excellence, ChatGPT can assist students in prewriting conception, outlining structure, expanding drafts, assessing coherence/flow, and identifying possible plagiarism. These interactive real-time features can help scaffold students throughout the writing process without AI directly generating content for the user. It can help teachers save time on repetitive drafting cycles while personalizing support. This also allows students to free-write with the opportunity to receive feedback that can help improve their writing, encouraging writing on topics that interest the student but might not be appropriate in an academic setting.

AI tools can also benefit language learners by providing personalized and immediate feedback on their language use, both in writing and speaking. For example, ChatGPT can introduce new vocabulary in context, provide definitions, and suggest synonyms, helping language learners to expand their lexicon and use words appropriately. It can also help students improve their grammar and syntax knowledge, as language learners can receive feedback on their grammatical errors as well as the cohesiveness and coherence of their writing. Students can also practice pronunciation in the target language using ChatGPT's speech recognition technology, which can help them improve their spoken language skills.

Using AI in Education for Collaboration

For collaborative work, ChatGPT can be easily accessed through video conferencing platforms such as Zoom. Instructors can simply share their screen with an open ChatGPT window and interact with it live, allowing the class to observe and participate. They can model constructive conversational prompts, search strategies, and follow-up questions. Then, students can be instructed to frame their own queries and evaluate ChatGPT's responses. This promotes critical thinking and technological literacy. Additionally, the whole-class can use the chat features in the screen-sharing platform and have students suggest text they want to use ChatGPT to understand. One person can be responsible for entering the information and sharing their screen with the results.

It is vital for students to understand that while ChatGPT collects some usage data for improvement purposes, it does not gather private personal information without consent, beyond what is required to have a Google account. In addition, there are many chatbots that do not use data entered for training and do not require additional personal data (beyond a Google account). Educators should verify that school policies permit AI tool utilization and inform students to avoid sharing identifiable details. Teachers can demonstrate positive usage principles that facilitate learning rather than banning student engagement with this rapidly emerging technology. Part of this process is to ensure that students understand why they are using ChatGPT or AI and what it means for them and their learning. When encouraging students to use ChatGPT, teachers should emphasize that all information entered into the system is viewable by someone, so users need to be mindful of what they share.

This is also an opportune time to establish rules for using AI and chatbots in learning. This is when educators should discuss academic honesty and the concerns surrounding issues like plagiarism and ethics. The definition of plagiarism is, according to Merriam-Webster, "to steal and pass off (the ideas or words of another) as one's own: use (another's production) without crediting the source" (Merriam-Webster.com). While a person can argue that AI is not "someone else", if you use AI to write for you, it is still using words that are not your own and portraying them as your own. Therefore, it is very important to teach about citing AI use and involvement in any work completed, as well as to focus on where the ideas are coming from. Overly using AI can also limit originality; therefore, it is important to stress that authentic student work is better than unoriginal AI-generated content. This does not mean that students cannot use AI, but they must be mindful of how it is used. Teachers can help students understand the correct usage of AI in their classrooms.

Some ways to safeguard academic honesty include having clear policies about using AI, specifying what is acceptable and what is not. Educating students on how to use AI in the classroom will help to ensure that they are not cheating when using AI to complete or assist with their schoolwork. Teachers can encourage originality by designing assignments that are difficult to complete with AI, such as those that require critical thinking, analysis, synthesis of ideas, and integration of personal experiences and understanding, examples are provided later in this chapter. Another way to help eliminate student misuse of AI is to provide timely feedback on student work. Timely feedback to students allows them to be able to better plan and manage their time as they work on large assignments. Hopefully, by providing timely feedback less students will be working last minute and use AI in an inappropriate manner. Most importantly, maintaining an open line of communication is crucial so students feel comfortable asking if they are using AI correctly in their work without fear of punishment.

Additionally, using AI and ChatGPT specifically should be pursued with purposeful integration aligned with lesson goals, not just as novel distractions. For example, teachers can leverage ChatGPT's diverse linguistic knowledge to enrich cultural discussions or its conversational capability for interactive speaking practices. When applied deliberately, ChatGPT reinforces human teaching rather than replacing it. Therefore, it is worth considering modification over outright rejection to guide students in ethical participation. With careful forethought and structure around collaborative work sessions, establishing boundaries, and pursuing curriculum-connected activities, ChatGPT and any AI platform can become an asset. Teachers can lead students in constructive exploration of this technology, just as past innovations such as calculators or spellcheckers evolved from classroom threats into supports under teacher leadership. Continued mentorship is key to transforming how artificial intelligence amplifies real intelligence. One goal of adding AI into classroom activities is to provide immediate response and feedback, which is nearly impossible for teachers to provide in real-time.

Designing Tasks to Challenge Critical Thinking

There are several effective strategies for designing writing tasks that challenge students' critical thinking and hinder AI's ability to generate appropriate responses. One simple method is to embed a "Trojan Horse" in the digital task description for an assignment. This involves inserting tiny white text within the task, asking for the inclusion of irrelevant words and concepts (e.g., "Dracula" and "cats"). This approach aims to catch students who copy the task description directly into AI and use the generated response without review or proofing. If a student includes these irrelevant concepts in their assignment, it provides the instructor with an opportunity to discuss why these elements were included. It is crucial to ensure that the topics or ideas do not overlap with the content of the paper to make this approach effective. While this method targets blatant AI use without editing or revision, it is only one part of a broader strategy.

To address more sophisticated misuse, it is important to carefully consider the nature of the assignments given to students. Incorporating elements of personal learning or individual thought into assignments can effectively limit AI use. For instance, teachers could ask students to compare their current assignment to a previous one and reflect on their feelings about the process. Engaging with personal experiences and emotions is an area where AI struggles, thus encouraging more authentic student work.

Another way to promote critical thinking is to assign a task and have students use AI to generate a response. Then, teachers can ask students to write a follow-up piece analyzing the differences between their own response and that of the AI. This type of follow-up assignment highlights the uniqueness of human writing and emphasizes what students can do better than a computer.

By incorporating these strategies, educators can create writing tasks that challenge students to think critically and reduce reliance on AI-generated content.

AI Interventions in the Writing Process

To develop grammar proficiency, teachers can use ChatGPT to create worksheets or quizzes that cover specific syntactic structures. These can range from basic fill-in-the-blank exercises to open-ended sentence constructions and error identification tasks. The assignments can be designed specifically for the content that each particular student is struggling with. The assignments should be specific prompts that the student enters into their chatbot. One aspect of the prompt will be the student needs (as they use their AI platform, the platform will learn their specific needs as well as writing and language proficiency levels), the specific content and format for the assignment, and how the information should be reported back to the student. If they are working independently, all feedback can go directly to the student in real time. Students can work through these personalized assignments, receiving automated scoring and feedback from ChatGPT. This might also mean printing or copying the assignment and turning it in to the teacher for review. This allows learners to strengthen their grammatical understanding at their own pace.

In the writing process itself, AI can be beneficial at various stages. Teachers should first identify which parts of the writing process they want students to complete independently and where AI assistance is acceptable. Transparency in this approach is crucial. Providing students with a checklist of writing steps, indicating which ones can involve AI assistance and what that might look like, can be very helpful.

During the prewriting and brainstorming phase, AI can assist with generating ideas, narrowing or widening the topic, finding related topics, and drafting a basic outline. In the drafting stage, AI can help organize ideas, suggest wording options (similar to a thesaurus), and provide feedback on drafts. As drafts become more complete, AI can assist with organization, cohesion and coherence checks, grammar and wording checks, citation and style checks, and suggestions for additional content.

Additionally, students can use AI to help draft multimedia aspects of assignments, such as starting a presentation or creating a how-to guide based on their paper's content. For academic writing, AI can ensure proper use of academic language and adherence to citation and style conventions. If research is needed, AI can help organize sources and provide proper citations.

However, it is important to note that many free AI chatbots (such as ChatGPT, Gemini, and Claude) are not effective at finding resources. Additionally, some AI chatbots, such as ChatGPT, can easily produce artificial hallucinations, which can potentially cause harm by spreading misinformation or leading to incorrect conclusions in research studies (Alkaissi & McFarlane, 2023). For research purposes, specialized AI-powered research tools can better find resources and related articles.

Ethical Use of AI in Writing Assignments

AI is not meant to replace the human element of writing but to enhance it. Understanding how to use AI appropriately in your context is crucial. The first step is to determine what is allowed regarding AI use and to be transparent about how you have used AI (if you have). This includes modeling good behavior by indicating when you have had help from AI, such as including a citation or a note explaining which AI tool you used and how you used it, and expecting the same from your students.

Educators should provide students with clear guidelines on when they can and cannot use AI in their assignments. This could be included in the rubric for each assignment or as a general guide for the class. The goal of ethical AI use is to ensure that AI is not being used to replace critical thinking. Critical thinking can be evaluated in many different ways, writing is just one of them. There may be times when writing is used in conjunction with other methods, such as in multimodal design. Like the transition from typewriters to word processors, we must consider the changes that AI will bring to the writing process.

One part of the transition to using AI for education is ensuring that our students' writing sounds human and connects with the topic on a deeper level. It is important for students to see and understand the differences between their writing and what AI can produce. AI can be beneficial in the writing process in several ways, such as editing for grammar and spelling and reviewing for cohesion and coherence. AI can quickly perform these tasks and provide feedback on its actions, aiding the learning process. The student will still need to review the feedback and suggestions on their writing from AI and make decisions about what should be changed and what they want to keep. This is the same process students should be used to for accepting grammar and spelling changes in Microsoft Word or Google Docs, but now the suggestions are coming from AI. An important part of the classroom conversation needs to discuss the author's voice, and how important it is for them to maintain their voice in their work.

Using AI to improve writing is a valuable application of this technology as a tool, similar to having a friend or a writing center review a draft and provide feedback. By integrating AI ethically and transparently, writers can enhance the writing process without compromising the integrity of the work.

Promoting Academic Integrity

A major concern among writing teachers regarding AI is plagiarism or academic honesty. To address this, we need to revisit our earlier definition of plagiarism and change the focus to claiming credit for work that is not one's own rather than using someone else's words as your own. This is particularly relevant since AI-generated content does not come from a specific "someone else," a point students often raise in their defense.

Detecting AI use is inherently challenging, as current AI detectors are unreliable. The idea of recognizing students' writing styles is also problematic because many students already use AI, making it difficult to distinguish between their original work and AI-assisted content. The most effective way to address AI-related plagiarism is to understand AI and help students understand it as well. By being clear about when and how AI can be used and how and when it is used, students can help the teacher see and understand their process. It is also possible to create quizzes from papers using the vocabulary a student used to create the quiz. Educators can have individual conferences with the students to discuss their ideas and vocabulary words. Teachers can also have their students sum their paper up, and evaluate how well they understood the concepts.

Educators should demonstrate AI's limitations, model proper usage, and teach students how to attribute AI appropriately in their work. Creating an AI usage checklist can help students disclose their use of AI and facilitate conversations about academic honesty. This checklist can be simple, listing various AI uses for students to check off, or more detailed, requiring explanations of how they used AI.

The first step in creating a code of academic integrity is to consider what you need to teach for your students to be successful and how AI fits into that plan. Once you have a general idea, you can have an open conversation with your students early on about integrating AI into the course. You can also invite students to participate in the process and help create a course policy that includes their input.

Outlining the ethical standards collaboratively and discussing how to uphold them are important steps. By involving students in both the policy creation and its enforcement, you can increase their buy-in and commitment to adhering to the established system.

Fostering a Shared Commitment to Academic Ethics

Involving students and educators in the collective creation and enforcement of academic ethics is essential. The focus should be on the authenticity of students' work and assessments. By implementing the approaches suggested in this chapter, the process becomes more manageable. However, there will still be instances where you might suspect a student of unethical AI use or be uncertain about their use of AI.

During these times, it is crucial to approach the conversation with the student thoughtfully. Teachers can:

- Have a discussion about the specific elements of the paper or project that make them suspect AI use
- See how well students understand the content that teachers question them about
- Ask directly if and how students used AI

- See if students omitted referencing the use of AI or if they intentionally left it out

Like other plagiarism issues students sometimes resist acknowledging wrongdoing, but often when provided with evidence they will admit to it. Unapproved AI use meetings will look much like other forms of plagiarism meetings. This process becomes smoother when you can refer to specific policies and AI rubrics established in your course, guiding the discussion towards how AI was used and ensuring transparency and accountability.

Shifting Focus to Assessment

Automated essay scoring powered by AI allows personalized feedback nearly instantaneously. AI can provide constructive comments on drafts based on rubrics. Students receive formative feedback within minutes, identifying weaknesses and guiding revisions. This complements peer reviews by offering an unbiased second opinion. By analyzing frequent issues across a class, teachers can tailor instruction more effectively.

Speech recognition AI provides immediate spoken language assessments. For example, the Flow by Wispr app (FlowVoice.ai) assesses fluency, pronunciation, and comprehension. This reduces teacher grading workload while providing detailed analytics for tracking progress. Regular low-stakes practice builds confidence. This app can be used on computers, tablets, and phones.

By automating routine grading, AI allows teachers to invest time in personalized interactions and creative lesson planning. However, AI assessment should augment rather than replace human evaluation. Balance is essential to avoid over-reliance on automated scores, which lack subjective judgment.

Transformative Role of AI in Assessment Practices

AI is here to stay, and it has already had a large impact on assignments and assessments. The authors of this chapter have heard a number of educators suggest it is time to go back to paper and pencil for writing tasks and assessments. This line of thinking is problematic as AI is only beginning to impact education, it makes more sense to argue for new approaches to writing assessment (Moorhouse, et al., 2023 & Pedersen, 2023). We do not know what this new approach will look like exactly in the future, but we want to make sure that we are preparing both ourselves as educators and our students for the world that they are in. AI allows us as teachers to give immediate personalized feedback to students in a way that was never possible before. In the past, early feedback for students was quite limited, because of a lack of teachers' time. Grades served as the final step, and teachers provided their comments to parents or directly to the students. Students often received basic feedback on report cards that indicated their performance as a student, sometimes getting the same comment from multiple teachers. As Learning Management Systems (LMS) became popular and tests were conducted in the LMS, it was also possible to provide basic feedback to wrong answers guiding the student to why it was wrong. These are all early primitive versions of computerized feedback, and AI can now provide this kind of feedback in seconds. AI can review content and provide nearly instant feedback on whatever issues you have asked it to review. This means each student could be prompting AI to give them feedback based on their own unique needs given to them by their teachers. This is an excellent way to use AI as a formative assessment tool. As a summative assessment tool, AI also has a role, especially when we look at multiple submissions from one student and look for themes or issues that the teacher has identified that the student has across their work. To do this, a teacher could enter all of their comments and feedback into AI and see what themes and overall performance indicators are identified. This could be done at the end of the course and based on the feedback the teacher has provided to the student on various assignments, creating a final report of the students' work.

Mitigating Excessive Reliance on AI

While we are focusing on the positive elements of AI, it is important to note that we do not want to create a generation that has dependence on AI and AI-created content. We want to create a generation of students who know how to use AI to make their work better, but do not rely on it to do their work for them.

Creating prompts that minimize dependence on AI-generated responses involves designing tasks and questions that encourage independent thinking, research, and personal reflection. Here are some strategies to achieve this:

1. **Encourage Critical Thinking:**
    a. **Questions:** Ask questions that can only be answered using multiple sources of information (synthesis) and connect to class content.
        i. Example: "How does the theme of power as discussed in class manifest in George Orwell's '1984'?"
        ii. Example: How do the strategies for learning vocabulary that we covered in class apply to understanding complex academic texts in English?
    b. **Tasks:** Use assignments that make students compare different sources of viewpoints to complete.
        i. Example: "Compare and contrast a paper you wrote with one AI created on the causes of World War I and World War II."
        ii. Example: "Read the text and reflect on Huong's experiences as an exchange student, and discuss how her experiences are similar to or different from your experiences as a language learner?"
2. **Promote Independent Research:**
    a. **Questions:** Have students invest time in researching information, especially completing forms provided to guide their investigation.
    b. Create questions that require specific key ideas or facts that will have to be looked up and require multiple sources for that information, including class lecture and discussion.
        i. Example: "What were the main causes of the American Revolutionary War according to at least three primary historical documents, and our course discussion?"
        ii. Example: "What are the most common errors made by English learners from your native language background, according to three different research articles/studies, discuss those errors based on class discussion?"

c. **Tasks:** Create assignments that ask for students to gather data or conduct experiments on their own.
    i. Example: "Conduct a survey on students' favorite outside of school activities, analyze the results, and prepare a presentation for class on your findings."
    ii. Example: "Conduct a survey on the most challenging aspects of learning English among your classmates. Analyze the results and prepare a presentation on strategies to overcome these challenges."

3. **Personal Reflection and Experience:**
    a. **Questions:** Ask for personal opinions, reflections, and experiences.
        i. Example: "Describe a time in the past when you felt your best. Describe why you felt so good, and what you learned about yourself from that process?"
        ii. Example: "Reflect on a movie, book, or song in English that had a significant impact on you. Why did it resonate with you, and how did it influence your understanding of the language and culture?"
    b. **Tasks:** Design assignments that have self-analysis or personal growth as an aspect.
        i. Example: "Write a reflective essay on your progress over the past year and set goals for the next one."
        ii. Example: "Write a reflective journal entry to evaluate the effectiveness of the strategies and techniques you've used for learning English. Which methods have worked best for you, and which ones do you plan to adjust or change moving forward?"

4. **Collaborative Work:**
    a. **Questions:** Create activities that require group work to complete.
        i. Example: "As a group, create a list of the most important skills for being successful in life, and propose a program to ensure that people can acquire those skills."
        ii. Example: "As a group, explore the impact of English language proficiency on career opportunities in a globalized world."
    b. **Tasks:** Assign group projects where each group member has a distinct role and responsibility (could be assigned by the teacher or the group).

    i. Example: "Working in a group, create a presentation about different books that you would like to read for class, with each member focusing on a different book"
    ii. Example: "As a group, create a collaborative podcast about famous landmarks in English-speaking countries, with each member taking a distinct role (researcher, interviewer, script-writer, editor, presenter, etc.)"

5. **Encourage Originality and Creativity:**
    a. **Questions:** Design questions that ask for creative or original thought and unique solutions.
        i. Example: "What would your dream future society look like?"
        ii. Example: "Imagine you have the ability to create a new English word. What would it be, and what would it mean? How would you introduce this word into everyday conversations?"
    b. **Tasks:** Create creative activities like writing a story, designing an experiment, or creating something visual (artwork).
        i. Example: "Write a short story using the themes from class that incorporates elements of fiction and imagery."
        ii. Example: "Write a digital storybook for children that introduces them to basic English vocabulary and concepts."
6. **Utilize Authentic Assessments:**
    a. **Questions:** Ground assessments and assignments to real-world problems and applications when possible.
        i. Example: "How can the community support the children living in it?"
        ii. Example: "What initiatives could schools take to better support immigrant students and families adjusting to a new educational system?"
    b. **Tasks:** Create projects that address real-world products or solutions.
        i. Example: "Identify and define a current social issue here at school and develop a plan to solve the issue."
        ii. Example: "Identify a cultural barrier that affects communication in your community and propose strategies to promote cultural understanding."
7. **Scaffold Learning:**

a. **Questions:** Design your education plan around progressively more challenging questions/activities/assignments that bring in prior knowledge.
    i. Example: "What are the basic principles of economics? How do we apply these principles to the current global market?"
    ii. Example: "Describe the role of technology in education today. How can English language learners use technology to enhance their language acquisition and communication skills?"
b. **Tasks:** Integrate older content into current exams and assignments.
    i. Example: "Use what we have learned about literary analysis to create a checklist for what makes a good book, and create a rubric for students to review books in their class libraries."
    ii. Example: "Apply your understanding of grammar rules and sentence structure to create an editing checklist for improving written English. Develop a rubric to assess peers' writing samples based on these criteria."

By using these strategies, educators can create tasks and assignments that foster independent thinking, encourage personal engagement, and minimize the reliance on AI-generated responses. Teachers might use only one strategy or multiple strategies within an assignment or assessment. It is important to think about each step of the process as there might be good ways to combine the strategies through the steps in the assignment. It is also a good idea to base assignments and assessments off of in-class learning, discussion, and activities whenever possible. This helps create a unique version of knowledge that AI will not be able to address in a response, but active learners will have no problems incorporating into their work.

AI Tools for Educators

AI offers significant benefits for educators, particularly in providing immediate feedback and scoring. This can greatly assist students before they submit assignments or assessments. Additionally, students can use AI to create self-study materials for major exams, incorporating timed aspects, withholding answers until completion, and providing basic feedback on their submitted materials. At the end of this chapter is a short list of websites that compile AI resources for education.

Several platforms offer grading assistance for educators, often requiring a subscription fee from the school, organization, or university. These resources can grade early drafts and provide feedback, reducing the workload for educators who might have too many students to review all drafts thoroughly. This process can be integrated into the planning stage, where all early drafts are reviewed by AI, graded according to a rubric, and the feedback is provided to students. The final version is then submitted to the instructor, along with the AI feedback, allowing the teacher to see what has been done and what AI has suggested.

Educators can also use AI to assist with various tasks. AI can create basic lesson plans that teachers can then tailor to their individual students' needs. It can modify existing lesson plans to differentiate instruction and suggest quick activities or interactive elements that align with the curriculum or standards. This can be much faster than searching for ideas online.

Moreover, AI can help teachers organize their schedules, write reports, and draft communications with parents and administrators. It can also assist with basic translation, which is particularly useful for teachers with students whose first language they do not know. The diverse applications of AI can benefit both students and educators, enhancing the overall educational experience.

While AI can significantly enhance efficiency, teachers' solid content knowledge is crucial to ensure accuracy and relevance of AI-generated materials. Teachers must carefully review AI-generated resources to make sure that the instructional content is accurate and meets the lesson objectives and needs of their students.

Designing Balanced Prompts and Lesson Plans

Throughout this chapter, the importance of balancing AI and student work to demonstrate genuine learning and understanding has been emphasized. As educators, it is crucial to thoughtfully plan and respond to AI integration in our classrooms. This approach will vary among teachers, subjects, and grade levels, reflecting the unique processes of each classroom. The key objective is to ensure that students are showcasing their own learning, not merely submitting AI-generated content.

To achieve this balance, assignments should thoughtfully integrate AI and student learning. AI should be used as a support tool, similar to existing resources, to provide assistance that the teacher may not be able to offer directly. This support can include editing, immediate feedback on students' work, and even generating art to illustrate their writing.

Encouraging critical thinking and reflection on the learning process remains paramount. By thoughtfully incorporating AI in a way that complements student work, we can enhance the educational experience without undermining the authenticity of student learning. The goal is to leverage AI as a supportive tool that enhances the resources and assistance available to students, allowing them to demonstrate their understanding and creativity effectively.

Showcasing Versatile AI Tools

AI overall is advancing so quickly that it would be impossible to keep up with the new tools and resources available. This section will focus on a few options for bringing AI into your classroom. This is by no means an exhaustive list and nor will you find an exhaustive list anywhere.

ChatGPT, developed by OpenAI, is a powerful language model based on the GPT-4 architecture. It is designed to understand and generate human-like text, making it a versatile tool for various applications. In education, ChatGPT offers numerous possibilities, ranging from personalized learning experiences to administrative support. This detailed exploration looks at the diverse applications of ChatGPT in education, highlighting its potential for use in teaching and learning.

One of the first big concepts of ChatGPT and other chatbots is personalized learning. ChatGPT can serve as a virtual tutor, providing personalized assistance to students. It is capable of answering questions on a wide range of subjects, offering explanations tailored to the student's level of understanding, and providing additional resources for further study. Since this can be done individually with a few prompt alterations, each student can receive the support level that they need from ChatGPT. Another key concept is the way ChatGPT can support writing and research. As students write and research assignments, they can use ChatGPT to help them brainstorm and organize their ideas, provide feedback on drafts with a focus on grammar, coherence, and style, and assist with citations and bibliographies, ensuring style is followed. One very valuable aspect of this is that the student can get this feedback at any time of day or night. This is extremely helpful for those that might not have access to a writing center or writing resource help, or those with difficult schedules.

A third way to enhance teaching and learning is in language learning itself. ChatGPT can act as a conversational partner to practice speaking (through voice extensions and new GPT features that continue to be developed) and writing. It provides instant translations and can explain language nuances to the user. ChatGPT can create endless exercises to improve vocabulary and grammar skills. One of the most unique aspects of this is cultural nuance. ChatGPT can answer questions about why things are done or referenced in a certain way in a specific place (like understanding the southern use of "bless his/her heart," which is different from other areas in the US), which can aid in improving language learners' pragmatic competence in the target language. Often, being able to ask ChatGPT quickly is a low-stress way for the learner to understand a concept or an intended meaning without having to ask.

The ability to talk to ChatGPT can be achieved through the use of version 4.0 or a browser extension called VoiceWave available for Google Chrome or Microsoft Edge. This capability offers numerous advantages, particularly for language learning and expanding resources for individuals with physical limitations that make typing difficult. With the extension, a student can hold a conversation with ChatGPT in different languages, though English is the most robust version in the system. There are various settings for input language, output language, voice, accent, and more.

One of the main advantages is the ability to work on pronunciation. ChatGPT can be prompted to provide basic feedback on pronunciation, helping students improve their spoken language skills. Another advantage is that everything said is typed on the screen. This feature benefits those who are not proficient typists, providing them with a typed version of what is spoken.

Additionally, this conversational capability can enhance accessibility for students with disabilities. For example, students with visual impairments or motor disabilities can interact with ChatGPT without needing to type, thus making learning more inclusive. Furthermore, the ability to use voice commands can support multitasking, allowing students to engage with educational content while performing other activities.

The real-time interaction provided by VoiceWave can also foster more engaging and dynamic learning experiences. Students can ask questions, seek clarification, and receive instant feedback, which can help reinforce learning and understanding. This immediate interaction can simulate a more natural conversational practice, making it especially useful for language learners aiming to develop fluency and conversational skills. This can also aid pragmatics development as students can work with scenarios that ask for appropriate responses and provide example interactions based on student input.

Moreover, the ability of many AI platforms to switch between languages and dialects can be particularly useful for students learning multiple languages or dialects, as they can switch to any language they would like to work on. This feature allows for a more personalized learning experience, accommodating diverse linguistic needs and preferences (Ekellem, 2024).

In addition to aiding learners, there are many benefits to teachers' use of ChatGPT, including administrative and pedagogical support. One of the biggest uses has already been discussed previously in this chapter, and that is lesson planning. Teachers can use ChatGPT to generate lesson plans and educational materials, customize lesson content to meet diverse learner needs, and create engaging activities and interactive learning experiences. Most state standards and benchmarks are part of the corpus ChatGPT uses, so you can write a lesson plan to your specific standards as well as to a specific format for the plan. For instance, you can tell it you would like a Sheltered Instruction Observation Protocol (SIOP) based plan and then add the standards for your state. Once that is done, you can ask it to add differentiation for your specific Individualized Education Plan (IEP) as needed. Then modifications can be made by the teacher to best address their specific learners and classroom needs. This is also a great way to create quick and easy substitute plans that many districts are requiring. It is important to note that teachers shouldn't completely rely on

AI-generated instructional resources and must check and improve them if needed to ensure that the created materials are accurate content-wise and serve the purpose of the specific lesson they are designed for.

ChatGPT can also provide assistance with grading and feedback by automatically grading objective assignments such as quizzes, offering constructive feedback on essays and open-ended responses, and helping teachers manage large volumes of student work effectively. A teacher could enter all their feedback for a particular student or class and look at overall themes as well as trends in their learning. Then the teacher could use ChatGPT to help write the report using that data.

As we discuss creating lesson plans, it is also important to note that ChatGPT can help enhance student engagement. ChatGPT can be used as an interactive learning tool. Educational chatbots can help guide students through learning modules, virtual assistants can provide real-time help during online courses, and ChatGPT can help create a gamified learning experience to make learning more fun. With changes to ChatGPT and the launch of their free 4.o version, using existing chatbots by all users is easier, but it is also possible to create your own chatbot for your educational context. ChatGPT also enhances collaboration and communication. It can help facilitate group discussions and brainstorming sessions (especially with new integration into Google Docs and search engines), help students organize and manage project tasks, and provide real-time support for questions and challenges as they come up. It is important to model these uses so students can see how to do this as they work independently with ChatGPT. It is also possible to provide some basic prompts to get students started with any AI platform.

No discussion of ChatGPT or AI is complete without talking about ethical considerations and best practices. This is a conversation that should occur with all students before giving permission to use any AI in their work. To maintain academic integrity, it is crucial that all students are educated on the ethical use of AI tools. Each class should develop clear guidelines on when and how to use ChatGPT in their work. All students and their work should be monitored to ensure originality and authenticity. This can be done in a variety of ways depending on your context but might include a statement of AI use, submission of AI prompts and feedback, and/or submission of an AI completed version of the prompt. Another aspect to educate students on is data privacy. Protecting student data is vital, so teachers need to ensure that ChatGPT usage complies with data privacy regulations (from the school, parents, and ChatGPT itself), inform students about what data is collected and how it is used, and implement measures to safeguard sensitive information. This might look like a guide to share with students the kind of information that is safe to enter and what they should not be entering into any AI system. These conversations should occur before using AI with students as well as during the process of using AI. It is important to ensure the proper ethical use of any AI system with students.

There are a lot of future prospects and challenges when using AI in the classroom. AI is constantly improving. This means that it should continuously improve in accuracy and understanding. It will be able to provide more sophisticated and nuanced educational support in the future, and it will become better at adapting to the changing needs of educators and students. This means that we will have to continue as educators to use and learn what the capabilities of AI are to ensure the best use in the classroom and on assignments. Right now, there are some limitations to ChatGPT, which include the potential for generating incorrect or misleading information - hallucinating (when it fabricates a resource that does not exist), challenges in understanding context-specific nuance in language, and, as previously discussed, the need for continuous monitoring to ensure appropriate use. As educators, we have always had to keep up with aspects of technology to be efficient in our teaching approach and use in the classroom. ChatGPT and AI will now be added to the list of technologies that we will have to keep up to date on. This does not mean that we will need to be experts in all aspects of technology or AI, but that we will need to know the basics to understand how to integrate and exclude AI use in our activities.

CONCLUSION

There is no specific timeline for integrating AI into education or your classroom, but it is already here. AI will continue to be integrated more and more into education in the next decade. This means teachers need to be educated in how to use AI, identify improper AI use, and teach students proper AI use. This chapter has provided many actionable steps and strategies for implementing AI in the classroom. It is important to note that AI will become part of a continuous cycle of learning and adaptation for teachers and students.

As educators, we need to focus on a collaborative approach that promotes integrity and innovative assessment. AI is a powerful ally in advancing student learning, but learning about AI and how to use it is also part of preparing students for the digital age. It is crucial to keep ethical use and misuse in mind, ensuring that students are aware of how to use AI responsibly and effectively.

By incorporating AI into our teaching practices, we can enhance personalized learning, provide timely feedback, and support diverse learner needs. For example, AI tools like ChatGPT can serve as virtual tutors, offer writing and research assistance, and facilitate language learning through conversational practice. These tools can help students brainstorm, organize their ideas, receive feedback on drafts, and improve their language skills, all while accommodating different learning styles and schedules.

Additionally, AI can support teachers in administrative tasks such as lesson planning, grading, and providing feedback. With AI's help, teachers can create customized lesson plans, generate educational materials, and offer differentiated instruction to meet individual student needs. AI can also assist in grading objective assignments and providing constructive feedback on essays, helping teachers manage large volumes of student work more efficiently.

Overall, the integration of AI into education is not just about using new tools but about fostering a culture of continuous learning and adaptation. By embracing AI and its potential, we can create more engaging, effective, and inclusive learning environments that prepare students for the future. As we integrate AI more into our classrooms the focus of education will likely need to shift from being product oriented, i.e. a paper or test, to being process oriented, focusing more on what is being learned and applied as part of the learning process.

REFERENCES

Al-Jarf, R. (2024). Students' assignments and research papers generated by AI: Arab instructors' views. *Journal of Computer Science and Technology Studies*, *6*(2), 92–98. DOI: 10.32996/jcsts.2024.6.2.11

Alam, A. (2023). Harnessing the power of AI to create intelligent tutoring systems for enhanced classroom experience and improved learning outcomes. In G. Rajakumar, Ke-Lin Du, & Álvaro Rocha (Eds.), *Intelligent Communication Technologies and Virtual Mobile Networks* (pp. 571–591). Springer Nature Singapore. DOI: 10.1007/978-981-99-1767-9_42

Alkaissi, H., & McFarlane, S. I. (2023). Artificial hallucinations in ChatGPT: Implications in scientific writing. *Cureus*, *15*(2). Advance online publication. DOI: 10.7759/cureus.35179 PMID: 36811129

Chomsky, N., Roberts, I., & Watumull, J. (2023, Mar 08). *Noam Chomsky: The false promise of ChatGPT: Guest essay.* Retrieved June 30, 2023, from https://www.nytimes.com/2023/03/08/opinion/noam-chomsky-chatgpt-ai.html

Condon, W. (2011). Reinventing writing assessment: How the conversation is shifting. *WPA. Writing Program Administration*, *34*(2), 162–183.

Correia, S. G., Lima, L. A. de O., Lourenço, E. M. da S. M., Filho, T. A. G., Melo, R. J. de, Manca, R. da S., Santos, A. M. dos, Abreu, A. V. N. de, Coelho, E. C. da S., & Santos, J. L. D. de M. (2024). Applicability of artificial intelligence in the teaching and learning process. *Seven Editora*, 651–661.

Ekellem, E. (2024). Enhancing multicultural and multilingual education through problem-based teaching with conversational AI: A ChatGPT perspective. *TechRxiv*. DOI: 10.36227/techrxiv.170593903.35081891/v1

Essel, H. B., Vlachopoulos, D., Tachie-Menson, A., Johnson, E. E., & Baah, P. K. (2022). The impact of a virtual teaching assistant (chatbot) on students' learning in Ghanaian higher education. *International Journal of Educational Technology in Higher Education*, *19*(1), 57. DOI: 10.1186/s41239-022-00362-6

Guillén-Yparrea, N., & Hernández-Rodríguez, F. (2024). Unveiling generative AI in higher education: Insights from engineering students and professors, *2024 IEEE Global Engineering Education Conference (EDUCON)*, Kos Island, Greece, pp. 1-5, DOI: 10.1109/EDUCON60312.2024.10578876

Hartono, W., Nurfitri, N., Ridwan, R., Kase, E., Lake, F., & Zebua, Y. R. (2023). Artificial intelligence (AI) solutions in English language teaching: Teachers-students perceptions and experiences. *Journal on Education, 6*(1), 1452 -1461. https://jonedu.org/index.php/joe/article/view/3101

Kasneci, E., Sessler, K., Küchemann, S., Bannert, M., Dementieva, D., Fischer, F., Gasser, U., Groh, G., Günnemann, S., Hüllermeier, E., Krusche, S., Kutyniok, G., Michaeli, T., Nerdel, C., Pfeffer, J., Poquet, O., Sailer, M., Schmidt, A., Seidel, T., & Kasneci, G. (2023). ChatGPT for good? On opportunities and challenges of large language models for education. *Learning and Individual Differences, 103*, 102274. DOI: 10.1016/j.lindif.2023.102274

Kayalı, B., & Balat, Ş. (2024). Assessment, evaluation, and feedback in online education with artificial intelligence-supported tools. In Bansal, R., Chakir, A., Hafaz Ngah, A., Rabby, F., & Jain, A. (Eds.), *AI algorithms and ChatGPT for student engagement in online learning* (pp. 124–135). IGI Global., DOI: 10.4018/979-8-3693-4268-8.ch008

Lo, C. K. (2023). What is the impact of ChatGPT on education? A rapid review of the literature. *Education Sciences, 13*(4), 410. DOI: 10.3390/educsci13040410

Louly, N.M. (2024). Application of AI tools in education - A conceptual framework. *Recent trends in Management and Commerce* 5(2), 1-7. https://doi.org/DOI: 10.46632/rmc/5/2/1

Mohmed, H. E. F., & Elballat, D. B. (2024). The attitudes of faculty staff members and their assistants towards students' use of AI tools in scientific research: The attitudes of faculty staff members and their assistants towards students' use of AI tools in scientific research. [IJHS]. *International Journal of Humanities and Social Science, 1*(1), 49–61. DOI: 10.69792/IJHS.24.1.5

Moorhouse, B. L., Yeo, M. A., & Wan, Y. (2023). Generative AI tools and assessment: Guidelines of the world's top-ranking universities. *Computers and Education Open*, *5*, 100151. DOI: 10.1016/j.caeo.2023.100151

Nye, B. D., Graesser, A. C., & Hu, X. (2014). AutoTutor and family: A review of 17 years of natural language tutoring. *International Journal of Artificial Intelligence in Education*, *24*(4), 427–469. DOI: 10.1007/s40593-014-0029-5

Open, A. I. (2024). ChatGPT (June 20 version) [Large language model]. https://chat.openai.com/chat

Pahi, K., Hawlader, S., Hicks, E., Zaman, A., & Phan, V. (2024). Enhancing active learning through collaboration between human teachers and generative AI. *Computers and Education Open*, *6*, 100183. Advance online publication. DOI: 10.1016/j.caeo.2024.100183

Pedersen, I. (2023). The rise of generative AI and enculturating AI writing in postsecondary education. *Frontiers in Artificial Intelligence*, *6*, 1259407. Advance online publication. DOI: 10.3389/frai.2023.1259407 PMID: 37635912

Perkins, M. (2023). Academic integrity considerations of AI Large Language Models in the post- pandemic era: ChatGPT and beyond. *Journal of University Teaching & Learning Practice*, *20*(2). Advance online publication. DOI: 10.53761/1.20.02.07

Pikhart, M. (2020). Intelligent information processing for language education: The use of Artificial Intelligence in language learning apps. *Procedia Computer Science*, *176*, 1412–1419. DOI: 10.1016/j.procs.2020.09.151 PMID: 33042299

Plagiarize. 2024. In Merriam-Webster.com. Retrieved September 24, 2024, from https://www.merriam-webster.com/dictionary/plagiarize

Ramineni, C., & Williamson, D. M. (2013). Automated essay scoring: Psychometric guidelines and practices. *Assessing Writing*, *18*(1), 25–39. DOI: 10.1016/j.asw.2012.10.004

Saeli, H., Rahmati, P., & Koltovskaia, S. (2023). Learner engagement with written corrective feedback: The case of automated writing evaluation. *Journal of Response to Writing*, *9*(2), 1. https://scholarsarchive.byu.edu/journalrw/vol9/iss2/1

Sung, G., Guillain, L., & Schneider, B. (2023). Can AI help teachers write higher quality feedback? Lessons learned from using the GPT-3 engine in a makerspace course. In Blikstein, P., Van Aalst, J., Kizito, R., & Brennan, K. (Eds.), *Proceedings of the 17th International Conference of the Learning Sciences - ICLS 2023* (pp. 2093–2094). International Society of the Learning Sciences., https://repository.isls.org//handle/1/10177 DOI: 10.22318/icls2023.904961

Tuomi, I. (2018). The impact of artificial intelligence on learning, teaching, and education. M., Cabrera, R., Vuorikari, & Y., Punie (Eds.), *Policies for the future*. Publications Office of the European Union.

Urlaub, P., & Dessein, E. (2022). From disrupted classroom to human-machine collaboration? The pocket calculator, Google Translate, and the future of language education. *Journal of Linguistics and Language Teaching*, *14*(1), 45–59.

U.S. Department of Education, Office of Educational Technology. (2023). *Artificial intelligence and future of teaching and learning: Insights and recommendations*. Washington, DC. Retrieved from https://tech.ed.gov

Wibowo, G., Gunawan, I., & Sunuantari, M. (2024). Social network analysis# ChatGPT on social media. *International Journal of Innovative Research in Multidisciplinary Education*, *3*(07), 1178–1186. DOI: 10.58806/ijirme.2024.v3i7n02

Xu, Y., Liu, X., Cao, X., Huang, C., Liu, E., Qian, S., & Zhang, J. (2021). Artificial intelligence: A powerful paradigm for scientific research. *Innovation (Cambridge (Mass.))*, *2*(4), 100179. DOI: 10.1016/j.xinn.2021.100179 PMID: 34877560

Yang, H., & Zhu, K. (2022). Research on AI-assisted grading of math questions based on deep learning, Proc. SPIE 12174, *International Conference on Internet of Things and Machine Learning (IoTML 2021)*, 121740X (22 April 2022); DOI: 10.1117/12.2628649

Zimotti, G., Frances, C., & Whitaker, L. (2024). The future of language education: Teachers' perceptions about the surge of AI writing tools. *Technology in Language Teaching & Learning*, *6*(2), 1–24. DOI: 10.29140/tltl.v6n1.1136

ADDITIONAL READING

Artificial Intelligence. Office of Educational Technology. (2024, July 17). https://tech.ed.gov/ai/

Eric, C. (n.d.). Control Alt Achieve: Transforming education with technology. https://www.controlaltachieve.com/

Futurepedia. (2024). *Find the best AI tools & software*. Boost Productivity. Embrace AI. https://www.futurepedia.io/

Gokcearslan, S., Tosun, C., & Erdemir, Z. G. (2024). Benefits, challenges, and methods of Artificial Intelligence (AI) chatbots in education: A systematic literature review. [IJTE]. *International Journal of Technology in Education*, *7*(1), 19–39. DOI: 10.46328/ijte.600

Haristiani, N. (2019). Artificial intelligence (AI) chatbot as language learning medium: An inquiry. *Journal of Physics: Conference Series*, *1387*(1), 012020. DOI: 10.1088/1742-6596/1387/1/012020

Kemble, J. (2024). *Ai in education*. This is the Moment Tech Tools for Educators. https://wakelet.com/wake/Cdz80q8LuBQrGQygpbz93

Lee, A. V. Y. (2024). Staying ahead with generative artificial intelligence for learning: Navigating challenges and opportunities with 5Ts and 3Rs. *Asia Pacific Journal of Education*, *44*(1), 81–93. DOI: 10.1080/02188791.2024.2305171

Mao, J., Chen, B., & Liu, J. C. (2023, November 11). *Generative artificial intelligence in education and its implications for assessment - Techtrends*. SpringerLink. https://link.springer.com/article/10.1007/s11528-023-00911-4

Miller, M. (n.d.). *AI in the classroom: 10+ tools for teachers*. Ditch That Textbook. Retrieved from https://ditchthattextbook.com/ai

Perkins, M. (n.d.-a). Academic integrity considerations of AI large language models in the post-pandemic era: ChatGPT and beyond. *Journal of University Teaching and Learning Practice*.https://open-publishing.org/journals/index.php/jutlp/article/view/635

Perkins, M., Furze, L., Roe, J., & MacVaugh, J. (n.d.-b). *The Artificial Intelligence Assessment Scale (AIAS): A framework for ethical integration of Generative AI in educational assessment. Journal of University Teaching and Learning Practice*.https://open-publishing.org/journals/index.php/jutlp/article/view/810

Wispr Flow. (2024). *WISPR flow: Effortless voice dictation*. Effortless Voice Dictation. https://www.flowvoice.ai/?trk=article-ssr-frontend-pulse_little-text-block

Zawacki-Richter, O., Marín, V. I., Bond, M., & Gouverneur, F. (2019). Systematic review of research on artificial intelligence applications in higher education: Where are the educators? *International Journal of Educational Technology in Higher Education*, *16*(1), 39. DOI: 10.1186/s41239-019-0171-0

Chapter 4
Overcoming Language Barriers With Artificial Intelligence

Hümeyra Yener
Ministry of Education, Sinop Education Directive, Turkey

Serdar Yener
https://orcid.org/0000-0003-1413-7422
Sinop University, Turkey

ABSTRACT

The impact of the unpredictable spread of artificial intelligence in education is also seen in language learning or language use. The use of AI to overcome or eliminate problems / challenges encountered in language learnings is getting more interest. This idea is also becoming more and more common. AI applications that focus on the problems faced in language learning can provide personalized learning environments. Through personalized learning models learning can be effective. In this study the problems encountered in terms of language learning will be mentioned. Then, the methods, techniques and applications based on AI which can be used to solve these problems will be mentioned. Besides theoretical approaches used to explain AI usage in language learning are presented. Popular AI based apps focusing on different language learning skills are described. Also limitations and suggestions for future work presented.

DOI: 10.4018/979-8-3693-5477-3.ch004

INTRODUCTION

Today, we are witnessing the unstoppable spread of technology. The emergence of Artificial Intelligence (AI), one of the latest developments in technology, has changed many areas of life. One of these dimensions is language learning, which is a challenge that almost every individual encounters. Learning a language requires a steady and challenging process. However, it is thought that artificial intelligence, which facilitates many aspects of life, can eliminate the difficulties of language learning. The positive results of the use of artificial intelligence in language learning and translation give hope for the future. AI can be used to overcome many language barriers that arise in multilingual and multicultural educational environments.

Education is becoming increasingly difficult in multicultural environments by the effect of globalization. The unique characteristics of multicultural environments require educators and students to have different perspectives. In this respect, the importance of this study lies in the difficulties posed by multicultural environments in language learning. In multicultural environment, personalized solutions or applications provide effectiveness. This also common for language teaching. Personalized solutions can also be used to overcome challenges in language teaching. Past experiences in the use of AI give hope for the future. With the help of AI, difficulties/challenges in language learning can be overcome with personalized methods.

The effectiveness of AI in language processing, language comprehension, and language proficiency development, personalized AI apps in language learning are some sub topics of this study. The study was conducted based on the literature review. In addition, AI apps in language learning were examined through case study method. Currently, the general features of AI apps used by learners in language learning are presented. The theoretical background of the study is based on several theories. This study on the use of artificial intelligence in overcoming barriers in language teaching is based on Input Hypothesis, Output Hypothesis and the Interaction Hypothesis. Supervised, unsupervised, and reinforcement learning models form the basis of artificial intelligence-based translation applications. These models are also mentioned in the study.

Problem Statement

Foreign language learning is a complex process that includes different dimensions and challenges such as personal characteristics, learning styles, motivation, cognitive processes, feedback, cultural factors, semantic understanding, personalization, pronunciation problems, and data privacy. Traditional methods often fall short of solving these issues and challenges, leading to inadequate learning outcomes. Artificial Intelligence (AI) technologies can be a viable tool to solve these issues and challenges. Looking at the current state of AI technologies, it is seen that their use in language learning topics and difficulties has been improved and new areas of use are being discovered. However, the potential of AI technologies to overcome foreign language learning issues and problems has not yet been fully explored. This study attempts to demonstrate the effectiveness of AI technologies in addressing the challenges of foreign language learning. It also aims to produce solutions based on AI technologies.

Significance of the Research

Foreign language learning is one of the main topics in the field of education and training all over the world. Recommending the use of AI technologies in language teaching, which is an issue that has not lost its importance from the past to the present, aims to close the gap between education and AI technologies. In addition, the research findings have rich content for both instructors, students and researchers. Presenting language teaching methods that differ according to personal characteristics through AI technologies can increase the effectiveness of language teaching by making language teaching immersive and enjoyable. It can also shed light on the solution of chronic language learning problems and issues.

LITERATURE REVIEW

Many approaches have been developed regarding the use of AI in education (Chen et al., 2022). AI, a machine-based algorithmic method, is widely used in the education sector to develop predictions, diagnoses, recommendations, and decisions about the future (Hwang et al., 2020). These smart applications, which are developed based on theories in education, provide technological developments, theoretical applications, personalized learning methods, learning feedback, and pedagogical effectiveness (Chen et al., 2022). Inequalities in education cause the educational inequalities/ gap among students to grow. In this respect, artificial intelligence can be used to eliminate the problems caused by educational inequalities. For example, artificial intelligence can be used to eliminate learning disabilities arising from students' past experiences, learning differences arising from students' personal characteristics, and deficiencies arising from situational factors (Roll and Wylie, 2016; Hinojo-Lucena et al., 2019). Seeing this effect, many countries have started to use artificial intelligence to increase the effectiveness of education in many institutions while working on the effective use of artificial intelligence in education (Srinivasan, 2022).

The impact of the unpredictable spread of artificial intelligence in education is also seen in language learning or language use (Son et al., 2023). The use of AI to overcome or eliminate problems / challenges encountered in language learnings is getting more interest. This idea is also becoming more and more common. AI applications that focus on the problems faced in language learning can provide personalized learning environments. In this study the problems encountered in terms of artificial intelligence in language teaching will be mentioned. Then, the methods, tecniques and applications based on AI can be used will be mentioned. Popular AI based apps focusing on different language learning skills are described. Also limitations and suggestions for future work presented.

1. Artificial Intelligence in Language Learning

Artificial intelligence describes technology which is used in tasks that require the use of human intelligence. AI is a type of computer software and performed to modelize human intelligence. Artificial intelligence uses people's behaviors, discourses, and experiences to generate projections for the future and present future states through prediction. Artificial intelligence uses many technologies such as statistics, machine learning, and deep learning. Different type of difficulties in language learning, are tried to be solved by using appropriate artificial intelligence softwares (IBM,

2022). Since the problems encountered in language teaching often require personalized interventions, artificial intelligence can be used effectively.

AI in language learning can be used to address the following challenges:

1. **Motivation:** Motivation is one of the main determinants in language teaching as well as in every learning process. When students' motivation is low, learning activity cannot be achieved. Therefore, measures should be taken to increase motivation in language teaching. It may be appropriate to use gamifying applications that will increase the motivation of students (Burke, 2016).
2. **Learning Styles:** Another problem encountered in language teaching is that students' learning styles are different. When you try to teach a foreign language to a student who has visual learning skills with auditory methods, you may not get the expected results. Therefore, methods suitable for the learning styles of the students should be chosen. effectiveness can be increased by using suitable learning methods for students' learning styles thorough AI applications (Chen, 2022).
3. **Cognitive Process: Students**' cognitive comprehension processes should be taken into account in language teaching. It may be hard to teach complex structured information to students. AI can ease it and can facilitate learning. In this way, students are prevented from experiencing stress and learning can be facilitated. Students can create cognitive schemes for language learning can be provided by artificial intelligence through seting up suitable learning environments.
4. **Personalization:** Students' personal characteristics affect their learning processes. For example, learning speeds, learning styles, psychological physical and physiological characteristics lead to learning differences. Through the use of artificial intelligence, personalized learning applications can be created for students with different characteristics (Chen, 2022).
5. **Feedback:** Feedback is an important tool for the development of learning. Informing students about their learning processes and providing support for their mistakes or deficiencies can increase the effectiveness of learning. Artificial intelligence applications

can provide feedback to students in skills such as speaking, writing, listening, and grammar in foreign language teaching (Barrot et al., 2023).

6. **Cultural Factors:** Cultural differences affect learning in language teaching, both in terms of source and target language. When the cultural lifestyles in which the target language is spoken do not match the student's culture, it becomes difficult for students to imagine. Learning slows down when students are unable to make logical constructs. Therefore, artificial intelligence applications can be used to reduce the impact of cultural differences. Students can be enabled to imaginage the target culture.
7. **Pronounciation Problems:** One of the biggest problems faced by students is the pronounciation problem. The solution of pronounciation problems faced by students in the classroom or individual students requires personalized education. Developing students' pronunciation skills requires hours of work. That's why teachers have the most problems with developing pronunciation. This problem experienced by teachers can be overcome by artificial intelligence applications. AI applications focused on pronunciation improvement can offer personalized tutorials (Huang et al., 2020).
8. **Semantic Understanding: Semantic** factors specific to the culture of the target language affect learning. Idioms, proverbs, anecdotes, jokes, and daily speech discourses used in the target language often slow down learning. Since students cannot form semantic meaning, their perception is weakened. Therefore, artificial intelligence can be used to facilitate semantic sense-making (Polaria et al., 2017).
9. **Data Privacy:** Another problem that students face in learning environments is data privacy. AI applications can enable students to improve their learning without using their personal knowledge.

In order to overcome the learning difficulties mentioned above, AI applications created by modeling human intelligence with software can be used. With the use of AI, personalized applications can be created in accordance with the proficiency level, cognitive processes, learning speed and learning style of the learners. In addition, methods can be developed to make the learning process fun.

There are many technologies and methods in which artificial intelligence is used in language teaching (Son et al., 2022).

1. Chatbox

Although the use of chatboxes goes back a long way, with the widespread use of artificial intelligence in recent years, it creates suitable learning environments for students with new forms (Wang et al., 2021). Chatboxes are generally used to describe software created to provide an online conversation environment within an organization or group. For example, chatboxes are used to provide instant information sharing of individuals working in different departments in a large enterprise. chatbox can be used in the production department of an enterprise to announce a problem related to production processes or to indicate a need. When employees enter a problem statement in the chatbox, other users react and the speech is continued to get solution (Fryer et al., 2017). The biggest contribution of Chatbox is that it provides instant information sharing. Messenger apps are examples of this. However, with the development of AI, many software developers, especially ChatGPT, provide users with a virtual chat environment. Students provide an input to the chatbox on any topic they want to learn. Chatbox provides the information requested by the user within the framework of the codes produced by the software developers by using open sources. It tries to answer students' questions using open resources on the internet platform. Students can write questions on any topic related to language learning in the chatbox. Chatbox can model a conversation in restaurant. Chatbox can accompany the students as if they were talking in the restaurant. Students can interact with the chatbox with both writing and speaking. That's because many chatboxes (Whatsapp, telegram, etc) are capable of automated speech recognition (ASR). In addition, ASR is also used on platforms such as ChatGPT platforms or Bing, which use artificial intelligence effectively. In this way, students can improve themselves not only by writing but also by speaking in the chatbox. However, it is considered that the use of voice-based chatbox may be more beneficial for the development of ponounciation skills of learners . Students feel comfortable which can help them develop faster when they find this speaking opportunities. Fear of speaking in public hinders the development of many students.

2. Automatic Speech Recognition (ASR)

Many different technologies are combined in the ASR method, which is used improve to understand students' speech and writing, to create feedback, to interact. Learners can interact with virtual partners in a foreign language with ASR, which combines different technologies such as language processing, voice recognition, speech transcription, notetaking, automatic transcribers, Today, especially those who go to different countries for touristic or business purposes can perform their daily dialogues in this way with the software they install on their smartphones. In these translation tools, which are used in airports, restaurants, museums and hotels, the spoken language can be transcribed, text translation can be generated and appropriate answers can be created. With ASR, students do not experience stress and learning is accelerated as they can get support when they need it. It can also be used anywhere without time and place restrictions. Currently, many virtual tools, especially google assistant, can be used for ASR purposes. Since ASR gives immediate feedback to users, it prevents users from experiencing stress. In addition, with the help of AI, ASR provides users with autonomous and personalized feedback. ASR can enable students to develop in many skills. For example, it can increase the capacity of frequently used vocabulary. In addition, they can increase their pronounciation capabilities. Perhaps one of the most beneficial uses is that it makes it easier for students to take notes. With speech recognition, when students or teachers speak, these speeches are transcribed. With the transcribed speaking performances, students' speaking skills can be evaluated. Mistakes made in speech can be revealed. By tracking the mistakes made by the students longitudinally, statistics can be created and used for machine learning. With the help of AI, students can be offered different activities through the use of appropriate data (Dai and Wu, 2023). ASR is a convenient method to provide personalized support to students. Software can be designed according to the needs and expectations of the students. Today, ASR is used in many industries. ASR can be used in communication with disabled persons, in translations of different languages in international diplomatic meetings, in the determination of dialects and dialects, and in the continuation of daily dialogues during visits of tourists to different countries. One of the most common applications in this regard is Google Assistant. When ASR is used with AI, supportive environments can be created to provide interaction environment for learners. Students do not experience stress during learning English with AI softwares using the ASR method. Their development can be faster because students can speak without stress. Tools such as the animated speaking environment provide students with relaxed speaking opportunities using ASR. The animated models used contribute to the development of the student by interacting with the learners like human. They create feedback to learners, correct their mistakes, and create new discours. Today, ASR uses common pronounciation models. However, when there are some dialects and incorrect pronounciation, the ASR method may not be effective. Therefore, students should have preliminary preparation and development in pronounciation.

3. Automated Writing Evaluation (AWE)

It can give clues about learners' learning of writing tasks in foreign language learning. The AWE method, which is based on automated causal discourse analysis, which identifies the mistakes made by students while writing and reveals which learning deficit the errors are caused by, strengthens the writing ability. In addition, with automated feedback, the instant evaluation of students' writing can be performed and errors are seen immediately. The corrections made by instructors by reading the texts of learners are both time-consuming and tiring. It can also be seen that teachers often do not give similar feedback to similar mistakes. AWE can ensure that feedback is standardized. Some software, such as Grammarly, uses the AWE method (Barrot et al., 2023). As can be seen from the example of Grammarly, students use AWE effectively with personalized learning in out-of-class environments. When we look at user experiences, the use of AWE is becoming more and more common. It is especially preferred because it provides autonomous learning. Regular use of software such as grammarly, which uses the AWE method, also includes self-correction options. AI functions in the AWE method based on the statistics/data of individuals' past spelling mistakes.

4. Natural Language Processing (NLP)

Natural Language Processing (NLP) is the study of understanding the language use of individuals. The NLP technique is used in many areas, especially translation, in language learning (Lee, 2023). The NLP technique is based on the interaction of machines and individuals in the use of language. With its language processing ability, NLP is used to identify the language used by individuals, to make sense of it contextually, to interpret it and to produce appropriate responses. NLP is used to support language teaching, to process students' feedback, to analyze student inputs, to develop architecture for facilitating learning, to produce learning materials according to the learning situation, and to determine the level of learning. In the learning process, NLP can facilitate due diligence and decision-making by determining the next step for both students and instructors. However, when studies are observed in general, it is seen that the level of awareness of both instructors and learners about NLP is low (Perez-Paredes et al, 2018). In language teaching, NLP can create conversation opportunities that will encourage students to use language. Or it can identify the texts written by the students, make sense of them and provide feedback. Based on this feedback, students' speaking skills or writing abilities can improve. Speech and writing recognition ability makes NLP stand out.

5. Data Driven Learning (DDL)

One technology that can be used to improve low proficiency learner' language learning is data driven learning (DDL), which is based on students' use of corpora. DDL based on using the corpora of language of learners. Learners' language corpora can be used in paragraph writing, reading tasks, scientific article writing to determine the level of the student and to design development program in language learnig. The words, phrases, idioms, and proverbs used by the learners shows level of corpora and give clues about the level of the students. With the datas obtained, the learning areas where the learners are inadequate can be identified and corrective suggestions can be developed. However, studies show that the positive effect of the DDL method on reading speed and lexicommatical size is limited (Hadley and Charles, 2017). Since the DDL method is based on students' previous knowledge and corpora, it can be more effective on their writing skills.

6. Computerized Dynamic Assessment

The CDA method, which is based on Vygotsky's zone of proximal development (ZPD) theory, is used to reveal the learning potential of the individual. Generally, while other methods aim to measure the knowledge and experience of individuals, CDA tries to reveal the level of cognitive development based on social interactions. Within the framework of the sociocultural approach, dynamic assessment is carried out by corrective feedback (CF) in the form of guiding the learners when they make mistakes or have difficulties, and correcting mistakes. Corrective feedback is based on the dynamic interaction between the learner and the instructor in the dynamic assessment process (Kamrood et al., 2021). Computerized type of dynamic assessment is also based on directing learners with corrective feedback when they make mistakes. For dynamic assessment without using a computer, each learner is paired with an instructor. For computerized dynamic assessment, learners are supported with computers. With the use of appropriate software, the difficulties faced by the students or the mistakes they have made can be overcomed with the AI software. With the use of appropriate software, students are ensured to develop dynamically. CDA also facilitates the workload of teachers as it provides personalized assessment support to learners during the development process of students. In addition, CDA gives students flexibility both physically and in terms of time. CDA can be used effectively in areas such as speaking, writing and listening to a foreign language. When evaluated in terms of the use of artificial intelligence, the development of students can be monitored longitudinally with the CDA method. With the longitudinal data, the developmental levels of the students can be followed. Statistics can be made of the mistakes made by the students. Learning goals and paths can be created based on students' experiences.

7. Intelligent Tutoring Systems (ITS)

Although it is similar to the CDA method, it has different features. In the CDA method, computers provide feedback dynamically, while in the ITS process, there is no obligation to provide dynamic feedback. In addition, ITS provides personalized support such as CDA. Students continue their development with the instructions given interactively with the ITS system. The ITS system provides efficiency in the EFL process. ITS can be used to support students' traditional language learning processes. ITS can be used as a mentor to reinforce and improve students' learning in the classroom. In the same way, ITS can be used to guide students who want to learn a foreign language with the help of standalone applications. ITS can be used for the development of learners of all age groups and learning levels. Past experiences can be used to predict the future projections or determine appropriate strategies with using AI based ITS. In addition, there are ITs that determine the needs of the learners and prepare teaching materials accordingly. ITS is used with many functions such as evaluating students' performances, detecting errors, giving feedback, and creating special worksheets for students. It can evaluate the mistakes made by students in areas such as grammar, reading, pronounciation, vocabulary and offer solution tools. It is seen that ITS is also used to enhance contextual and situational factors for learners. Cultural-specific informations can also be provided through ITS to learners. Especially in classrooms with a large number of students, the ITS system reduces the workload of instructors. Although studies on individualized feedback have improved ITS, more studies are needed.

8. Translation Tools.

One of the first uses of artificial intelligence is the language translation. Translation processes that take time and energy have been facilitated by AI. In particular, AI based translation applications use users' past experiences, cultural and semantic factors which can enhance effectiveness. The development of translation tools that translate pages of text in seconds continues. In order to use translation tools effectively, the input texts or documents must be qualitative and in appropriate grammatical structure in the source language. When the grammar structure is appropriate, translation tools can be run effectively. Otherwise, there may be problems in using translation tools. The most used tool in translation tools is Google translate. In addition, text or document translation functions of Microsoft Office tools are widely used.

Artificial Intelligence and Personalized Learning

One of the biggest problems faced by learners in foreign language learning is the differentiation of individual factors. The effectiveness of learning is based on individual factors, situational factors, organizational factors. These factors affect the success of learning in an interactive way. People's temperament and character traits affect their learning styles. Individuals' cognitive schemas, learning styles, and learning speeds necessitate personalized training. It is not possible for a teacher to interact one-on-one with each student in todays learning environments. While learners who can afford cost of private lessons can have this opportunity, it is impossible for other learners who can not afford. AI can be used to overcome this problem. AI supported software suitable for learners with different learning characteristics can be used effectively. Software suitable for learners ' characteristics can create learning program and curriculum based on students' feedback. AI-based software can increase the success of the learning process according to students' strengths and weaknesses and other situational factors (Choi, 2016). There are many personalized learning platforms developed based on artificial intelligence. There are more and more platforms to meet the needs defined within the framework of this concept called personalized language learning (PLL). PLL platforms increase the opportunities for autonomous learning tailored to learners ' individual characteristics. PLL platforms can be used to overcome challenges defined as motivation, learning styles, cognitive process, personalization, feedback, cultural factors, pronounciation problems, semantic understanding, data privacy (Choi, 2016; Lu et al., 2018). PLL platforms can contribute to learners by providing autonomy, increasing their motivation, and providing feedback. Some of the commonly used PLL platforms are presented below:

1. **Google Translate**: Google Translate tools have long been one of the most widely used software all over the world. In the past, in the first versions, they were used for literal translation (word-for-word), but later it has been developed to perform translation for context, idiomatic expressions, the overall message, communicative translation and interpretative translation. With the use of artificial intelligence, all these functions can be achieved with using open source and the resources provided by the developers to meet requirements. Using Natural Language Processing (NLP) technology, Google translate software contributes closing language gaps. AI leverages open sources and code to eliminate incompatibilities in both the target and source languages. Currently, the latest version of Google translate software can translate in nearly 150 languages. In addition, with data, image and audio processing technologies, verbal, textual and formal data can be input the platform. In addition, one of the most used features by individuals is the so-called speech mode, which can provide real-time instant translation (Lee, 2023).
2. **DeepL**: One of the biggest problems faced by software that provides translation services is that they translate directly based on word for word (literal) translation without considering context and content analysis. Translation softwares that translates texts or documents through content and context processing can increase the quality. DeepL software is a software produced to eliminate these problems encountered in the Translate process. Using a method called Neural Machine Translation (NMT), DeepL translates sentences or texts taking with using their contextual and contextual characteristics (Lee, 2023). NMT ensures the accuracy and validity of translations. In addition, culture-specific products such as idioms, proverbs, and sayings in the target or source language can be effectively translated through DeepL. Although it does not support the 150 languages that Google Translate supports, it can be used effectively in several languages.
3. **ChatGPT: ChatGPT,** one of the most widely used artificial intelligence software, is an AI based interaction robot based on the chat method. There are several versions of ChatGPT. In the generally used free version, ChatGPT can respond to users by scanning the resources of the database it has. Although these resources are not up-to-date,

they can generally provide users with highly accurate information. In addition, up-to-date open sources are widely used in paid versions. ChatGPT models people's speech and responses, creating responses similar to human responses. Machine learning algorithms are used to generate answers similar to ChatGPT human answers. ChatGPT, which is a functional interaction platform for students learning a foreign language, provides students with excellent answers and appropriate questions in terms of grammar and content, meeting the expectations. One of the most important benefits for students is that it provides feedback. Feedback, on the other hand, ensures that effective and healthy learning (Lee, 2023).

4. **Duolingo**: Duolingo, one of the most specialized artificial intelligence software in PLL, offers students the opportunity to learn in approximately 30 languages. Basically, it can provide learning effectiveness with its individual learning models created according to the characteristics of each language, cultural characteristics, and personal characteristics of the learner. Since Duolingo focuses only on language, it is based on language learning theories and learning theories. From the first interaction of the student, the teaching process of the student is continued with the models developed according to the learning level. It uses animations, reminders and psychological supports to increase the motivation and participation of the student. Since Duolingo focuses only on foreign language teaching, it can produce solutions for each of the problem topics in language teaching, such as motivation, learning styles, cognitive process, personalization, feedback, cultural factors, pronounciation problems, semantic understanding, data privacy. According to the statistics of the mistakes made by the students, the next processes can also be planned.
    2. **Rosetta Stone**: Another software that is similar to Duolingo is Rosetta Stone. It is a software that provides the necessary learning materials for personalized language learning and is based on AI technology. Rosetta Stone software provides learning material in around 24 different languages and often specializes in grammar and vocabulary. In addition, with its ASR it improves pronunciation through interactive lessons with learners. In addition, with native speakers, learners' development is realized with live lessons and

feedback can be created. The software ensures that motivation is maintained by constantly reminding students. In addition, a reminder is made to provide appropriate inputs at the appropriate time, regarding the physiological learning characteristics of learners.

3. **Langotalk:** Providing an interactive learning environment based on artificial intelligence technology, Langotalk supports language teaching in more than 30 languages. Langotalk software tries to keep students' motivation at a certain level through games, tests, and chats. It provides continuous feedback to students through instantaneous interactions. Continuous feedback ensures that learning is effective. The development process of the student is monitored instantly and adaptation is facilitated. It also gives students individual assignments on language learning to spread the learning.
4. **Talkpal.ai:** Talkpal.ai, which creates chat environments with voice, image and text inputs, was developed by GPT. Based on the AI technology developed by GPT, Talkpal.ai creates fluent and interesting speech content to ensure that the student's motivation is continuous. The instant and accurate feedback provided by the software ensures that learning is fast.
5. **Speak.com:** The Speak.com software, which focuses on the development of students' speaking skills, provides live interactions with native speakers. In addition, it is supported by virtual interactions. Students can have the opportunity to talk about any topic or situation in chat rooms with native speakers. Speak.com software prepares tools and content to eliminate students' speech errors or deficiencies with using AI based technologies. Students' speech is analyzed to reveal pronunciation, intonation and fluency of speech. According to the results of the analysis, learning programs are developed to focus on deficiencies.
6. **WordTap:** WordTap tries to improve students' vocabulary with interactive learning methods and processes based on AI technology. Wordtap provides continuous feedback, ensuring that students' learning is in control. Through entertaining and motivating processes and providing feedback, students are constantly reflected. Students also adapt to education through these processes. A healthy adaptation process can enhance students' self-confidence. Wordtap also

produces exercises that will enable students to practice. Students' vocabulary improves through the exercises provided by wordtap.

7. **Linguabot:** Another software to increase the development of students' speaking skills is based on Linguabot artificial intelligence technology. It allows students to improve their speaking skills online wherever and whenever they want. Linguabot enables students to grow by providing interactive conversation opportunities. Speaking skills are improved with animations and constant reminder messages that will increase the motivation of the students.

The common feature of the above-mentioned platforms is that they are based on AI technology. In addition, these platforms focused on the challenges defined as motivation, learning styles, cognitive process, personalization, feedback, cultural factors, pronounciation problems, semantic understanding, and data privacy. Learning models developed based on the development of students contribute to the development of the learning process with feedback, motivational tools and animations. The feature of all applications is the development of PLL I.

Theoretical Framework

The theoretical framework of the research can be based on several theories related to language learning and artificial intelligence. Theories can provide logical explanations for the relationship of AI in eliminating problems encountered in language teaching.

- **Input Hypothesis**: It is thought that the motivation of individuals will increase with regular input by AI softwares and learning can occur. Within the framework of the input theory developed by Krashen (1982), AI applications that focus on the difficulties faced by individuals in foreign language learning force individuals to develop according to their characteristics. In this way, the individual will get the motivation to learn with the desire to succeed.
- **Output Hypothesis**: In language teaching, the student's verbal, text and visual outputs are important determinants in terms of evaluation of language learning. Learning can be of high quality when stu-

dents' practices in the language learning process are evaluated and feedback is provided. Output theory was developed by Swain (1985) and recommends that learners should produce to improve. The more output students provide while learning a language, the more opportunities for assessment are created. Students' output can be spoken dialogues, written texts, or visual outputs. Learning platforms based on artificial intelligence can increase students' outcomes. It is ensured that the participation of the students is increased and they are more active.

- **Interaction Hypothesis**: The interaction theory developed by Long (1996) suggests that development can be achieved in the fields of understanding, reading, listening and speaking through the interaction between the learner and the instructor. With the interaction process, feedback is given instantly through negotiation between the learner and the instructor, and the outputs are evaluated instantly. The interaction model, which could be realized with the physical one-to-one interaction of the learner and the instructor in the past, can be provided through applications based on artificial intelligence today. The development process of the student takes place in a controlled manner through the negotiation process.

METHODOLOGY

The study was conducted based on a literature review. In addition, the case study method was used to present the AI softwares used in the field according to its features. The problems faced by students in the process of learning a foreign language have been revealed through a literature review. In addition, researches on the use of artificial intelligence technologies in solving the problems encountered were also scanned. Research on the use and effectiveness of AI in other areas was also reviewed. In addition, the techniques used by AI in language teaching have been revealed through the literature review. Literature review was also used for the theories used in language teaching. All software currently used in the case study method is defined. In the case study method, visual, text and verbal processing tools used by artificial intelligence technologies are also defined.

The Future of Artificial Intelligence in Language Learning

Artificial intelligence is increasingly being used. In addition, new applications are produced to solve the problems encountered. It is used in many technologies along with AI to produce more personalized products. Contextual richness can be achieved by creating realistic scenarios through AI. For example, artificial intelligence for the use of foreign languages in the hospital environment can facilitate learning by creating virtual hospital environments and health scenarios. Currently, technologies such as ASR and AWE are used to support AI, but in the future, applications can be created to assess the emotions or predictions of learners. Enriched discourses can be created using artificial intelligence in virtual reality environments. However, some problems may arise with the use of AI in language teaching. The problems that may be encountered with the use of artificial intelligence in language teaching can be technological, individual and pedagogical.

Technological Challenges

- **Speech Recognition**: While AI is already enabling students to interact using ASR technology, there are still dimensions to be improved. For example, there is a need for improvement in the understanding of different local languages, dialects, dialects and accents (Huang et al., 2020).
- **Semantic Understanding**: Failure to fully evaluate some variables specific to both the source and target culture in language teaching can make learning difficult. The variables of the target culture complicate the learning process. It is often not possible for AI to process and respond to many different variables at the same time (Poria et al., 2017).
- **Data Privacy**: Most artificial intelligence applications work with the entry of users' personal information. In this case, users' past behavior and statistics can be stored. This may lead to a breach of personal data or its sharing with others.

Individual Challenges

- **Motivation**: While artificial intelligence uses many tools to increase and maintain the motivation of students, it is also difficult to motivate the new generation. For this, it can be difficult to find new tools to motivate the new generation.
- **Learning Styles**: Although the learning styles of individuals are different, new differences are also identified. It can be difficult for AI to create strategies for the new differences encountered.
- **Cognitive Load**: Students' cognitive processes also differ with the developing technology. It can also be difficult for AI to react to changing cognitive processes.

Pedagogical Challenges

- **Personalization**: One of the biggest factors in learning is individual differences. Although the learning styles, learning levels and forms of the students are different, differences in other dimensions are also observed today. It is becoming difficult to use artificial intelligence effectively in new areas of differences.
- **Feedback**: Feedback is a very important determinant for both learning and individual development. However, with the widespread use and integration of technology, traditional forms of feedback may become dysfunctional. In this case, artificial intelligence may be insufficient to create new forms of feedback.
- **Cultural Sensitivity**: Cultural tools and differences are gradually transformed. AI may not be able to react to evolving cultural differences.

RESULTS

In this study, the problem areas encountered in foreign language learning are presented. Problems faced in foreign language learning can be overcome with applications created with the use of artificial intelligence technologies. Foreign language learning programs based on AI technologies can solve learners' problems as in skills of comprehension, speaking, listening and pronunciation. These practices can increase the effectiveness of foreign language education. Effectiveness in learning a foreign language can be seen in students' exam results, reports, and interpersonal interactions. It can increase students' self-confidence and reduce their prejudices against foreign languages. The use of applications based on AI technologies can also reveal potential problem areas. AI can also create new opportunities for solving the problems that will arise with the use of new technologies. Comprehensive studies can also provide sub-problems. In general, software based on AI technologies;

Provide learning activity: It ensures that the goals set in the learning process are achieved. It allows to achieve the goals set in speaking, listening, writing and comprehension.

Provide learning efficiency: It ensures the efficient use of time, energy, financial resources and other physical resources used in foreign language teaching.

Increases Multiculturalism and Multilingualism: Overcoming the problems encountered in foreign language teaching with the use of artificial intelligence accelerates and facilitates the adaptation process of individuals in multicultural and multilingual environments. This could lead to new studies. It increases intercultural and interdisciplinary studies and enables individuals to get closer to each other.

Creates Personalized Learning Opportunities: Most of the problems encountered in foreign language learning are based on individual factors. Individual factors require personalized approaches. Research in foreign language teaching will demonstrate how AI can provide personalized learning experiences by adapting to each student's individual needs and learning styles. This includes personalized learning paths, adaptive learning materials, and examples of personalized feedback.

Develops Resilience Ability to Foreign Language Learning: When solutions are sought with up-to-date technologies based on AI in foreign language teaching, the required experience is gained for the problems that may be encountered in the future. With the experience gained and the capacity to use AI, individuals and organizations gain resilience capability.

The use of the transformative power of AI in foreign language teaching can improve students' learning without being affected by time, place and other constraints. As the quality of learning a foreign language increases, the level of internationalization of individuals, organizations and countries may increase. Intercultural studies and cooperation develop. In the long run, it ensures the development of foreign trade and increases the gross national product and per capita income of the countries. As both practitioners and students use artificial intelligence in the language learning process, the spread and inclusivity of artificial intelligence will increase.

There may be difficulties that the use of artificial intelligence will bring. Due to the lack of physical infrastructure, it is not possible to use artificial intelligence tools without having the minimum required technologies. Physical disparities between countries can also create disparities in the use of AI. In addition, AI requires intensive interaction with technology. Intense technology interaction can also lead to an increase in negative types of stress, such as technostress. On the other hand, as emphasized in different parts of the study, the unique characteristics of cultures necessitate the personalization of software. Such personalization efforts require time and financial resources. This can be a challenge.

Limitations

This study, which deals with solving the problems encountered in foreign language learning based on artificial intelligence, has a number of limitations. First, cultural nuances and contextual characteristics can prevent AI applications from being used in any environment. Culture-specific idioms, proverbs, sayings, and other literary tools can reduce the effectiveness of the use of artificial intelligence. On the other hand, artificial intelligence applications require a lot of personal data to be entered. While some artificial intelligence applications can be used without using personal data, many applications require the entry of some information, such as credentials and email. With the use of personal data, statistics of many of our virtual behaviour can be recorded. Recording personal data can be problematic. The use of artificial intelligence technologies requires minimum subfrastructures. Therefore, users need to have a basic technological and cognitive background. In the absence of minimum requirements, it is not possible to use the mentioned artificial intelligence applications. AI applications use user statistics and past data to develop program training for the future. Therefore, the data must be qualified and of high quality. When qualified data is not provided, the effectiveness of applications may decrease.

REFERENCES

Barrot, J. S. (2023). Using automated written corrective feedback in the writing classrooms: Effects on L2 writing accuracy. *Computer Assisted Language Learning*, *36*(4), 584–607. DOI: 10.1080/09588221.2021.1936071

Burke, B. (2016). *Gamify: How gamification motivates people to do extraordinary things*. Bibliomotion, Inc. DOI: 10.4324/9781315230344

Chen, C. M. (2022). Personalized E-learning system with self-regulated learning assisted mechanisms for promoting learning performance. *Expert Systems with Applications*, *41*(2), 225–238.

Chen, X., Zou, D., Xie, H., Cheng, G., & Liu, C. (2022). Two Decades of Artificial Intelligence in Education: Contributors, Collaborations, Research Topics, Challenges, and Future Directions. *Journal of Educational Technology & Society*, *25*(1), 28–47.

Dai, Y., & Wu, Z. (2023). Mobile-assisted pronunciation learning with feedback from peers and/or automatic speech recognition: A mixed-methods study. *Computer Assisted Language Learning*, *36*(5–6), 861–884. DOI: 10.1080/09588221.2021.1952272

Fryer, L. K., Ainley, M., Thompson, A., Gibson, A., & Sherlock, Z. (2017). Stimulating and sustaining interest in a language course: An experimental comparison of chatbot and human task partners. *Computers in Human Behavior*, *75*, 461–468. DOI: 10.1016/j.chb.2017.05.045

Hadley, G., & Charles, M. (2017). Enhancing extensive reading with data-driven learning. *Language Learning & Technology*, *21*(3), 131–152.

Hinojo-Lucena, F.-J., Aznar-Díaz, I., Cáceres-Reche, M.-P., & Romero-Rodríguez, J.-M. (2019). Artificial intelligence in higher education: A Bibliometric study on its impact in the scientific literature. *Education Sciences*, *9*(1), 51. DOI: 10.3390/educsci9010051

Huang, J. T., Li, J., Yu, D., Deng, L., & Gong, Y. (2020). Recent advances in deep learning for speech research at Microsoft. In *2013 IEEE International Conference on Acoustics, Speech and Signal Processing* (pp. 8604-8608). IEEE.

Hwang, G. J., Xie, H., Wah, B. W., & Gašević, D. (2020). Vision, challenges, roles and research issues of Artificial Intelligence in Education. *Computers and Education: Artificial Intelligence, 1*, 100001. DOI: 10.1016/j.caeai.2020.100001

Kamrood, A. M., Davoudi, M., Ghaniabadi, S., & Amirian, S. M. R. (2021). Diagnosing L2 learners' development through online computerized dynamic assessment. *Computer Assisted Language Learning, 34*(7), 868–897. DOI: 10.1080/09588221.2019.1645181

Lee, S. M. (2023). The effectiveness of machine translation in foreign language education: A systematic review and meta-analysis. *Computer Assisted Language Learning, 36*(1–2), 103–125. DOI: 10.1080/09588221.2021.1901745

Pérez-Paredes, P., Guillamón, C. O., & Jiménez, P. A. (2018). Language teachers' perceptions on the use of OER language processing technologies in MALL. *Computer Assisted Language Learning, 31*(5–6), 522–545. DOI: 10.1080/09588221.2017.1418754

Poria, S., Cambria, E., Bajpai, R., & Hussain, A. (2017). A review of affective computing: From unimodal analysis to multimodal fusion. *Information Fusion, 37*, 98–125. DOI: 10.1016/j.inffus.2017.02.003

Poria, S., Cambria, E., Bajpai, R., & Hussain, A. (2017). A review of affective computing: From unimodal analysis to multimodal fusion. *Information Fusion, 37*, 98–125. DOI: 10.1016/j.inffus.2017.02.003

Roll, I., & Wylie, R. (2016). Evolution and revolution in artificial intelligence in education. *International Journal of Artificial Intelligence in Education, 26*(2), 582–599. DOI: 10.1007/s40593-016-0110-3

Shute, V. J. (2008). Focus on formative feedback. *Review of Educational Research, 78*(1), 153–189. DOI: 10.3102/0034654307313795

Son, J., Ružić, N. K., & Philpott, A. (2023). Artificial intelligence technologies and applications for language learning and teaching. *Journal of China Computer-Assisted Language Learning*. Advance online publication. DOI: 10.1515/jccall-2023-0015

Srinivasan, V. (2022). AI & learning: A preferred future. *Computers and Education: Artificial Intelligence*, *3*, 100062.

Sweeney, L. (2013). Discrimination in online ad delivery. *ACM Queue; Tomorrow's Computing Today*, *11*(3), 10–29. DOI: 10.1145/2460276.2460278

Sweller, J. (1988). Cognitive load during problem solving: Effects on learning. *Cognitive Science*, *12*(2), 257–285. DOI: 10.1207/s15516709cog1202_4

Wang, J., Hwang, G.-W., & Chang, C.-Y. (2021). Directions of the 100 most cited chatbot-related human behavior research: A review of academic publications. *Computers and Education: Artificial Intelligence*, *2*, 100023. DOI: 10.1016/j.caeai.2021.100023

Chapter 5
Personalized Adaptive Language Learning in AI-Powered High-Immersion Virtual Reality

Eunkyoung Elaine Cha
https://orcid.org/0009-0001-5946-2440
University of Georgia, USA

Yongluan Ye
University of North Texas, USA

Regina Kaplan-Rakowski
https://orcid.org/0000-0002-6769-7784
University of North Texas, USA

Prerna Choubey
University of North Texas, USA

ABSTRACT

The integration of artificial intelligence (AI) and virtual reality (VR) into

DOI: 10.4018/979-8-3693-5477-3.ch005

education is growing, expediting the optimization of personalized adaptive language learning (PALL). This chapter discusses the foundations of personalized adaptive learning, explaining its importance for language learners. The potential of AI in language learning and an overview of VR–assisted language learning are presented with a particular focus on the potential of AI embedded into VR, which enables PALL experiences. The role of AI-enhanced high-immersion VR is explained with examples of providing language learners with individualized and contextualized learning environments through immersive real-world based scenarios and simulations. The chapter pinpoints current challenges and future avenues for exploration.

INTRODUCTION

Personalized adaptive learning (PAL) has been gaining attention as an instructional design and pedagogical approach that enables a learning environment to be personalized and tailored to individual learners with diverse needs. The implementation of PAL in educational settings may facilitate learning processes, simultaneously challenging pedagogical practices (Bingham et al., 2016; Taylor et al., 2021). As of 2024, PAL has become increasingly feasible given the rapid advances in Artificial Intelligence (AI), computing power, data analytics techniques, and machine learning, thereby experiencing a surge in its popularity (Tang et al., 2021; Zawacki-Richter et al., 2019). AI can be defined as a technology that allows computers to learn, simulate, and perform human-like functions, which has been applied to diverse fields such as machine learning, deep learning and neural nets, quantum computing, learning analytics, and data mining (Chen et al., 2020; Cope et al., 2021). While PAL has been applied to various subject areas, its incorporation into the language learning context has been growing, considering the demands for individualized language learning in the era of globalization (Chen et al., 2021). The purpose of this chapter is to present the case of personalized adaptive language learning (PALL) with its particular focus on AI-powered high-immersion virtual reality (VR), which is known as an immersive space where learners can develop authentic, situated, and experiential learning experiences. First, this chapter will briefly overview the background and foundations of PAL, explaining its importance for language learners. Second, the chapter will discuss the role of AI in language education, especially highlighting its progress within the area of generative AI. Third, the overview of VR-assisted language learning will be presented with a particular focus on the role of AI embedded into VR, which enables PAL experiences. Fourth, we will provide some examples of PAL opportunities within VR. Finally, the chapter will pinpoint current challenges and future avenues for exploration.

BACKGROUND

Personalized Adaptive Learning

Technology–enhanced learning environment has pushed forward the optimization of personalized learning and adaptive learning. The advancement of smart devices and emerging technologies such as virtual reality (VR) and artificial intelligence (AI) led to the growing integration of personalized and adaptive learning into various educational settings. Personalized learning and adaptive learning are two distinct concepts yet closely related to each other (Lin et al., 2013; Peng et al., 2019; Xie et al., 2019). The US Department of Education Office of Educational Technology (2010) defined personalized learning as "instruction that is paced to learning needs, tailored to learning preferences, and tailored to the specific interests of different learners" (p. 12). Personalized learning has been considered as a student–centered approach, which emphasizes the need for centering students as an active learner at the core of learning and providing instructions tailored to individual learning needs (Bernard et al., 2019; Lee et al., 2018; Lee et al., 2022). With diverse technology tools being introduced and incorporated into learning, technology–supported personalized learning was further discussed with the emphasis on student–centered teaching and the voice of students (Schmid et al., 2022). The paradigm of personalized learning has also been dramatically changed as computational algorithms, AI models, big data, and learning analytics were integrated into diverse applications and software available through different smart and wearable devices, which accelerated the use of individualized instructions and learning contents tailored to the learning pace of individuals.

Adaptive learning, on the other hand, has emerged as an approach to adjusting learning contents based on the learner's prior knowledge (Huang & Shiu, 2012). Shemshack and Spector (2020) highlighted that adaptive learning is mostly discussed in the technology–enhanced learning environment where the learning contents are adjusted to the existing knowledge of learners, whereas personalized learning is a broader term referring to the adjustment of learning based on different needs, interests, and goals of individual learners. Given that personalized learning and adaptive learning are often being used interchangeably, attention to defining the combined concept of personalized adaptive learning (PAL) has been growing.

With the technology advancement and use, PAL extends the discussion of pedagogical approaches to learner-centered individualized learning by identifying learner's needs and providing tailored support and feedback (Taylor et al., 2021). Peng et al. (2019) defined PAL as a "technology–empowered effective pedagogy which can adaptively adjust teaching strategies timely based on real–time monitored (enabled by smart technology) learners' differences and changes in individual characteristics, individual performance, and personal development" (p. 6). PAL can make the learning process of individual learners to be more effective and efficient, providing appropriate learning contents (Costa et al., 2021), instructions (Connor et al., 2018; Hammerschmidt-Snidarich et al., 2019), and timely feedback (You et al., 2019) while enhancing learners' engagement (Arroyo et el., 2014), self-efficacy (Rachels & Rockinson-Szapkiw, 2018), competency and skills (Alrawashdeh et al., 2024; Hsieh et al., 2012; Hsu et al., 2013). Furthermore, Xie et al. (2019) discussed promising aspects of PAL in their review, illuminating the role of up-to-date technologies that enable the use of critical data sources, such as individualized and contextualized learning data, which serve as the key parameters to facilitate PAL. Xie et al. also envisioned that collaborative and immersive learning environments afforded by wearable devices and VR technology may broaden the field where PAL can be applied.

Personalized Adaptive Learning for Language Learners

The incorporation of technology has also led to the increasing prevalence of the application of PAL in language learning (Slavuj et al., 2017; Xie et al., 2019). Until 2024, the research attention has been unevenly divided between different language competencies and various aspects of PAL (Chen et al., 2021). While vocabulary, grammar, and reading skills attracted the most attention (Chen et al., 2021; Slavuj et al., 2017), personalized recommendation, mobile-assisted personal adaptive language learning, and personalized feedback have also garnered interest within PAL research (Chen et al., 2021).

Integrating PAL into language learning, different personalized adaptive language learning (PALL) affordances and learning theories were employed to promote learners' language competencies. One such application of PALL is to provide personalized recommendations for learning various language competencies. The recommendations can be based on learners' current language abilities and demographic information, such as gender, age, and location. Researchers have explored an effective design of PALL in which vocabulary recommendations and feedback were provided to individual learners based on their existing vocabulary knowledge and ability (Chen & Chung, 2008), interests and personal learning goals (Heilman et al., 2013; Hsu et al., 2013), and physical location (Wu et al., 2014). All these studies produced pivotal findings suggesting the effectiveness of the PALL in improving learners' language competencies.

The application of PALL has been effectively tailored to various contexts and purposes. For example, some successful PALL designs aimed to support learners to practice using the target language by focusing on learners' memory circle and retrieval of existing language knowledge (Chen & Chung, 2008; Kohnke et al., 2019). PALL was also integrated into game-based learning environments to enhance motivation, increase engagement, and reduce anxiety (Jung & Graf, 2008; Kohnke et al., 2019; Wei et al., 2018). In such environments, the PALL approach supported individual learning experiences by evaluating the learners' language abilities and providing materials or tasks with the appropriate difficulties tailored to individual learners (Slavuj et al., 2017).

Specifically, Hooshyar et al. (2018) evaluated learners' vocabulary knowledge by comparing them with pre-established learning objectives and generated personalized learning game contents to support individual learners' alphabet and vocabulary learning. Su et al. (2014) have also found positive effects of PALL in helping learners improve their pronunciation and interpersonal speaking skills with recursive conversation games, where individual learners were prompted to practice unfamiliar words and sentences. Given the increasing accessibility of mobile devices (e.g., smartphones, tablets), game-based learning environments are widely explored and designed using the PALL approach to integrate them into such devices (Chen et al., 2021).

Theories within Personalized Adaptive Language Learning

Theories explaining the positive effect of PALL on learning include the involvement load hypothesis (Hulstijn & Laufer, 2001), zone of proximal development (Kinginger, 2002), spaced learning (Kim & Webb, 2022), and situated learning (Lave & Wenger, 1991). The involvement load hypothesis postulates that learners' intrinsic need can increase their motivation (Hulstijn & Laufer, 2001). Within PALL, the learning environment can be personalized and contextualized based on individual learners' existing knowledge and interests, which may promote their intrinsic need to gain knowledge while leading them to be highly motivated.

Moreover, many personalized recommendation designs in PALL are based on the zone of proximal development theory, which argues that learning can be optimized when the content and skill are one level more complex than learners' current knowledge and abilities (Kinginger, 2002). Having personalized learning contents through the design of PALL, individual learners can engage in activities and tasks customized to their current stages of learning while keeping a balance between their existing knowledge, ability, and appropriate level of challenge.

Spaced learning is another theory that informs effective PALL design, which suggests distributing the learning content and practice into multiple repeating sections throughout the learning process, instead of one whole intense section, for better learning outcomes (Zou et al. 2021). Furthermore, situated learning theory argues that learning is a process aiming to adapt to a community, which is situated in the sociocultural context (Clancey, 1995). In PALL, learners are often situated in a learning context where they engage in social and cultural interactions within real-world based situations and scenarios to acquire and practice target languages (Li et al., 2022; Warschauer, 2005).

AI AND PERSONALIZED ADAPTIVE LANGUAGE LEARNING

AI in Education

While PAL focuses on individualized instruction customized to learners' unique needs and abilities, AI amplifies this capability by processing big data to create adaptive learning environments that respond to learners in real time. The development of AI has progressed considerably since its conceptual beginnings in the 1950s, evolving from basic algorithms capable of performing simple tasks to complex systems that emulate human cognitive functions (Cope et al., 2021). Substantive investments in AI technology (Thormundsson, 2023) and policy statements aiming to advance and standardize the use of AI have been growing in various fields (European Commission, 2018; UNESCO, 2022) including education (Zawacki-Richter et al., 2019).

Artificial Intelligence in Education (AIED) aims to improve educational processes and learning outcomes by optimizing the management of educational systems (Celik et al., 2023). Earlier efforts in the 1960s included mainly *weak* or *narrow AI* which relied on systems that are pre-programmed by humans (Holmes et al., 2019). Such systems are controlled and predictable, prone to limitations such as the inability to learn from experiences or adapt to new, unforeseen situations. As a result, *weak AI* cannot improve performance or extend capabilities beyond the specific tasks for which they were originally designed. This inflexibility of *weak AI* contrasts with *strong AI*, which is able to identify relationships and patterns that may facilitate learning across a range of situations, including PAL (Clark, 2020).

The incorporation of AI in PAL can create customizable learning experiences for the learners. Digital tools and systems are used to create individual learning paths for students based on their strengths, weaknesses, and pace of learning, facilitating adaptive learning environments (Becker et al., 2018; Taylor et al., 2021). Educators and learners widely use AI applications (Kaplan-Rakowski, Grotewold, et al., 2023), with some variation between K-12 and university settings including tools and technologies such as teaching robots, intelligent tutoring systems, and adaptive learning systems (Wang et al., 2015). The advancement in AI is accelerating the adoption of personalized learning approaches, which may have been difficult and uneconomical in traditional learning settings (Magomadov, 2020). Advanced adaptive technologies are increasingly becoming available providing learners with customized learning environments using the compilation of information such as learners' prior knowledge and academic achievement, which can benefit learners with diverse socioeconomic backgrounds and special needs (Al-Badi et al., 2022).

The adoption of AI in delivering personalized education by profiling the academic history and development of students and educators could be beneficial. Communication is also an integral part of student-teacher interaction that could be enhanced with the help of AI (Wang et al., 2015). AI-driven educational systems and platforms often employ autonomous scoring, and assessment, and intelligent agents—such as learner-support chatbots—to facilitate communication among learners and instructors, thereby creating a collaborative learning environment (Holmes et al., 2019).

AI in Language Learning

Differences in language learning skills and patterns of individual learners have gained much attention (Ellis, 2021; Woo & Choi, 2021). The emergence of Intelligent Computer Assisted Language Learning (ICALL) as a subfield of Computer Assisted Language Learning (CALL; Kannan & Munday, 2018; Woo & Choi, 2021) focuses on applying AI concepts, techniques, algorithms, and technologies to CALL, especially for natural language processing (NLP), user modeling, expert systems, and intelligent tutoring systems (Woo & Choi 2021). Such application of AI is promising for PALL, as it predicts and adapts to the massive learner data creating a learning environment tailored to individual language learners (Pérez-Paredes et al., 2018; Yang et al., 2024). For example, Chen et al. (2021) provided an example of the three-dimensional (3D) face recognition techniques that are commonly combined with automatic speech recognition (ASR) to provide PALL experience based on individual characteristics.

Off-the-shelf AI tools that are not designed specifically for education have also been incorporated and showed some potential in helping learners develop language skills. In a study by Obari et al. (2020), 30 college students in Japan used cloud-based AI assistants, such as Google Mini and Amazon Alexa, for their English language learning. Compared with their 29 counterparts who used non-AI materials focused on standardized English test practice and vocabulary learning, the participants who used AI improved more in a third-party standardized English test. The participants considered the AI tool to be most helpful in helping them develop their listening skills, followed by their speaking skills. Studies have also confirmed the potential of AI in enhancing language ability and competencies by optimizing language learning experiences and increasing autonomy, motivation, engagement, and effectiveness (Obari et al., 2020; Pokrivcakova, 2019; Woo & Choi, 2021).

Research has explored different types and uses of AI. The development of machine learning, which is a subset of AI, generates systems that can learn from and make decisions based on data (Pavlik, 2023). The Generative AI (GAI), a specific type of AI that includes models such as ChatGPT, leverages these ML techniques to generate human-like text based on vast datasets. The 2022 launch of ChatGPT—a freely available generative AI tool— escalated both interest and the use of GAI (Lampropoulos et al., 2024), quickly allowing teachers to embrace its potential (Alm & Ohashi, 2024; Kaplan-Rakowski, Grotewold, et al., 2023). GAI can analyze patterns of how humans communicate, and based on these patterns and prompts, it can generate output. This capability could help enable GAI to create interactive and personalized learning experiences that could address individual learners' needs.

In the context of language learning, the spike in the implementation of AI has been providing increased opportunities to develop learning environments where language skills and competencies can be practiced with attention to the preferences, needs, learning pace, and language level of individual learners. One such learning environment is high-immersion VR.

AI-POWERED HIGH-IMMERSION VR FOR PERSONALIZED ADAPTIVE LANGUAGE LEARNING

High-immersion VR for Language Learning

In addition to AI, VR has also increasingly been used to support language learning (Dhimolea et al., 2022). High-immersion virtual reality is defined as "a computer-generated 360° virtual space that can be perceived as being spatially realistic, due to the high immersion afforded by a head-mounted device" (Kaplan-Rakowski & Gruber, 2019, p. 552). High-immersion VR contrasts with low-immersion VR (experienced on a 2D monitor) in the intensity of immersion and the embodiment (Kaplan-Rakowski & Gruber, 2019). Although both types of VR may benefit language learning, this chapter focuses specifically on high-immersion VR. To experience high-immersion VR, users need to wear a VR headset (see Figure 1) that facilitates isolation from the real world (Dhimolea et al., 2022), simultaneously enhancing immersion and the sense of presence within the virtual environment (Kaplan-Rakowski, Cockerham, & Ferdig, 2023; Kaplan-Rakowski & Gruber, 2023; Ye & Kaplan-Rakowski, 2024).

Figure 1. Depiction of high-immersion VR

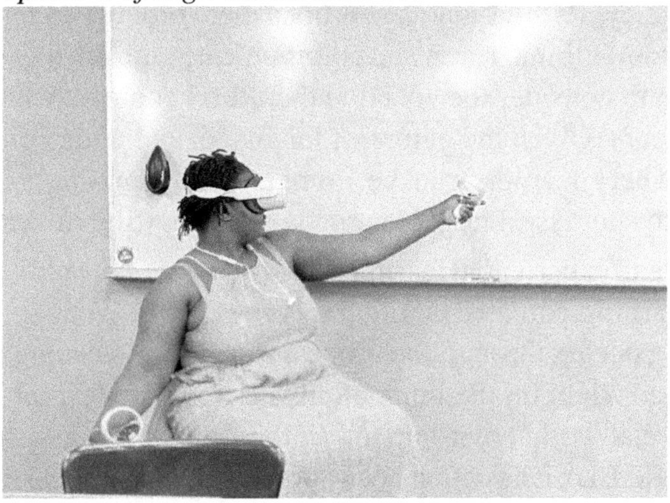

Note. User interacting within high-immersion VR.

VR offers enhanced engagement in contextualized language learning scenarios for practicing various language skills and competencies (Kaplan-Rakowski, 2024); for example, reading (Kaplan-Rakowski & Gruber, 2023), listening (Ye & Kaplan-Rakowski, 2024), speaking (Dooly et al., 2023; Gruber & Kaplan-Rakowski, 2020; Thrasher, 2022, 2023; Xie et al., 2019; Yang et al., 2020), or grammar (Huang et al., 2023; Xie et al., 2019).

The immersive nature and interactivity of VR can create simulations of the real world where learners can participate in kinesthetic, embodied, situated exploration, and experiential learning in authentic contexts (Chun et al., 2022; Petersen et al., 2022; Sharrab et al., 2023; Vázquez et al., 2018). Moreover, VR allows learners to interact and collaborate with learners, instructors, and practitioners beyond the boundaries of their physical locations (Sharma & Dash, 2023; Sharrab et al., 2023).

Experiential and Situated Learning in VR-Assisted Language Learning

Along with AI technology, VR can create interactive and context-rich language learning experiences, maximizing the potential of PALL. Language consists of three major components, which are form (e.g., phonology, morphology, syntax), content (e.g., semantics), and use (pragmatics; Bloom & Lahey, 1978). Language is not a mere product, but a process and a symbolic tool to think, learn, and communicate with others, which makes it inevitable to consider the social and cultural contexts where language learning occurs. Given the nature of language, authentic communicative situations where learners can be immersed in input–rich contexts can contribute to successful target language learning (Shih & Yang, 2008).

Situated and experiential learning environments can facilitate the target language learning. Situated learning theory (Lave & Wenger, 1991) posits that learning occurs through the process of making meaning in the social world. It sheds light on the interactions between the learner and the surrounding social world environment. In the field of VR-assisted language learning (VRALL), it has often been adopted as a theoretical framework to create authentic learning content and environment for language learning. The immersive learning environment in VR allows learners to interact with their surrounding virtual social world as they engage in language learning activities. Specifically, VR applications designed primarily for language learning can provide learners with authentic communicative contexts, situating and immersing them in real-world scenarios (Christoforou et al., 2019; Shih & Yang, 2008). Situated and immersed learning experiences using VR are claimed to have a positive impact on learners' engagement in language learning, increasing their sense of presence (Alfadil, 2020; Dhimolea et al., 2022; Lee, 2019; Pack et al., 2020).

Experiential learning is another frequently used theoretical framework in VRALL, especially given that learners are exposed to real-world scenarios and simulations in VR, contributing to their target language development. Kolb's (1984, 2015) experiential learning model posits that experience is the key element of learning and development and that knowledge is obtained from the transformation of both objective and subjective experiences. The VR learning environment provides learners with opportunities to actively interact with their virtual surroundings, going beyond reading a text and watching a video to experience the simulated world and scenarios.

For instance, Vázquez et al. (2018) suggested a positive effect of VR on the vocabulary retention rate of second language learners through kinesthetic learning in virtual environments. Park (2018) also showed that immersive experiences and simulated tasks facilitated through VR could improve learners' linguistic competence. Mirzaei et al. (2020) further explored how VR experiences could foster cultural awareness of language learners. In their experimental study, 37 English learners used VR to create real-world based, culturally responsive scenarios and practice communicative skills. Findings revealed that authentic VR scenarios and contextual experiences enhanced learners' motivation and engagement in learning other cultures and supported learners in developing cross-cultural competence.

AI-POWERED HIGH-IMMERSION VR FOR PERSONALIZED ADAPTIVE LANGUAGE LEARNING

Although research on VR-based learning consistently demonstrates that learners report high presence, engagement, and enhanced motivation (Huang et al., 2010; Kaplan-Rakowski, Cockerham, & Ferdig, 2023; Kaplan-Rakowski & Gruber, 2023; Makransky et al., 2019; Ye & Kaplan-Rakowski, 2024), some learners also expressed a need for more feedback and guidance in their VR learning experience (Wang et al., 2021). AI-supported PAL incorporated within VR may meet this need, mirroring its success in real-world applications. For self-guided learners or as a supplement to instructors, pedagogical agents in VR can collaborate with learners in VR and provide timely feedback and guidance (Chun et al., 2022; Tai & Chen, 2021). For example, Hussain et al. (2024) used Ready Me player, a versatile avatar library, and Oculus Lip Sync to turn an AI chatbot into a life-like pedagogical agent who can support immigrant workers in VR safety simulations. Machine-learning AI can further assist instructors by collecting and analyzing learner behavioral data in VR to generate behavioral patterns to guide instructional decisions (Porwol et al., 2023).

One of the affordances of VR is that it can provide authentic simulations of real-world scenarios (Kaplan-Rakowski, 2024), such as making appointments at a doctor's office, inquiring about merchandise at a store (Lee, 2019; Tai & Chen, 2022), enjoying meals while chatting on a Parisian terrace (Thrasher, 2022), or giving a class presentation (Gruber & Kaplan-Rakowski, 2020). Although until 2023 language practice simulations in such scenarios were impossible, their limitation was that they used *narrow AI* models using pre-programmed interactions.

As of 2024, however, thanks to the surge of GAI possibilities, language practice in such scenarios can be facilitated by the incorporation of AI-conversational partners. By conversing with AI chatbots, students can receive immediate feedback on their speaking accuracy and pronunciation. At the same time, they can check their listening comprehension skills.

Research in the area of AI embedded within VR is only beginning to emerge, but some initial findings are already available. For example, in a study by Thrasher et al. (2024), 54 high school language learners shared their perceptions of interacting with AI-empowered agents. Overall, the participants' experience was positive. Most students enjoyed AI-enriched activities and the ability to explore VR environment settings. Participants shared that AI helped them learn foreign phrases and sentences which "felt like a real conversation." Moreover, most students were able to understand what the AI bot said.

Although the participants' initial experiences were positive, the implementation of AI within VR has also encountered some challenges. For instance, in the same study (Thrasher et al., 2024), participants had concerns about some technical issues (e.g., the microphone not picking up the speech) or classroom issues ("Talking with everyone in the room is challenging"). Teachers wanting to implement AI speaking practice activities should be aware of such challenges and adjust; for instance, by selecting a higher-quality microphone to help mitigate audio-related issues. Additionally, students may need to be more generously spaced out to reduce the competition of various sounds within a small classroom space. VR application designers wishing to embed AI-powered activities should benefit from such findings by Thrasher et al. to adjust AI activities to diminish further issues.

Example of AI–Powered VR App

Although the number of VR apps has been increasing, as of 2024, few pedagogically sound language learning apps exist. One instance of a language learning app that implements GAI in free-flowing conversations in VR is *Immerse*. *Immerse* provides a variety of language practice options including opportunities to practice speaking with an AI-powered conversational partner. Language learners can converse with a chatbot on various topics (e.g., ordering food, talking about hobbies, receiving advice from a doctor) in English, French, or Spanish in dozens of settings such as a sports resort, a fast-food bar, or a restaurant.

As described in Chun et al., (2024), when wanting to practice speaking, learners go to a selected setting and approach an AI-empowered avatar by starting a conversation (see Figure 2) and completing a list of tasks designed for role-play (see Figure 3). After learners choose a task, the AI-empowered conversational partner initiates the conversation and waits for the learners to respond. While exchanging verbal information with the chatbot, learners receive feedback, thereby enhancing their language skills and boosting their confidence. When all the tasks are completed, the conversation terminates. The reduction in immediacy and shifting focus from form to meaning can reduce foreign language anxiety (Ebadi & Azizimajd, 2024; La & Li, 2011). Although the feedback from the AI-empowered practice helps keep the conversation on target, it does not explain knowledge, such as the language form. Therefore, instructions from teachers are still necessary to develop learners' language knowledge.

Figure 2. Screenshot of AI–Powered Conversational Partner

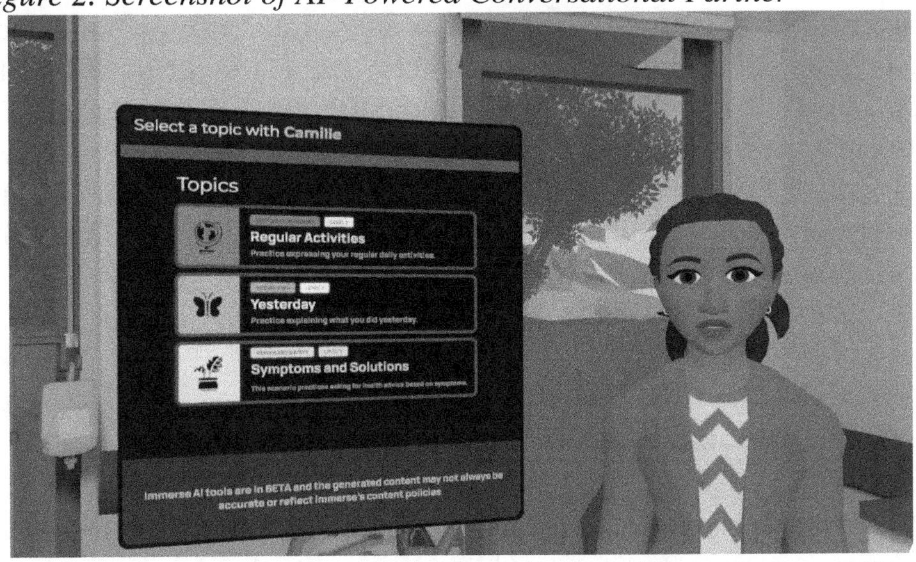

Note. Tasks available with the conversational partner in a hospital. Screenshot of Immerse.

Figure 3. Screenshot of AI–Powered Conversational Partner

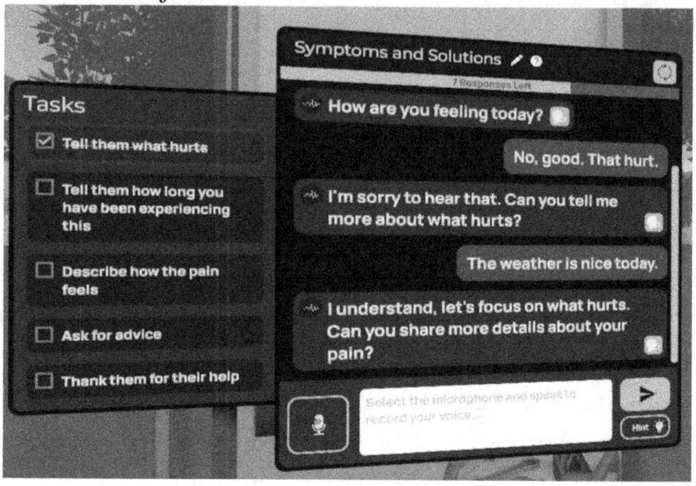

Note. Conversational partner guiding users to focus on the tasks. Screenshot of Immerse.

The conversational partner listens to the learner's input and responds appropriately even when the learner's sentences are not entirely correct. Being AI-empowered, it can interpret minimal language input effectively. Moreover, it can scaffold the learner throughout the conversation. If the learner strays off the topic, the AI-empowered avatar politely guides them back to the target topic. Learners can also ask additional questions, for example, asking how to say a certain thing in the target language. The AI-empowered chatbot responds accordingly, thereby acting as a language tutor. This approach is designed to facilitate language learning in a low-anxiety context, simultaneously providing a realistic and interactive learning environment for language students.

OPPORTUNITIES, CHALLENGES, AND POSSIBLE SOLUTIONS

Applying AI in VR can reduce many barriers caused by the current common classroom settings, enabling learners to develop language and cultural competence in a more cost-effective way. AI-powered VR applications including *VirtualSpeech AI, SpeakPro, Engagely* are making the language learning process easier and fun for the learners with their new features. These applications with the help of AI are incorporating NLP that makes it possible for the learners to interact with virtual tutors and helps generate human-like responses making the conversation much more realistic in nature. The AI integration of these applications has PAL, as AI can customize the difficulty level and content for the learner profiles based on their proficiency levels, making the learning process more effective. The speech recognition feature makes the learning process seamless as AI can recognize accents, pronunciation, grammatical errors and can provide real-time feedback to the learners. VR thus allows learners to experience and explore authentic target language environments, practicing languages under the guidance of AI (Mirzaei et al., 2018; Thrasher et al., 2024). While AI has considerably developed NLP and speech recognition, its inaccuracy in recognizing the variations in human conversations (especially when it comes to cultural references, unfamiliar accents, humor or sarcasm) leaves a lot of room for improvement. That is, to implement this technology, several problems inherent in AI and VR need to be solved.

VR embedded with AI may provide learners with opportunities to develop their language skills and sociocultural knowledge through situated and experiential learning (Chun et al., 2022; Chun et al., 2024; Shih & Yang, 2008). Language proficiency can be described as the ability to meet communication objectives using the target language (ACTFL, 2024). Therefore, language learning needs to go beyond the three major components (form, content, and use), and include sociocultural knowledge that is sometimes expressed non-verbally (Atkinson, 2002; Kramsch, 2014; Mirzaei et al., 2018).

For instance, learning how to greet people in different languages not only involves learning verbal expressions, such as "hello", "konichiwa", or "hola", but also non-verbal signs of whether one should wave, bow, or kiss the other person on the cheek. Although observation of these culturally appropriate communications can be done through watching and analyzing videos (Wong, 2000), VR technology paired with AI can provide a more hands-on and immersive option (Ma, 2021). Specifically, learners may have the chance to participate in individual conversations that flow naturally with AI partners to solve realistic problems contextualized in VR (Thrasher et al., 2024). Moreover, when programmed properly, AI partners can also demonstrate culturally appropriate non-verbal communication in these conversations (Mirzaei et al., 2018). These AI partners can further serve as tutors helping learners to correct grammatical and pronunciation errors while gathering data for analysis (Yun et al., 2023). Such personalized practice and data analytics can free instructors to better focus on learners' progress, plan effective instructions accordingly, and guide generative activities, such as reflections and discussions, a key step of situated and experiential learning (Kolb, 2015; Lave & Wenger, 1991).

However, implementing AI-embedded VR technology can remain challenging for language educators (Akgun & Greenhow, 2022; Hanson & Shelton, 2008). Favorably, researchers and practitioners offer solutions to some of these issues. The first challenge is the lack of necessary teacher training to use the technology effectively (Kaplan-Rakowski, Dhimolea, & Khukalenko, 2023; Khukalenko et al., 2022). Even when teachers are motivated to use VR for language learning, they need proper training on topics, such as instructional design and problem-shooting (Kaplan-Rakowski, Papin, & Hartwick, 2023). Therefore, when opting to use VR applications with AI, teachers should participate in VR training offered by school districts or VR companies.

The second challenge involves environmental resources, such as VR equipment and classroom setups (Fransson et al., 2020; Thrasher et al., 2023). When using expensive VR devices, safe and organized storage and timely charging are important, which may require appliances, such as mobile charging carts. Moreover, when using AI in VR for speaking practice, classrooms need to be arranged to allow students ample space, ensuring the absence of background noise that could interfere with speech recognition (Thrasher et al., 2024).

Third, the cost of the devices remains to be a concern. Although affordable VR headsets exist (e.g., Google Cardboard), higher quality devices (e.g., Oculus 3) provide a better VR experience. In addition to the equipment cost, VR apps with AI may be associated with some costs and may regular subscriptions, which may exceed the budgets of many schools (Chun et al., 2022).

Fourth, despite the immense potential of AI in language learning, there have also been concerns regarding data security and privacy issues (Akgun & Greenhow, 2022). With the extensively increased use of AI, the need for reinforcement of privacy policies and informed consent practices has been emphasized (Kannan & Munday, 2018; Woo & Choi 2021). Research using AI raised questions on which and where collected data will be stored, and who will have access to them (Regan & Jesse, 2019). Although data collection and storage may be inevitable for diverse purposes including research, prioritizing data privacy is necessary. More discussion and considerations are needed to develop guidelines and regulations on how to collect and access student learning data, what data can be collected, and how to protect the data (Chen et al., 2021).

FUTURE AVENUES FOR RESEARCH AND APPLICATION

Future research may extend the discussion of the pedagogical implications of integrating AI and VR into language learning contexts. For example, AI language learning tools have the potential to support learners in understanding different cultures, customs, traditions, and social norms through interactive and real-life scenarios (Chen et al., 2021; De la Vall & Araya, 2023). Along with the potential of enhancing the cultural quotient, these AI tools can also help analyze students' language proficiency levels and learning patterns, provide customized learning content, and adapt to the learning pace of individual learners, ensuring their personalized learning experiences (Chen et al., 2021). Moreover, Porter and Grippa (2020) highlighted the capacity of AI-powered tools capable of providing timely personalized feedback to students by recognizing the areas of improvement and tracking their progress in their language learning. These AI-powered language learning applications can also incorporate innovations such as NLP, speech recognition, and gamification, enhancing PAL experiences by understanding user needs and behavior (Pokrivcakova, 2019). Specifically, AI has potential for language learning, with the advancements in NLP and its capability for supporting networked learning and handling massive data (Kannan & Munday, 2018). Considering these aspects of using AI for language learning, further research can explore how to integrate it into actual learning settings, which may vary depending on diverse language learning contexts. For example, Schmidt and Strasser (2022) suggested different ways of using AI technology to support foreign language learning and teaching, illustrating both potentials (e.g., machine translation, writing tools with linguistic versatility, tailored feedback, ubiquitous learning experience, entertainment) and challenges (e.g., limited cultural sensitivity, redundant feedback mechanisms, data privacy, limited capability of understanding pragmatics) of integrating AI into language education. More evidence is necessary for evaluating the effectiveness and efficiency of AI-enhanced language learning.

CONCLUSIONS

The current chapter discussed how emerging technologies, particularly AI and VR, facilitated PAL approaches in the context of language learning. The integration of PAL into language learning has a positive impact on improving both learning and affective outcomes. It provides learners with contents and instructions tailored to individual learners based on their existing knowledge and unique needs, as well as timely feedback, which is critical in developing language skills (Connor et al., 2018; Costa et al., 2021; Hammerschmidt-Snidarich et al., 2019; You et al., 2019). On the other hand, it can enhance learners' engagement, motivation, and self-efficacy (Arroyo et al., 2014; Rachels & Rockinson-Szapkiw, 2018). The advancement of AI technology in education expedited such promising aspects of PALL.

Creating situated and experiential learning environments is necessary in language learning, given that learners' exposure to the input rich contexts and authentic communicative situations may effectively contribute to their successful target language learning (Shih & Yang, 2008). In VR, learners can immerse themselves in real-world scenarios and simulations, allowing them to experience a situated and contextualized language learning environment, leading to a more effective and efficient learning process (Christoforou et al., 2019; Park, 2018; Vázquez et al., 2018). Specifically, learners can engage in kinesthetic and embodied learning in authentic contexts using high-immersion VR, which provides an increased immersion and sense of presence (Chun et al., 2022; Makransky et al., 2019).

Although the application of AI to VR may not be new, the effect of AI-powered high-immersion VR on language learning remains to be explored. Despite its potential in situating learners into realistic scenarios and simulations, elevating the sense of presence and perceived immersion, challenges and concerns with its use and pedagogical affordances need to be solved. Teachers may experience difficulties in implementing it into their instructions without sufficient training. Limited time and space given to educators in schools and higher education institutions can lower the accessibility of such technologies. Moreover, its affordability can be challenging due to the high cost of VR devices and software. Data security and privacy issues are also constantly discussed topics in the context of AI usage and its integration into education. Given the recent extensive use of AI and the ongoing discussion about the potential of VR in language learning, future studies addressing these challenges and issues are recommended.

REFERENCES

Akgun, S., & Greenhow, C. (2022). Artificial intelligence in education: Addressing ethical challenges in K-12 settings. *AI and Ethics*, *2*(3), 431–440. DOI: 10.1007/s43681-021-00096-7 PMID: 34790956

Al-Badi, A., Khan, A., & Eid-Alotaibi, . (2022). Perceptions of learners and instructors towards artificial intelligence in personalized learning. *Procedia Computer Science*, *201*, 445–451. DOI: 10.1016/j.procs.2022.03.058

Alfadil, M. (2020). Effectiveness of virtual reality game in foreign language vocabulary acquisition. *Computers & Education*, *153*, 103893. Advance online publication. DOI: 10.1016/j.compedu.2020.103893

Alm, A., & Ohashi, L. (2024). A worldwide study on language educators' initial response to ChatGPT. *Technology in Language Teaching & Learning*, *6*(1), 1–23. DOI: 10.29140/tltl.v6n1.1141

Alrawashdeh, G. S., Fyffe, S., Azevedo, R. F. L., & Castillo, N. M. (2024). Exploring the impact of personalized and adaptive learning technologies on reading literacy: A global meta-analysis. *Educational Research Review*, *42*, 100587. Advance online publication. DOI: 10.1016/j.edurev.2023.100587

Arroyo, I., Woolf, B. P., Burelson, W., Muldner, K., Rai, D., & Tai, M. (2014). A multimedia adaptive tutoring system for mathematics that addresses cognition, metacognition and affect. *International Journal of Artificial Intelligence in Education*, *24*(4), 387–426. DOI: 10.1007/s40593-014-0023-y

Atkinson, D. (2002). Toward a sociocognitive approach to second language acquisition. *Modern Language Journal*, *86*(4), 525–545. DOI: 10.1111/1540-4781.00159

Becker, S. A., Brown, M., Dahlstrom, E., Davis, A., DePaul, K., Diaz, V., & Pomerantz, J. (2018). *NMC horizon report: 2018 higher education edition*. EDUCAUSE Publications., https://library.educause.edu/resources/2018/8/2018-nmc-horizon-report

Bernard, R. M., Borokhovski, E., Schmid, R. F., Waddington, D. I., & Pickup, D. I. (2019). Twenty-first century adaptive teaching and individualized learning operationalized as specific blends of student-centered instructional events: A systematic review and meta-analysis. *Campbell Systematic Reviews*, *15*(1–2), e1017. Advance online publication. DOI: 10.1002/cl2.1017 PMID: 37131463

Bingham, A. J., Pane, J. F., Steiner, E. D., & Hamilton, L. S. (2016). Ahead of the curve: Implementation challenges in personalized learning school models. *Educational Policy*, *32*(3), 454–489. DOI: 10.1177/0895904816637688

Bloom, L., & Lahey, M. (1978). *Language development and language disorders*. John Wiley & Sons, Inc. https://doi.org/DOI: 10.7916/D8QZ2GQ5

Celik, I., Dindar, M., Muukkonen, H., & Jarvela, S. (2022). The promises and challenges of artificial intelligence for teachers: A systematic review of research. *TechTrends*, *66*(4), 616–630. DOI: 10.1007/s11528-022-00715-y

Chen, C. M., & Chung, C. J. (2008). Personalized mobile English vocabulary learning system based on item response theory and learning memory cycle. *Computers & Education*, *51*(2), 624–645. DOI: 10.1016/j.compedu.2007.06.011

Chen, L., Chen, P., & Lin, Z. (2020). Artificial intelligence in education: A review. *IEEE Access : Practical Innovations, Open Solutions*, *8*, 75264–75278. DOI: 10.1109/ACCESS.2020.2988510

Chen, X., Zou, D., Xie, H., & Cheng, G. (2021). Twenty years of personalized language learning: Topic modeling and knowledge mapping. *Journal of Educational Technology & Society*, *24*(1), 205–222. https://www.jstor.org/stable/26977868

Christoforou, M., Xerou, E., & Papadima-Sophocleous, S. (2019). Integrating a virtual reality application to simulate situated learning experiences in a foreign language course. In F. Meunier, J. Van De Vyver, L. Bradley, & S. Thouësny (Eds.), *CALL and complexity – short papers from EUROCALL 2019* (1st ed., pp. 82–87). Research-publishing.net. https://doi.org/DOI: 10.14705/rpnet.2019.38.990

Chun, D., Kaplan-Rakowski, R., Ovsiannikova, U., Thrasher, T., & Yuan, Y. (2024 forthcoming). AI-mediated high-immersion virtual reality for language learning. In Lan, Y. J., Qi, G., & Chun, D. (Eds.), *AI-mediated language education in the metaverse era*. Springer.

Chun, D. M., Karimi, H., & Sañosa, D. J. (2022). Traveling by headset: Immersive VR for language learning. *CALICO Journal, 39*(2), 129–149. DOI: 10.1558/cj.21306

Clancey, W. J. (1995) A tutorial on situated learning. In Self, J. (Ed.), *International Conference on Computers and Education (Taiwan)* (pp.49–70). AACE

Clark, D. (2020). *Artificial intelligence for learning: How to use AI to support employee development*. KoganPage.

Connor, C. M., Mazzocco, M. M. M., Kurz, T., Crowe, E. C., Tighe, E. L., Wood, T. S., & Morrison, F. J. (2018). Using assessment to individualize early mathematics instruction. *Journal of School Psychology, 66*, 97–113. DOI: 10.1016/j.jsp.2017.04.005 PMID: 29499792

Cope, B., Kalantzis, M., & Searsmith, D. (2021). Artificial intelligence for education: Knowledge and its assessment in AI-enabled learning ecologies. *Educational Philosophy and Theory, 53*(12), 1229–1245. DOI: 10.1080/00131857.2020.1728732

Costa, R. S., Tan, Q., Pivot, F., Zhang, X., & Wang, H. (2021). Personalized and adaptive learning: Educational practice and technological impact. *Texto Livre: Linguagem e Tecnologia, 14*(3), 1–11. DOI: 10.35699/1983-3652.2021.33445

De la Vall, R. R. F., & Araya, F. G. (2023). Exploring the benefits and challenges of AI-language learning tools. *Int. J. Soc. Sci. Humanit. Invent, 10*(1), 7569–7576. DOI: 10.18535/ijsshi/v10i01.02

Dhimolea, T. K., Kaplan-Rakowski, R., & Lin, L. (2022). A systematic review of research on high-immersion virtual reality for language learning. *TechTrends, 66*(5), 810–824. DOI: 10.1007/s11528-022-00717-w

Dooly, M., Thrasher, T., & Sadler, R. (2023). "Whoa! Incredible!": Language learning experiences in virtual reality. *RELC Journal*, *54*(2), 321–339. DOI: 10.1177/00336882231167610

Ebadi, S., & Azizimajd, H. (2024). Investigating the effects of speaking tasks in clubhouse on EFL learners' speaking and foreign language speaking anxiety. *Computer Assisted Language Learning*, •••, 1–33. https://doi-org.libproxy.library.unt.edu/10.1080/09588221.2024.2371381. DOI: 10.1080/09588221.2024.2371381

Ellis, R. (2021). A short history of SLA: Where have we come from and where are we going? *Language Teaching*, *54*(2), 190–205. DOI: 10.1017/S0261444820000038

European Commission. (2018, April 25). *Artificial intelligence for Europe*. COM (2018) 237 final. https://eur-lex.europa.eu/legal-content/EN/TXT/?uri=COM%3A2018%3A237%3AFIN

Fransson, G., Holmberg, J., & Westelius, C. (2020). The challenges of using head mounted virtual reality in K-12 schools from a teacher perspective. *Education and Information Technologies*, *25*(4), 3383–3404. DOI: 10.1007/s10639-020-10119-1

Gruber, A., & Kaplan-Rakowski, R. (2020). Use experience of public speaking practice in virtual reality. In Zheng, R. (Ed.), *Cognitive and affective perspectives on immersive technology in education* (pp. 235–249). IGI Global., DOI: 10.4018/978-1-7998-3250-8.ch012

Hammerschmidt-Snidarich, S. M., Edwards, L. M., Christ, T. J., & Thayer, A. J. (2019). Leveraging technology: A multi-component personalized system of instruction to teach sight words. *Journal of School Psychology*, *72*, 150–171. DOI: 10.1016/j.jsp.2018.12.005 PMID: 30819460

Hanson, K., & Shelton, B. E. (2008). Design and development of virtual reality: Analysis of challenges faced by educators. *Journal of Educational Technology & Society*, *11*(1), 118–131. https://www.jstor.org/stable/jeductechsoci.11.1.118

Heilman, M., Collins-Thompson, K., Callan, J., Eskenazi, M., Juffs, A., & Wilson, L. (2010). Personalization of reading passages improves vocabulary acquisition. *International Journal of Artificial Intelligence in Education, 20*(1), 73–98. DOI: 10.3233/JAI-2010-0003

Holmes, W., Bialik, M., & Fadel, C. (2019). *Artificial intelligence in education: Promises and implications for teaching and learning*. Center for Curriculum Redesign.

Hooshyar, D., Yousefi, M., Wang, M., & Lim, H. (2018). A data-driven procedural-content-generation approach for educational games. *Journal of Computer Assisted Learning, 34*(6), 731–739. DOI: 10.1111/jcal.12280

Hsieh, T.-C., Wang, T.-I., Su, C.-Y., & Lee, M.-C. (2024). A fuzzy logic-based personalized learning system for supporting adaptive English learning. *Journal of Educational Technology & Society, 15*(1), 273–288. https://www.jstor.org/stable/10.2307/jeductechsoci.15.1.273

Hsu, C.-K., Hwang, G.-J., & Chang, C.-K. (2013). A personalized recommendation-based mobile learning approach to improving the reading performance of EFL students. *Computers & Education, 63*, 327–336. DOI: 10.1016/j.compedu.2012.12.004

Huang, H. M., Rauch, U., & Liaw, S. S. (2010). Investigating learners' attitudes toward virtual reality learning environments: Based on a constructivist approach. *Computers & Education, 55*(3), 1171–1182. DOI: 10.1016/j.compedu.2010.05.014

Huang, S.-L., & Shiu, J.-H. (2012). A user-centric adaptive learning system for e-learning 2.0. *Journal of Educational Technology & Society, 15*(3), 214–225. https://www.jstor.org/stable/jeductechsoci.15.3.214

Huang, X., Zou, D., Cheng, G., Chen, X., & Xie, H. (2023). Trends, research issues and applications of artificial intelligence in language education. *Journal of Educational Technology & Society, 26*(1), 112–131. DOI: 10.30191/ETS.202301_26(1).0009

Hulstijn, J. H., & Laufer, B. (2001). Some empirical evidence for the involvement load hypothesis in vocabulary acquisition. *Language Learning, 51*(3), 539–558. DOI: 10.1111/0023-8333.00164

Hussain, R., Sabir, A., Lee, D., Zaidi, S. F. A., Pedro, A., Abbas, M. S., & Park, C. (2024). Conversational AI-based VR system to improve construction safety training of migrant workers. *Automation in Construction, 160,* 105315. Advance online publication. DOI: 10.1016/j.autcon.2024.105315

Jung, J., & Graf, S. (2008). An approach for personalized web-based vocabulary learning through word association games. *Proceedings of 2008 International Symposium on Applications and the Internet,* Finland, 325–328. IEEE. http://dx.doi.org/DOI: 10.1109/SAINT.2008.63

Kannan, J., & Munday, P. (2018). New trends in second language learning and teaching through the lens of ICT, networked learning, and artificial intelligence. *Círculo de Lingüística Aplicada a la Comunicación, 76,* 13–30. DOI: 10.5209/CLAC.62495

Kaplan-Rakowski, R. (2024). High-immersion virtual reality for pragmatics development. In Chapelle, C. A., Taguchi, N., & Kadar, D. (Eds.), *The encyclopedia of applied linguistics* (2nd ed.). Wiley-Blackwell.

Kaplan-Rakowski, R., Cockerham, D., & Ferdig, R. E. (2023). The impact of sound andimmersive experience on learners using high-immersion virtual reality and table: A mixed-methods study. *British Journal of Educational Technology*, *55*(4), 1560–1582. DOI: 10.1111/bjet.13417

Kaplan-Rakowski, R., Dhimolea, T. K., & Khukalenko, I. S. (2023). Language teachers' beliefs about using high–immersion virtual reality. *Education and Information Technologies*, *28*(10), 12505–12525. DOI: 10.1007/s10639-023-11686-9

Kaplan-Rakowski, R., Grotewold, K., Hartwick, P., & Papin, K. (2023). Generative AI and teachers' perspectives on its implementation in education. *Journal of Interactive Learning Research*, *34*(2), 313–338. https://www.learntechlib.org/p/222363/. DOI: 10.70725/815246mfssgp

Kaplan-Rakowski, R., & Gruber, A. (2019). Low-immersion versus high-immersion virtual reality: Definitions, classification, and examples with a foreign language focus. *Proceedings of the Innovation in Language Learning International Conference 2019,* Florence, 552–555.

Kaplan-Rakowski, R., & Gruber, A. (2023). An experimental study on reading in high-immersion virtual reality. *British Journal of Educational Technology, 55*(2), 541–559. DOI: 10.1111/bjet.13392

Kaplan-Rakowski, R., Papin, K., & Hartwick, P. (2023). Language teachers' perceptions and use of extended reality. *CALICO Journal, 40*(1), 1–23. DOI: 10.1558/cj.22759

Khukalenko, I. S., Kaplan-Rakowski, R., An, Y., & Iushina, V. D. (2022). Teachers' perceptions of using virtual reality technology in classrooms: A large-scale survey. *Education and Information Technologies, 27*(8), 11591–11613. DOI: 10.1007/s10639-022-11061-0 PMID: 35603316

Kim, S. K., & Webb, S. (2022). The effects of spaced practice on second language learning: A meta-analysis. *Language Learning, 72*(1), 269–319. DOI: 10.1111/lang.12479

Kinginger, C. (2002). Defining the zone of proximal development in US foreign language education. *Applied Linguistics, 23*(2), 240–261. DOI: 10.1093/applin/23.2.240

Kohnke, L., Zhang, R., & Zou, D. (2019). Using mobile vocabulary learning apps as aids to knowledge retention: Business vocabulary acquisition. *Journal of Asia TEFL, 16*(2), 448–767. DOI: 10.18823/asiatefl.2019.16.2.16.683

Kolb, D. A. (1984). *Experiential learning: Experience as the source of learning and development*. Prentice-Hall, Inc.

Kolb, D. A. (2015). *Experiential learning: Experience as the source of learning and development* (2nd ed.). Pearson Education, Inc.

Kramsch, C. (2014). Language and culture. *AILA Review, 27*(1), 30–55. DOI: 10.1075/aila.27.02kra

Lai, C., & Li, G. (2011). Technology and task-based language teaching: A critical review. *CALICO Journal, 28*(2), 498–521. DOI: 10.11139/cj.28.2.498-521

Lampropoulos, G., Ferdig, R. E., & Kaplan-Rakowski, R. (2024). A social media data analysis of general and educational use of ChatGPT: Understanding emotional educators. *SSRN*. http://dx.doi.org/DOI: 10.2139/ssrn.4468181

Lave, J., & Wenger, E. (1991). *Situated learning: Legitimate peripheral participation*. Cambridge University Press. DOI: 10.1017/CBO9780511815355

Lee, A. (2019). Using virtual reality to test academic listening proficiency. *Korean Journal of English Language and Linguistics*, *19*(4), 688–712. DOI: 10.15738/kjell.19.4.201912.688

Lee, D., Huh, Y., Lin, C.-Y., & Reigeluth, C. M. (2018). Technology functions for personalized learning in learner-centered schools. *Educational Technology Research and Development*, *66*(5), 1269–1302. DOI: 10.1007/s11423-018-9615-9

Lee, D., Huh, Y., Lin, C.-Y., & Reigeluth, C. M. (2022). Personalized learning practice in U.S. learner-centered schools. *Contemporary Educational Technology*, *14*(4), ep385. Advance online publication. DOI: 10.30935/cedtech/12330

Li, F., Fan, S., & Wang, Y. (2022). Mobile-assisted language learning in Chinese higher education context: A systematic review from the perspective of the situated learning theory. *Education and Information Technologies*, *27*(7), 9665–9688. DOI: 10.1007/s10639-022-11025-4

Lin, C. F., Yeh, Y.-C., Hung, Y. H., & Chang, R. I. (2013). Data mining for providing a personalized learning path in creativity: An application of decision trees. *Computers & Education*, *68*, 199–210. DOI: 10.1016/j.compedu.2013.05.009

Luck, M., & Aylett, R. (2000). Applying artificial intelligence to virtual reality: Intelligent virtual environments. *Applied Artificial Intelligence*, *14*(1), 3–32. DOI: 10.1080/088395100117142

Ma, L. (2021). An immersive context teaching method for college English based on artificial intelligence and machine learning in virtual reality technology. *Mobile Information Systems*, *2021*(1), 2637439. Advance online publication. DOI: 10.1155/2021/2637439

Magomadov, V. S. (2020). The application of artificial intelligence and Big Data analytics in personalized learning. *Journal of Physics: Conference Series*, *1691*(1), 012169. Advance online publication. DOI: 10.1088/1742-6596/1691/1/012169

Makransky, G., Terkildsen, T. S., & Mayer, R. E. (2019). Adding immersive virtual reality to a science lab simulation causes more presence but less learning. *Learning and Instruction*, *60*, 225–236. DOI: 10.1016/j.learninstruc.2017.12.007

Mirzaei, M. S., Meshgi, K., & Nishida, T. (2020). A situation creation system to enable experiential learning in virtual worlds for developing cross-cultural competencies. In K.-M. Frederiksen, S. Larsen, L. Bradley, & S. Thouësny (Eds.), *CALL for widening participation: Short papers from EUROCALL 2020* (1st ed., pp. 233–239). Research-publishing.net. https://doi.org/DOI: 10.14705/rpnet.2020.48.1194

Mirzaei, M. S., Zhang, Q., Van der Struijk, S., & Nishida, T., (2018). Language learning through conversation envisioning in virtual reality: A sociocultural approach. *Future-proof CALL: Language learning as exploration and encounters-short papers from EUROCALL*, 207–213. http://dx.doi.org/DOI: 10.14705/rpnet.2018.26.838

Obari, H., Lambacher, S., & Kikuchi, H. (2020). The impact of using AI and VR with blended learning on English as a foreign language teaching. In K.-M. Frederiksen, S. Larsen, L. Bradley & S. Thouësny (Eds.), *CALL for widening participation: short papers from EUROCALL 2020 (pp. 253-258).* Research-publishing.net. https://doi.org/DOI: 10.14705/rpnet.2020.48.1197

Pack, A., Barrett, A., Liang, H.-N., & Monteiro, D. V. (2020). University EAP students' perceptions of using a prototype virtual reality learning environment to learn writing structure. *International Journal of Computer-Assisted Language Learning and Teaching, 10*(1), 27–46. DOI: 10.4018/IJCALLT.2020010103

Park, M. (2018). Innovative assessment of aviation English in a virtual world: Windows into cognitive and metacognitive strategies. *ReCALL, 30*(2), 196–213. DOI: 10.1017/S0958344017000362

Pavlik, J. V. (2023). Collaborating with ChatGPT: Considering the implications of generative artificial intelligence for journalism and media education. *Journalism & Mass Communication Educator, 78*(1), 84–93. DOI: 10.1177/10776958221149577

Peng, H., Ma, S., & Spector, J. M. (2019). Personalized adaptive learning: An emerging pedagogical approach enabled by a smart learning environment. *Smart Learning Environments, 6*(9), 9. Advance online publication. DOI: 10.1186/s40561-019-0089-y

Pérez-Paredes, P., Ordoñana Guillamón, C., & Aguado Jiménez, P. (2018). Language teachers' perceptions on the use of OER language processing technologies in MALL. *Computer Assisted Language Learning, 31*(5-6), 522–545. DOI: 10.1080/09588221.2017.1418754

Petersen, G. B., Petkakis, G., & Makransky, G. (2022). A study of how immersion and interactivity drive VR learning. *Computers & Education, 179*, 104429. Advance online publication. DOI: 10.1016/j.compedu.2021.104429

Pokrivcakova, S. (2019). Preparing teachers for the application of AI-powered technologies in foreign language education. *Journal of Language and Cultural Education, 7*(3), 135–153. DOI: 10.2478/jolace-2019-0025

Porter, B., & Grippa, F. (2020). A platform for AI-enabled real-time feedback to promote digital collaboration. *Sustainability (Basel), 12*(24), 10243. Advance online publication. DOI: 10.3390/su122410243

Porwol, L., Pereira, A. G., & Dumas, C. (2023). Transforming e-participation: VR-dialogue – building and evaluating an AI-supported framework for next-gen VR-enabled e-participation research. *Transforming Government, 17*(2), 233–250. DOI: 10.1108/TG-12-2021-0205

Rachels, J. R., & Rockinson-Szapkiw, A. J. (2018). The effects of a mobile gamification app on elementary students' Spanish achievement and self-efficacy. *Computer Assisted Language Learning, 31*(1–2), 72–89. DOI: 10.1080/09588221.2017.1382536

Regan, P. M., & Jesse, J. (2019). Ethical challenges of edtech, big data and personalized learning: Twenty-first century student sorting and tracking. *Ethics and Information Technology, 21*(3), 167–179. DOI: 10.1007/s10676-018-9492-2

Schmid, R., Pauli, C., Stebler, R., Reusser, K., & Petko, D. (2022). Implementation of technology-supported personalized learning—Its impact on instructional quality. *The Journal of Educational Research, 115*(3), 187–198. DOI: 10.1080/00220671.2022.2089086

Schmidt, T., & Strasser, T. (2022). Artificial intelligence in foreign language learning and teaching: A call for intelligent practice. *Anglistik, 33*(1), 165–184. DOI: 10.33675/ANGL/2022/1/14

Sharma, P., & Dash, B. (2023). AI and VR enabled modern LMS for students with special needs. *Journal of Foreign Language Education and Technology, 8*(1), 1–15.

Sharrab, Y., Almutiri, N. T., Tarawneh, M., Alzyoud, F., Al-Ghuwairi, A.-R. F., & Al-Fraihat, D. (2023). Toward smart and immersive classroom based on AI, VR, and 6G. *International Journal of Emerging Technologies in Learning, 18*(2), 4–16. DOI: 10.3991/ijet.v18i02.35997

Shemshack, A., & Spector, J. M. (2020). A systematic literature review of personalized learning terms. *Smart Learning Environments, 7*(1), 33. Advance online publication. DOI: 10.1186/s40561-020-00140-9

Shih, Y.-C., & Yang, M.-T. (2008). A collaborative virtual environment for situated language learning using VEC3D. *Journal of Educational Technology & Society*, *11*(1), 56–68. https://www.jstor.org/stable/10.2307/jeductechsoci.11.1.56

Slavuj, V., Meštrović, A., & Kovačić, B. (2017). Adaptivity in educational systems for language learning: A review. *Computer Assisted Language Learning*, *30*(1–2), 64–90. DOI: 10.1080/09588221.2016.1242502

Su, P. H., Wu, C. H., & Lee, L. S. (2014). A recursive dialogue game for personalized computer-aided pronunciation training. *IEEE/ACM Transactions on Audio, Speech, and Language Processing*, *23*(1), 127–141. DOI: 10.1109/TASLP.2014.2375572

Tai, T. Y., & Chen, H. H. J. (2021). The impact of immersive virtual reality on EFL learners' listening comprehension. *Journal of Educational Computing Research*, *59*(7), 1272–1293. https://doi.org/https://doi.org/10.1177/0735633121994291. DOI: 10.1177/0735633121994291

Tang, K.-Y., Chang, C.-Y., & Hwang, G.-J. (2023). Trends in artificial intelligence-supported e-learning: A systematic review and co-citation network analysis (1998–2019). *Interactive Learning Environments*, *31*(4), 2134–2152. DOI: 10.1080/10494820.2021.1875001

Taylor, D. L., Yeung, M., & Bashet, A. Z. (2021). Personalized and adaptive learning. In Ryoo, J., & Winkelmann, K. (Eds.), *Innovative learning environments in STEM higher education* (pp. 17–34). Springer International Publishing., DOI: 10.1007/978-3-030-58948-6_2

The American Council on the Teaching of Foreign Languages (ACTFL). (2024). *The ACTFL proficiency guidelines 2024*. ACTFL. https://www.actfl.org/uploads/files/general/Resources-Publications/ACTFL_Proficiency_Guidelines_2024.pdf

Thormundsson, B. (2023, July 7). *AI corporate investment worldwide 2015-2022*. Statista. https://www.statista.com/statistics/941137/ai-investment-and-funding-worldwide/#statisticContainer

Thrasher, T. (2022). The impact of virtual reality on L2 French learners' language anxiety and oral comprehensibility: An exploratory study. *CALICO Journal*, *39*(2), 219–238. DOI: 10.1558/cj.42198

Thrasher, T. (2023). Meeting in the metaverse: Language learners' insights into the affordances of virtual reality. In D. Cockerham, R. Kaplan-Rakowski, W. Foshay & M. J. Spector (Eds.), *Reimagining education: Studies and stories for effective learning in an evolving digital environment* (pp. 179–194). Educational Communications and Technology: Issues and Innovations. Springer. https://doi.org/DOI: 10.1007/978-3-031-25102-3_17

Thrasher, T., Kaplan-Rakowski, R., Chun, D., & Sadler, R. (2023). Virtual reality: "Awesome", "OK", or "Not so good" for language learning? In B. Bédi, Y. Choubsaz, K. Friðriksdóttir, A. Gimeno-Sanz, S. Björg Vilhjálmsdóttir & S. Zahova (Eds.), *CALL for all Languages - EUROCALL 2023 Short Papers* (pp. 15–18). https://doi.org/DOI: 10.4995/EuroCALL2023.2023.16948

Thrasher, T., Kaplan-Rakowski, R., Ovsiannikova, U., Meyr, J., & Yuan, Y. (2024). "I can talk to Spanish speakers in Illinois!": Student perspectives on AI-avatar role plays in virtual reality. *WorldCALL2023: Conference Proceedings.*https://doi.org/DOI: 10.22492/issn.2759-1182.2023.18

UNESCO. (2022). *Recommendation on the ethics of artificial intelligence*. UNESCO. https://unesdoc.unesco.org/ark:/48223/pf0000381137

U.S. Department of Education, Office of Educational Technology. (November, 2010). Transforming American education: Learning powered by technology. National education technology plan 2010. https://www.ed.gov/sites/default/files/netp2010.pdf

Vázquez, C., Xia, L., Aikawa, T., & Maes, P. (2018). Words in motion: Kinesthetic language learning in virtual reality. *In 2018 IEEE 18th International Conference on advanced learning technologies (ICALT)* (pp. 272–276). IEEE. https://doi.org/DOI: 10.1109/ICALT.2018.00069

Wang, D., Han, H., Zhan, Z., Xu, J., Liu, Q., & Ren, G. (2015). A problem solving oriented intelligent tutoring system to improve students' acquisition of basic computer skills. *Computers & Education*, *81*, 102–112. DOI: 10.1016/j.compedu.2014.10.003

Wang, Y., Grant, S., & Grist, M. (2021). Enhancing the learning of multi-level undergraduate Chinese language with a 3D immersive experience - An exploratory study. *Computer Assisted Language Learning*, *34*(1–2), 114–132. DOI: 10.1080/09588221.2020.1774614

Warschauer, M. (2005). Sociocultural perspectives on CALL. In Egbert, J., & Petrie, G. (Eds.), *CALL research perspectives* (pp. 41–52). Lawrence Erlbaum.

Wei, C.-W., Kao, H.-Y., Lu, H.-H., & Liu, Y. C. (2018). The effects of competitive gaming scenarios and personalized assistance strategies on English vocabulary learning. *Journal of Educational Technology & Society*, *21*(3), 146–158. https://www.jstor.org/stable/26458514

Wong, J. (2000). "Applying" conversation analysis in applied linguistics: Evaluating English as a second language textbook dialogue [Electronic Version]. In *TESOL Convention, Vancouver, BC*.

Woo, J. H., & Choi, H. (2021). Systematic review for AI-based language learning tools. *arXiv preprint arXiv:2111.04455*. https://doi.org//arXiv.2111.04455DOI: 10.48550

Wu, T. T., Huang, Y. M., Chao, H. C., & Park, J. H. (2014). Personalized English reading sequencing based on learning portfolio analysis. *Information Sciences*, *257*, 248–263. DOI: 10.1016/j.ins.2011.07.021

Xie, H., Chu, H.-C., Hwang, G.-J., & Wang, C.-C. (2019). Trends and development in technology-enhanced adaptive/personalized learning: A systematic review of journal publications from 2007 to 2017. *Computers & Education*, *140*, 103599. Advance online publication. DOI: 10.1016/j.compedu.2019.103599

Yang, H., Gao, C., & Shen, H. (2024). Learner interaction with, and response to, Ai-programmed automated writing evaluation feedback in EFL writing: An exploratory study. *Education and Information Technologies, 29*(4), 3837–3858. https://doi-org.libproxy.library.unt.edu/10.1007/s10639-023-11991-3. DOI: 10.1007/s10639-023-11991-3

Ye, Y., & Kaplan-Rakowski, R. (2024). An exploratory study on practicing listening comprehension skills in high–immersion virtual reality. *British Journal of Educational Technology, 55*(4), 1651–1672. DOI: 10.1111/bjet.13481

You, X., Li, M., Xiao, Y., & Liu, H. (2019). The feedback of the Chinese learning diagnosis system for personalized learning in classrooms. *Frontiers in Psychology, 10*, 1751. DOI: 10.3389/fpsyg.2019.01751 PMID: 31611827

Yun, C.-O., Jung, S.-J., & Yun, T.-S. (2024). Interactive learning tutor service platform based on artificial intelligence in a virtual reality environment. In B. J. Choi, D. Singh, U. S. Tiwary, & W.-Y. Chung (Eds.), Intelligent Human Computer Interaction (pp. 367–373). Springer., , IHCI 2023.DOI: 10.1007/978-3-031-53827-8_32

Zawacki-Richter, O., Marín, V. I., Bond, M., & Gouverneur, F. (2019). Systematic review of research on artificial intelligence applications in higher education–where are the educators? *International Journal of Educational Technology in Higher Education, 16*(1), 1–27. DOI: 10.1186/s41239-019-0171-0

Zou, D., Wang, M., Xie, H., Cheng, G., Wang, F. L., & Lee, L. K. (2021). A comparative study on linguistic theories for modeling EFL learners: Facilitating personalized vocabulary learning via task recommendations. *Interactive Learning Environments, 29*(2), 270–282. DOI: 10.1080/10494820.2020.1789178

Chapter 6
Preparing for Tomorrow:
AI Literacy in English Language Teaching

Ivana Krsmanović
Faculty of Technical Sciences, University of Kragujevac, Čačak, Serbia

Dagmar Anna Archan
CAMPUS 02 UAS Graz, Austria

ABSTRACT

The paper underscores the significance of incorporating Artificial Intelligence (AI) literacy into English language instruction to adapt to the changing educational landscape. Utilizing a comprehensive mixed-methods research design, a survey was administered among 115 English Language Teaching (ELT) educators from various geographical locations worldwide. The findings indicate a high level of self-reported AI literacy among educators, with strong competencies in detecting, understanding, and applying AI. The findings further reveal that a small percentage of educators have received training in AI application in ELT, and among those who have, perceived benefits were reported as low. Although a number of teachers expressed concern about the reliability, transparency, and potential negative impacts on teaching quality and student outcomes when considering the use of AI in ELT, the findings confirmed that utilizing AI

DOI: 10.4018/979-8-3693-5477-3.ch006

tools in language education, such as customized feedback and automated assessment, can offer various benefits for learners.

INTRODUCTION

Since 1989, when the *International Journal of Artificial Intelligence* was first published, how to utilize Artificial Intelligence (AI) for learning and teaching practices has become the core field of interest of researchers engaged in AI in education (AIED) (Holmes et al., 2022, p. 19). While, on the one hand, research in AI in Education has demonstrated the effectiveness of various AI tools for learners and teachers alike (Cardona et al., 2023, p. 1), numerous concerns have been expressed regarding AI potentially overtaking teachers' jobs (Gentile et al., 2023; Edmett et al., 2023; Popenici & Kerr, 2017) and eventually jeopardizing the educational system as it is, causing unrepairable consequences, on the other hand. Despite ongoing disputes, everyday practice in universities and schools has confirmed the increasing popularity of AI tools among both student and teaching populations.

In that sense, AI literacy of teachers emerges as a major pillar of all future AI in Education. However, not all educators seem to be equally affected by these rapid advancements. It looks like educators specializing in Information and Communication Technology (ICT) have exhibited a more intuitive grasp of AI, due to their educational background, while the broader teaching population, after initial scepticism regarding the potential of AI to enrich learning/teaching experiences, often prompts the adoption of more rudimentary approaches to the discipline. So, to address the unmet priorities found in contemporary classrooms, these educators seek AI-enhanced approaches that can provide safe, effective and scalable outputs, even without an in-depth understanding of AI. However, despite aspirations that AI in education can significantly enhance the learning experience, enable personalized teaching, and strengthen academic results, it looks like many of these educators have a sense of still ''being in the dark''. One way in which these issues might be addressed, as the Council of Europe suggests, is by encouraging all teachers of subjects ranging from the sciences to the humanities and arts, and not just the

ICT or computer science teachers, to explore the potential uses, benefits, impacts, challenges and risks of AI in their subject areas (Holmes et al., 2022, p. 31). Incorporating AI topics into school curricula is viewed as a strategic initiative to prepare the next generation (Chiu & Chai, 2020; Zhao et al., 2022).

As AI continues to gain prominence in education, it is crucial to examine its implementation within English Language Teaching and Learning contexts, particularly focusing on the AI literacy of EL educators. The digital age is revolutionizing our learning and teaching methods and introducing a plethora of new tools that can support us in many ways. In the field of English Language Teaching, the current landscape of research indicates a growing recognition of the importance of AI literacy among educators and a willingness to incorporate AI into teaching practices (Sharma & Bozkurt, 2024; Yang et al., 2020). The question remains: Are we adequately prepared for this transformative shift in education, and if not, how can we prepare?

What further complicates the matter is the fact that the application of AI in English language teaching has already demonstrated promising outcomes in enriching the learning environment (Jiang, 2023; Mukhallafi, 2020), so we must not be (too) late. More precisely, ChatGPT, a language-based AI model, has gained significant prominence in ELT research as a writing assistance tool that can increase the motivation of learners to learn English (Mauban, 2024; Tica & Krsmanović, 2024; Alharbi, 2023; Koraishi, 2023; Ali et al., 2023; Godwin-Jones, 2022). Although ''AI in ELT is still in its infancy'' (Saradgah & Sa'di, 2022, p. 351), concerns arise that a lack of proficiency in using AI-powered tools in teaching English might widen the gap in learning and teaching opportunities. At the same time, EL educators might feel inadequate, so they should become digitally literate, master AI tools and increase employability as a result (Zhai, 2022).

LITERATURE REVIEW

Relevant studies underscore the imperative for English language teacher education to integrate AI literacy, revealing a significant gap in training and preparation among educators worldwide. For example, the British Council's report on *Artificial Intelligence and English Language Teaching: Preparing for the Future* (Edmett et al., 2023, p. 19) states that, since English language learning is likely to be the most common discipline for AI use in education, English language teacher education and training must include a focus on AI literacy. This report also emphasizes that 54% of English educators feel that have not been adequately trained to incorporate AI in their teaching (Edmett et al., 2023, p. 30). The findings of this study included more than 1,000 ELT educators from 15 countries who confessed that they are ill-prepared for the increased use of AI and that their existing teacher education and continuing professional development (CPD) provision was seen as lacking when it comes to teachers' digital literacies (Edmett et al., 2023, p. 52). In that sense, continued research and endeavours are essential to bridge the gap between AI technology and educational practices to ensure the effective implementation and utilization of AI in teaching.

Research into AI literacy us still in its infancy and it is not surprising that no generally valid definition of AI literacy has been developed (Ng et al., 2021). Wang et al. (2020) define AI literacy as follows: "to be aware of and comprehend AI technology in practical applications; to be able to apply and exploit AI technology for accomplishing tasks proficiently; and to be able to analyze, select, and critically evaluate the data and information provided by AI, while fostering awareness of one's own personal responsibilities and respect for reciprocal rights and obligations" (Wang et al., 2020, p. 3). According to their definition, AI literacy consists of the ability of using AI applications to fulfil tasks in a targeted manner, taking a critical view of their output and being aware of their responsibilities when using AI tools. As a result, they define four areas of competence: awareness, usage, evaluation and ethics (cf. Wang et al., 2020). Awareness describes the ability to identify and understand AI technologies, while usage refers to the ability to utilise and apply AI technologies in such a way that tasks can be successfully completed (i.e. having access to AI applications, mastering the operation of AI applications and integrating AI tools). Evaluation deals with the ability to analyse AI applications, select the right AI applications for a specific purpose and critically assess their results. Ethics refers to the ability to recognise and assess responsibilities and risks associated with the use of AI technologies.

To describe AI competences, Ng et al. (2021) conducted a comprehensive literature review on digital literacy and found that AI literacy is often defined based on the concept of digital literacy. They summarise four sub-areas that contribute to AI literacy (cf. Ng et al., 2021, p. 4): know and understand AI, use and apply AI, evaluate and create AI and AI ethics (fairness, transparency and safety in dealing with AI). This definition is somewhat broader than that of Wang et al. as it also includes the creation of AI applications.

Long and Magerko (2020) define AI literacy as follows: "a set of competencies that enables individuals to critically evaluate AI technologies, communicate and collaborate effectively with AI, and use AI as a tool online, at home, and in the workplace" (Long & Magerko, 2020, p. 2). Like Ng et al., they see digital literacy and the ability to use it responsibly and comprehensibly as a prerequisite for AI literacy, but not the ability to program AI (Long & Magerko, 2020, p. 2; Wang et al., 2020, 1).

Yet, despite AI literacy among EL educators being a key predictor of successful implementation of AI tools in everyday teaching and practice, a plethora of research has primarily focused on the effects of AI on learning outcomes. These studies have investigated various aspects, such as the personalization of learning experiences (Moybeka, 2023), automated writing evaluation (Almehmadi, 2024), the efficiency of language acquisition, and the enhancement of student engagement and motivation (Sumakul et al., 2022; Mukhallafi, 2020), while often overlooking the crucial role of educators' proficiency with AI technologies. Indeed, numerous research studies have highlighted the potential benefits of employing AI technologies in ELT and and emphasized the need for developing teachers' digital competencies and acquiring essential skills for the twenty-first century (Choukaier, 2024; Sharma & Bozkurt, 2024; Ng et al., 2023; Bozkurt, 2023; Moybeka, 2023; Vera, 2023; Black, 2023; Sumakul et al., 2022; Mukhallafi, 2020).

The current landscape of research indicates a growing recognition of the importance of AI literacy among educators and a willingness to incorporate AI into teaching practices (Dincer & Bal, 2024; Alhalangy & AbdAlgane, 2023; Black, 2023; Ng et al., 2023). However, although a number of studies indicate that EL educators perceive AI technologies as opportunities to enhance language teaching and practice (Mabuan, 2024; Dincer & Bal, 2024; Koraishi, 2023), only few research studies have examined how prepared teachers are to effectively implement and manage these technologies in the classroom. Further studies are needed to explore the AI literacy proficiency of EL educators.

RESEARCH OBJECTIVES

The proposed study aims to provide insights into the readiness of English language educators to embrace AI technologies in their teaching practices, offering implications for teacher training programs, curriculum development, and the future of ELT pedagogy in the era of AI. The goal of the research study is to assess EL educators' AI literacy level first, and then evaluate their attitudes towards AI implementation in teaching practices, and their needs for further training and development in that sense.

Firstly, it is hypothesized (H1) that English language teachers with higher levels of AI literacy will demonstrate greater confidence and willingness to adopt AI technologies in their classrooms. Secondly, (H2) it is anticipated that teachers who perceive AI as a threat to their profession may exhibit resistance towards incorporating AI tools into their teaching practices. Lastly, (H3) the study posits that educators with extensive training in AI and educational technology will be more adept at leveraging AI tools to enhance language learning outcomes.

Methodology, Sampling and Instrument

This research explores the intersection of Artificial Intelligence (AI) and English Language Teaching (ELT) through a comprehensive, exploratory mixed-methods design.

The instrument utilized in this study comprises five parts to comprehensively assess various aspects related to Artificial Intelligence (AI) literacy among English language lecturers. The first part consists of a demographic questionnaire comprising six questions aimed at gathering essential background information about the participants. Following this, the second part employs the Meta AI Literacy Scale (MAIL), developed by Carolus et al. (2023), which consists of 34 statements (within 9 constructs) designed to measure AI literacy based on well-founded competency models (Carolus et al. in particular refer to Ng et al.´s concept of AI literacy) and psychological change- and meta-competencies. This scale offers a robust framework for evaluating participants' proficiency in understanding and utilizing AI technologies, and it was validated for reliability. Lastly, part three explores training and professional development issues through 4 questions, and part four focuses on benefits and challenges of AI in English language classrooms. Finally, part five deals with Pearson's correlation.

A 1-5 point Likert scale was employed in this study to assess various dimensions related to AI literacy and its application in ELT. This scale allows participants to indicate their level of agreement or disagreement with given statements, ranging from 1 (strongly disagree) to 5 (strongly agree). Results are interpreted with means categorized as follows: 1.00-1.79 (very low); 1.80-2.59 (low); 2.60-3.39 (moderate); 3.40-4.19 (high); 4.20-5.00 (very high). The reliability of the scale was assessed using the Cronbach's alpha coefficient, resulting in a Cronbach's Alpha of 0.95 for the entire instrument, 0.93 for the MAIL scale, and 0.88 for the AI-related questions in Part 3.

The study involved a sample of N=115 English Language Teaching (ELT) educators from diverse geographical locations worldwide. The sampling method used in the study aligns with the concept of purposeful sampling. The survey instrument was prepared using Google Forms and disseminated through various channels, including personal networks of ELT educators in the EU and beyond, as well as educational/research groups on social media platforms such as Facebook, Linked-in, and Twitter. The analysis of the collected data involved both quantitative and qualitative methods. Quantitatively, correlations between AI literacy levels and attitudes towards AI integration were examined, along with the impact of professional development on AI adoption. The qualitative analysis entails thematic coding of responses regarding perceived benefits and challenges of AI integration, as well as narratives surrounding attitudes towards AI in ELT. The collected data underwent analysis using SPSS software for statistical and inferential analysis, with a Pearson coefficient analysis.

RESULTS AND DISCUSSION

Part 1: Demography (Q1-6)

To provide a comprehensive understanding of the participants, an analysis of the demographic data was conducted to contextualize their backgrounds and experiences. The demographic analysis based on the provided data reveals a distribution across different age groups (Q1). The majority of the sample falls within the age range of 31-50 years, with 30.4% aged 31-40 and 46.1% aged 41-50. Additionally, there is a notable percentage of individuals aged 51-65, comprising 13.9% of the population. The younger population, aged 20-30, represents 7.8% of the total, indicating a smaller but still relevant segment. Those aged 65 and over constitute 1.7% of the population.

The demographic analysis also reveals insights into gender distribution and the professional background of the educators. The demographic data provided indicates a distribution of gender identities within the sample (Q2), with females comprising the majority at 72.2%, followed by males at 25.2%, and other gender identities at 2.6%. The data provided on the highest level of education attained by the respondents (Q3) reveals a diverse educational landscape. The majority of English language educators hold a Master's degree (MA) at 46.6%, followed by those with a Doctorate (PhD) at 33.9%, and individuals with a Bachelor's degree (BA) at 18%. A smaller percentage of educators are currently pursuing a PhD at 1.5%.

As far as current employment status is concerned (Q4), the distribution is as follows: a substantial majority of respondents are engaged full-time (87.8%). Part-time positions constitute 7.8%, reflecting a notable but comparatively smaller segment. The adjunct category accounts for only 1.7% of professionals, whereas retired educators comprise 2.6% of the sample. The distribution of years of professional service or teaching experience among individuals (Q5) is as follows: 42.6% have more than 20 years of experience, 33% have 11-20 years of experience, 15.7% have 5-10 years of experience, and 8.7% have less than 5 years of experience.

Finally, regarding the country of teaching (Q6), the respondents currently teach in 41 countries, with some of them working in multiple regions, including Serbia, Bosnia and Herzegovina, Japan, China, Indonesia, Poland, Austria, Kazakhstan, Ecuador, Philippines, Tanzania, Colombia, Pakistan, Norway, UAE, Egypt, Japan, Canada, Montenegro, Belgium, India, Bangladesh, Nepal, North Macedonia, Portugal, Spain, Morocco, Italy, Scotland, Vietnam, Thailand, Zimbabwe, Taiwan, France, South Korea, Korea, Israel, Bulgaria, South Africa, Russia, Iraq.

Part 2: AI Literacy (Q7)

The second part of the questionnaire (Q7) consisted of MAIL scale (MAILS) utilized to measure EL educators' AI literacy and perceptions through 34 ''I can'' statements (Carolus et al., 2023). The statements were grouped into 9 constructs for easier data processing. The analysis covers various dimensions such as application, detection, understanding, creation of AI, and other related competencies.

Table 1. Descriptive statistics for the MAIL questionnaire

Descriptive Statistics - MAILS					
Q7	N	Minimum	Maximum	Mean	Std. Deviation
Apply_AI	106	1.00	5.00	3.4355	1.13519
Detect_AI	111	1.00	5.00	3.4204	1.03837
Understand_AI	108	1.00	5.00	3.4491	1.06206

continued on following page

Table 1. Continued

Descriptive Statistics - MAILS					
Q7	N	Minimum	Maximum	Mean	Std. Deviation
Create_AI	115	1.00	5.00	1.6739	.96324
Learning	115	1.00	5.00	2.6754	1.04524
AI_Emotion_regulation	115	1.00	5.00	3.6145	.99471
AI_Ethics	115	1.00	5.00	3.4986	.98959
AI_Problem_Solution	115	1.00	5.00	2.7536	1.11002
AI_Persuasion_literacy	115	1.00	5.00	3.5652	1.11622

The findings of the MAIL scale reveal that the respondents scored high on the following categories: Application of AI, Detection of AI, Understanding of AI, AI Emotion regulation, AI Ethics, AI Problem solutions, AI Persuasion Literacy (Table 1). These results underscore educators' proficiency in applying AI technologies in their everyday practices, adeptness in recognizing AI applications, and a heightened awareness of ethical considerations in AI use. Also, the results imply that EL educators display a proactive stance against AI influencing daily decisions, highlighting awareness and the ability to prevent such influence when necessary. These findings indicate that educators demonstrate a high level of (self-reported) AI literacy. The highest mean score observed is for Emotion regulation associated with AI (Mean = 3.61, SD = 0.74), which indicates that educators generally feel that they can manage their emotional responses when interacting with AI in everyday tasks. This encompasses controlling frustration and anxiety when dealing with AI, as well as handling euphoria that arises when using AI tools. Conversely, the lowest mean score is for the creation of AI (Mean = 1.67, SD = 0.99), indicating a significant gap in educators' ability to develop AI technologies, which underscores the need for targeted training and resources in this critical area.

Furthermore, the respondents demonstrated moderate competences in constructs AI Problem Solving and AI Learning with Mean=2.75 and Mean=2.67, respectively. These findings indicate that EL educators perceive themselves as moderately literate to leverage AI in problem-solving scenarios and keeping up with the rapid changes in the AI domain introducing novelties on a daily basis. Finally, the lowest scored construct was Create AI. The ability to create AI stands out with a very low mean of 1.67, and a standard deviation of 0.96. This indicates that creating AI technologies is a significant challenge for most educators, suggesting a need for enhanced training and resources to elevate their proficiency and confidence in AI creation.

Overall, these findings demonstrate what we would call somehow expected but realistic perspective among educators regarding their AI literacy, having in mind how recent language-based AI tools have been introduced on a more global scale. This indicates that these respondents are well aware of both their current knowledge and areas where they require further understanding. The moderate to high scores across most dimensions indicate a generally positive but cautious attitude towards AI, with significant variability pointing to a need for targeted professional development and support to address the gaps in AI literacy and application. The low score in AI creation emphasizes the need for more comprehensive training programs to equip educators with the skills needed to develop and innovate with AI technologies effectively. However, as we have seen in reviewing different definitions of AI literacy, creating AI is not necessarily the most important part of AI literacy. We believe that educators can successfully use AI technology in English language teaching, even if they are not able to create AI applications themselves, if other criteria (awareness, use, evaluation and ethics as defined by cf. Wang et al., 2020; cf. Ng et al., 2021, p. 4) are met.

Part 3: Training and Professional Development (Q8-Q11)

To address the hypotheses posed in this study, we were explored the educators' preparedness and perspectives regarding AI technologies in education. When asked whether they received any formal training or professional development related to AI technologies in education (Q8), a significant proportion, 46.1% of respondents confessed to had not received any kind of formal training in AI technologies (Figure 1). This finding underscores a notable gap in preparedness for integrating advanced technologies into educational practices. Furthermore, 28.7% of respondents indicated they had minimal training, suggesting basic familiarity with AI concepts but lacking in-depth knowledge or skills. Another 20.9% reported moderate training, indicating a more substantial level of preparation, likely including practical applications and pedagogical strategies involving AI.

Interestingly, a smaller percentage of educators (2.6%) reported having received extensive training in AI technologies. This group likely includes educators who have undergone comprehensive professional development programs focusing extensively on AI applications in education. Moreover, only 1.7% of respondents reported expert-level training in AI technologies. This suggests a very specialized and advanced level of proficiency, possibly involving mastery of AI tools, advanced applications, and research in educational contexts. Altogether, these two groups make only up only 4.3% of respondents, highlighting a stark contrast with the majority who have received little to no training.

Figure 1. Educators' level of training in AI

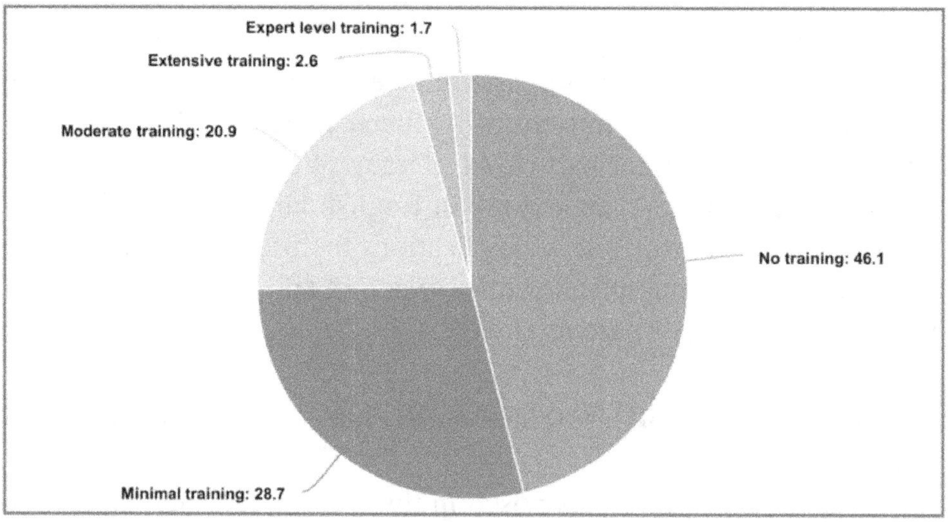

The follow-up question (Q9), "If yes, how has this training influenced your approach to integrating AI in your teaching?" elicited intriguing responses that reveal a diverse range of perspectives among educators (Figure 2). Of the 46.1% of respondents who had received AI-related training, only a quarter (26.1%) considered it to be ''extremely beneficial'' (18.3%) or ''very beneficial'' (7.8%) for their approach to integrating AI into their teaching. This is somewhat surprising, as it means that for 75%

of respondents, the training they received did not improve the integration of AI technology in their teaching. There could be several reasons for this, for example, the workshop they attended were poorly structures, too generic, did not meet their specific needs, or they would have needed more intensive training. Alternatively, they may have decided not to use AI tools in their teaching because it would have taken too much time to prepare, or because they did not feel competent enough to integrate AI technologies. This issue needs to be explored further in order to design training opportunities that meet the needs of teachers and lead to the desired outcome.

On the other hand, 19.1% of respondents found the training “slightly beneficial,” and 14.8% rated it as “moderately beneficial.” These figures indicate that while some educators saw some value in the training, it was not transformative enough to significantly impact their teaching practices. This might point to a need for more tailored and practical training sessions that address the specific challenges and opportunities of integrating AI in EL T education. Finally, 18.3% of educators found the training “very beneficial,” and 7.8% rated it as “extremely beneficial.” These numbers, though smaller, highlight that effective training programs do exist and can significantly enhance educators' ability to integrate AI tools in their teaching.

Figure 2. Educators' impression on the usefulness of prior training in AI

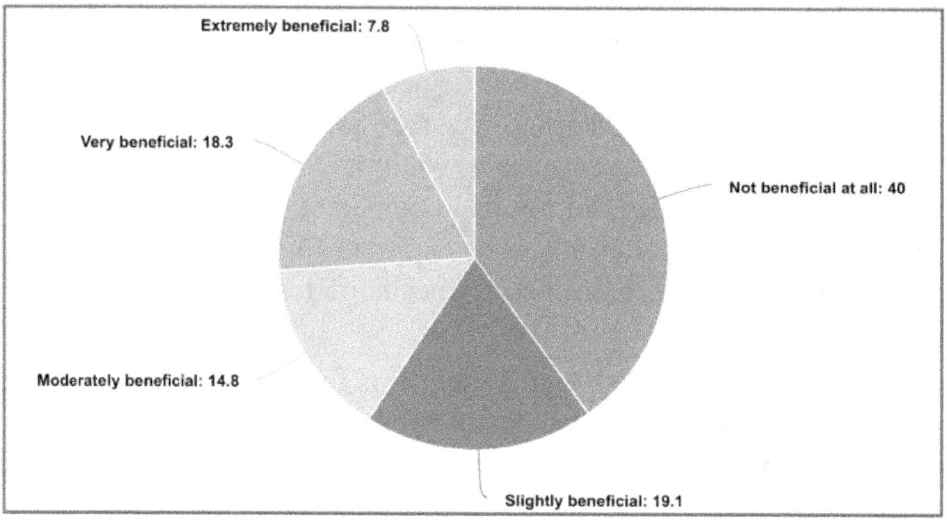

Figure 3. Educators' interest in future AI training and development opportunities

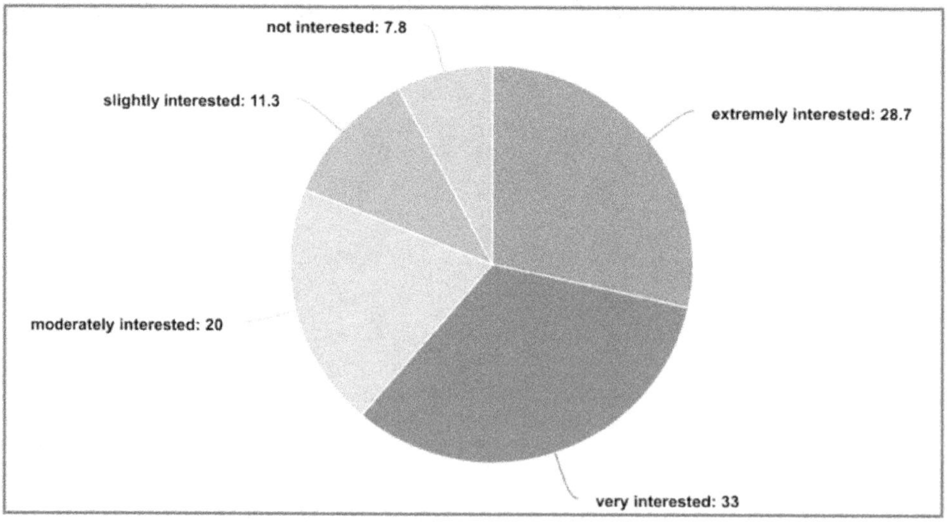

Q10 focused on opportunities for further training, so we asked the respondents ''Would you be interested in participating in professional development opportunities focused on AI literacy for English language teachers?'' Notably, 28.7% of respondents indicated they were extremely interested, and an additional 33% reported being very interested (Figure 3). This combined 61.7% reflects a robust eagerness among educators to enhance their AI literacy, suggesting a recognition of the importance of AI technologies in modern language teaching. Moderate interest was expressed by 20% of respondents, indicating that while they acknowledge the potential benefits of AI training, they may require additional incentives or reassurances about the relevance and applicability of such training to their specific teaching contexts. On the other hand, 11.3% of respondents were only slightly interested, and 7.8% were not interested at all in AI-focused professional development. This minority may include educators who are either skeptical about the efficacy of AI in education, feel overwhelmed by the prospect of integrating new technologies, or believe their current pedagogical approaches are sufficient without the incorporation of AI tools.

Figure 4. Educators' experimenting with AI tools in ELT, based on recommendations

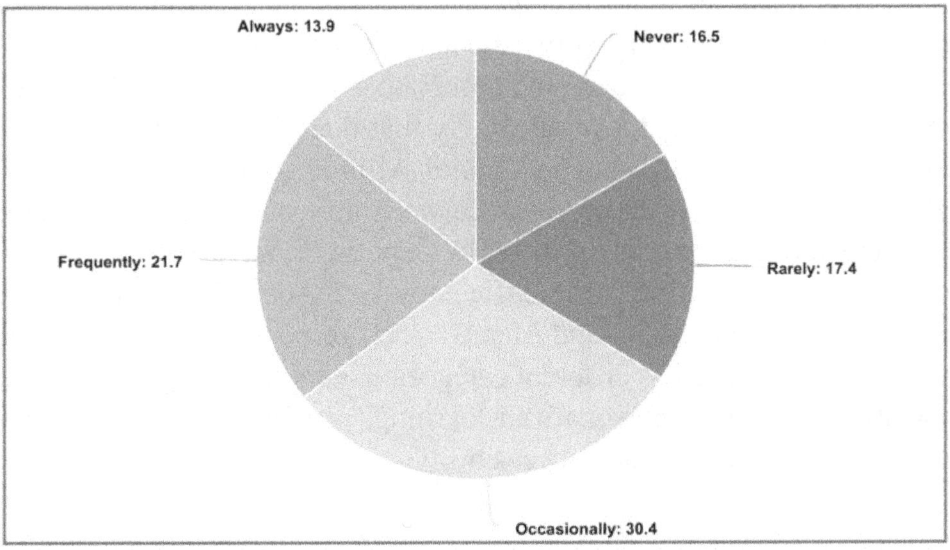

The responses to whether educators have experimented with or utilized AI-powered tools in their language teaching (Q11), even without formal training, provide a comprehensive view of their informal engagement with AI technologies. The data (Figure 4) indicate a diverse spectrum of engagement with AI-powered tools among educators. While a notable percentage (34%) of educators either never or rarely use AI tools, a larger segment (66%) reports varying degrees of regular utilization, from occasional to always. This trend suggests that informal networks and peer recommendations play a critical role in encouraging the adoption of AI technologies. The largest group of respondents reported using AI tools occasionally (30.4%). This indicates a moderate level of engagement, where educators might be selectively incorporating AI tools into their teaching practices as opportunities arise, likely influenced by specific needs or positive recommendations from peers.

Part 4: Perceived Benefits/Challenges of AI Integration in ELT Classroom (Q12-Q14)

To investigate the potential benefits of challenges of AI in ELT we asked the respondents to rate the perceived benefit of each potential advantage of AI integration in English language teaching and learning from their experience, by offering a list of 10 potential benefits with brief explanations (Q12). The results from the descriptive statistics (Table 2) reveal a certain consistency and, overall, imply that there is a generally positive attitude towards the various benefits of AI in language learning among educators. Notably, all categories received high scores, with means above 3.49, indicating a generally positive perception of AI's potential benefits. However, categories of Time Efficiency and Accessibility scored the highest with Means=3.93 and Means=3.91, respectively. The relatively high mean scores across different categories suggest a recognition of AI's potential to enhance personalized learning, provide adaptive feedback, and increase efficiency and accessibility.

Table 2. Descriptive statistics for perceived benefits of AI in ELT

Descriptive Statistics					
Perceived benefits	**N**	**Minimum**	**Maximum**	**Mean**	**Std. Deviation**
[1. Personalized Learning: AI can tailor learning materials and activities to individual student needs, enhancing engagement and comprehension.]	115	1	5	3.64	1.208
[2. Adaptive Feedback: AI-powered systems can provide immediate feedback on language exercises, helping learners identify and correct errors more effectively.]	115	1	5	3.84	1.144
[3. Enhanced Language Practice: AI language-learning apps offer interactive activities and simulations for students to practice speaking, listening, reading, and writing skills.]	115	1	5	3.87	1.159
[4. Accessibility: AI technologies can provide language instruction to learners with disabilities, offering alternative formats and adaptive features to accommodate diverse needs.]	115	1	5	3.91	1.089
[5. Time Efficiency: AI tools can automate routine tasks such as grading assignments and generating lesson plans, allowing teachers to focus more on individualized instruction and student support.]	115	1	5	3.93	1.183
[6. Language Assessment: AI-driven assessment tools can accurately evaluate language proficiency, providing insights into learners' strengths and areas for improvement.]	115	1	5	3.63	1.216
[7. Immersive Learning Experiences: Virtual reality (VR) and augmented reality (AR) applications powered by AI can create immersive language-learning environments, enhancing engagement and retention.]	115	1	5	3.59	1.176
[8. Language Translation Support: AI translation tools can assist learners in understanding texts written in unfamiliar languages, facilitating comprehension and vocabulary acquisition.]	115	1	5	3.61	1.190
[9. Real-time Language Assistance: AI chatbots and virtual assistants can provide learners with instant support and clarification on language-related queries, fostering independent learning.]	115	1	5	3.73	1.172
[10. Data-Driven Insights: AI analytics can analyze learner performance data to identify patterns and trends, enabling teachers to make informed decisions about instructional strategies and interventions.]	115	1	5	3.63	1.134

Q13 was designed to evaluate EL educators' attitudes towards AI regarding potential challenges. The data reflect educators' concerns regarding the integration of AI technologies in language teaching and learning (Table 3). Notably, all challenges received relatively high mean scores, with most above 3.6, indicating a broad recognition of these issues among educators. However, three categories (out of 10) scored above 4, namely Professional Development Needs (M=4.10), Quality Control (M=4.03), and Technological Literacy Gap (M=4.02). Standard deviation in each of these three categories is below 1, which indicates that most of the responses are clustered around the mean value, with only fewer extreme values.

The highest mean score of M=4.10 and a standard deviation below 1 (SD=0.977) indicates a strong consensus among educators on the necessity for comprehensive and continuous professional development programs.

In other words, educators require not only initial training but also regular updates to stay abreast of rapid advancements in AI. A mean score of M=4.03 for the Quality Control category reflects significant concerns about maintaining the quality and accuracy of AI-generated content and resources. Educators are aware of the potential for mediocre or inaccurate instructional materials produced by AI systems. Similarly, M=4.02 for Technological Literacy Gap indicates a strong concern about the technological literacy gap among both educators and students which can hinder the effective utilization of AI tools in language education. These findings indicate that addressing the technological literacy gap is crucial for the successful adoption of AI technologies and are compliant with the results from similar studies (Hieu & Thao, 2024; Alhalangy & AbdAlgane, 2023).

Table 3. Descriptive statistics for perceived challenges of AI in ELT

Perceived challenges	N	Minimum	Maximum	Mean	Std. Deviation
[1.Technical Dependence: Over-reliance on AI technologies may undermine educators' autonomy and creativity in designing language instruction, potentially leading to disengagement and dependency among learners.]	114	1	5	3.61	1.134
[2. Equity and Access: Unequal access to AI tools and resources may exacerbate existing disparities in language education, disadvantaging learners from under-served communities or low-resource settings.]	115	1	5	3.86	.990
[3. Privacy Concerns: AI systems that collect and analyze learner data may raise privacy concerns, particularly regarding the storage and sharing of sensitive information without adequate safeguards.]	115	1	5	3.83	1.102
[4. Bias and Cultural Sensitivity: AI algorithms may perpetuate biases or cultural stereotypes in language instruction materials, negatively impacting learner perceptions and cultural understanding.]	115	1	5	3.69	1.029
[5. Human Interaction: Excessive reliance on AI technologies may diminish opportunities for authentic human interaction and communication in language learning, hindering interpersonal skills development.]	114	1	5	3.89	1.140
[6. Technological Literacy Gap: Some learners and educators may lack the necessary technological literacy to effectively utilize AI tools in language instruction, leading to underutilization or misuse of these resources.]	115	1	5	4.02	.946
[7. Quality Control: The proliferation of AI-generated content and resources may compromise the quality and accuracy of language instruction materials, necessitating rigorous vetting and validation processes.]	115	1	5	4.03	.964
[8. Ethical Dilemmas: Ethical considerations surrounding AI use in language teaching, such as data privacy, consent, and algorithmic transparency, may pose challenges for educators and institutions.]	115	1	5	3.98	1.017
[9. Professional Development Needs: Educators may require ongoing training and support to develop the skills and confidence necessary to integrate AI technologies effectively into language instruction.]	114	1	5	4.10	.977

continued on following page

Table 3. Continued

Perceived challenges	N	Minimum	Maximum	Mean	Std. Deviation
[10. Cost and Sustainability: Implementing AI solutions in language education may require significant financial investment and ongoing maintenance costs, posing challenges for resource-constrained institutions and educators.]	115	1	5	3.74	1.155
Valid N (list-wise)	113				

Other categories that scored high means in the potential challenges section are Ethical Dilemmas M=3.98, Human Interaction M=3.89, Equity and Access M=3.86, and Privacy Concerns M=3.83.

The near-4.0 mean score indicates that ethical issues are a prominent concern among educators. The high score suggests that educators are acutely aware of the potential ethical pitfalls of AI, such as biases in algorithms, data misuse, and lack of transparency in how AI decisions are made. This is also connected to the necessity of establishing Quality Control protocols mentioned earlier that would not only ensure the accuracy and reliability of AI-generated content but also address these ethical concerns by promoting transparency, accountability, and fairness in AI applications in ELT.

The high mean for the category of Human Interaction M=3.89 reflects concerns that AI technology may reduce opportunities for authentic human interaction, which is essential for developing interpersonal skills and fostering meaningful teacher-student relationships. There is evidence that AI cannot provide neither meaningful and in-depth feedback (Holmes et al., 2019) nor a warm, socially welcoming educational setting and care a human teacher can give. It is, therefore, reasonable to conclude that the pedagogical and human value of teaching, through the establishment of human connections between a learner and a teacher, brings additional benefits, such as tracking students' progress more effectively, providing personalized emotional support, and fostering a sense of community and belonging in the classroom. As no tool can replace human educators, it is necessary to balance AI use with traditional teaching methods so that the personal aspect of teaching remains intact. Equity and unequal Access to AI technology still remains a challenge for a huge number of EL educators (M=3.86). Overall, these findings suggest that, while educators see potential benefits in AI, they are also acutely aware of the challenges that need to be addressed to realize its potential.

To further test the hypotheses that teachers who perceive AI as a threat to their profession may exhibit resistance towards incorporating AI tools into their teaching practices, we asked EL educators to rate 5 statement to assess the level of comfort and trust in AI tools. We argue that trust in AI-powered tools is a pivotal factor in the successful integration of these technologies into English Language Teaching (ELT), so educators' comfort levels with AI can significantly influence their willingness to adopt and effectively use these tools in their classrooms. The survey data (Table 4) reveals varying degrees of comfort among educators when it comes to using AI-powered tools in language teaching, highlighting the importance of fostering trust and confidence in these technologies.

Table 4. Comfort levels of EL educators in using AI-Powered tools in language teaching

On a scale of 1 to 5, how comfortable are you with using AI-powered tools in your language teaching?					
		Frequency	**Percent**	**Valid Percent**	**Cumulative Percent**
Valid	1 - Not at all comfortable: I lack trust in AI apps and feel uneasy using them.	9	7.8	7.8	7.8
	2 - Uncomfortable: I feel hesitant or uneasy when using AI apps.	7	6.1	6.1	13.9
	3 - Neutral: I have no strong feelings either way about using AI apps.	30	26.1	26.1	40.0
	4 - Comfortable: I use them sometimes with ease and feel generally confident in their functionality.	44	38.3	38.3	78.3
	5 - Very comfortable: I am highly at ease with AI tools and frequently use them in various contexts.	25	21.7	21.7	100.0
	Total	115	100.0	100.0	

The largest group of respondents feel generally confident in using AI tools (38.3%), indicating that they use them sometimes with ease. This comfort level suggests a growing familiarity and acceptance of AI in language teaching. A substantial proportion of educators are highly at ease with AI tools (21.7%), frequently using them in various contexts. This high comfort level likely reflects extensive experience and positive outcomes from AI use. Overall, a high percentage of 60% of EL educators are either comfortable or very comfortable with the use of AI in their teaching practice. Also, a significant portion of educators have no strong feelings either way about using AI apps (26.1%). This neutrality indicates an openness to AI but also a lack of strong conviction, enthusiasm, or training. This group, with targeted support and positive experiences, can easily be turned into either proponents or skeptics of AI in education, depending on their subsequent experiences and training.

Finally, as far as EL educators who are not comfortable with the use of AI tools are concerned, a small but notable percentage of educators lack trust in AI apps, feeling uneasy about their use (7.8%). Similarly, the group of educators hesitant or uneasy when using AI tools makes 6.1% of the sample. This indicates that, altogether, around 15% of EL educators lack trust or feel uneasy when using AI. While they may recognize the potential benefits, their discomfort suggests a need for more targeted training and reassurance about the efficacy and safety of AI applications in education.

Part 5: Correlation

The correlations between various factors related to AI technologies and language teaching and learning provide valuable insights into the potential impact of AI in educational settings. The data reveals significant correlations between different aspects of AI and language education, indicating the interconnected nature of these variables (Table 5).

Table 5. Pearson's correlations

Correlations												
		Apply_AI	**Detect_AI**	**Understand_ AI**	**Create_AI**	**Learning**	**AI_ Emotion_ regulation**	**Group_ Benefits**	**Group_ Challenges**	**Q9 - AI potential to enhance ELT**	**Q13 - formal training in AI**	**Q16 - AI experimenting**
Apply_AI	Pearson Correlation	1	.618**	.841**	.232*	.732**	.486**	.544**	.169	.456**	.203*	.435**
	Sig. (2-tailed)		.000	.000	.017	.000	.000	.000	.087	.000	.037	.000
	N	106	103	101	106	106	106	106	104	106	106	106
Detect_AI	Pearson Correlation	.618**	1	.779**	.318**	.474**	.458**	.318**	.102	.111	.101	.256**
	Sig. (2-tailed)	.000		.000	.001	.000	.000	.001	.289	.247	.289	.007
	N	103	111	105	111	111	111	111	109	111	111	111
Understand_AI	Pearson Correlation	.841**	.779**	1	.294**	.660**	.516**	.432**	.163	.255**	.258**	.367**
	Sig. (2-tailed)	.000	.000		.002	.000	.000	.000	.095	.008	.007	.000
	N	101	105	108	108	108	108	108	106	108	108	108
Create_AI	Pearson Correlation	.232*	.318**	.294**	1	.478**	.173	.123	-.007	.124	.437**	.342**
	Sig. (2-tailed)	.017	.001	.002		.000	.065	.191	.939	.186	.000	.000
	N	106	111	108	115	115	115	115	113	115	115	115

continued on following page

Table 5. Continued

Correlations												
		Apply_AI	Detect_AI	Understand_ AI	Create_AI	Learning	AI_ Emotion_ regulation	Group_ Benefits	Group_ Challenges	Q9 - AI potential to enhance ELT	Q13 - formal training in AI	Q16 - AI experimenting
Learning	Pearson Correlation	.732**	.474**	.660**	.478**	1	.408**	.410**	.148	.368**	.342**	.512**
	Sig. (2-tailed)	.000	.000	.000	.000		.000	.000	.117	.000	.000	.000
	N	106	111	108	115	115	115	115	113	115	115	115
AI_Emotion_ regulation	Pearson Correlation	.486**	.458**	.516**	.173	.408**	1	.207*	.288**	.052	-.007	.140
	Sig. (2-tailed)	.000	.000	.000	.065	.000		.027	.002	.584	.939	.135
	N	106	111	108	115	115	115	115	113	115	115	115
Group_Benefits	Pearson Correlation	.544**	.318**	.432**	.123	.410**	.207*	1	.167	.513**	.194*	.272**
	Sig. (2-tailed)	.000	.001	.000	.191	.000	.027		.077	.000	.038	.003
	N	106	111	108	115	115	115	115	113	115	115	115
Group_Challenges	Pearson Correlation	.169	.102	.163	-.007	.148	.288**	.167	1	-.052	.016	-.063
	Sig. (2-tailed)	.087	.289	.095	.939	.117	.002	.077		.587	.866	.505
	N	104	109	106	113	113	113	113	113	113	113	113

continued on following page

Table 5. Continued

Correlations												
		Apply_AI	Detect_AI	Understand_ AI	Create_AI	Learning	AI_ Emotion_ regulation	Group_ Benefits	Group_ Challenges	Q9 - AI potential to enhance ELT	Q13 - formal training in AI	Q16 - AI experimenting
AI potential to enhance ELT	Pearson Correlation	.456**	.111	.255**	.124	.368**	.052	.513**	-.052	1	.190*	.453**
	Sig. (2-tailed)	.000	.247	.008	.186	.000	.584	.000	.587		.042	.000
	N	106	111	108	115	115	115	115	113	115	115	115
Formal training in AI	Pearson Correlation	.203*	.101	.258**	.437**	.342**	-.007	.194*	.016	.190*	1	.444**
	Sig. (2-tailed)	.037	.289	.007	.000	.000	.939	.038	.866	.042		.000
	N	106	111	108	115	115	115	115	113	115	115	115

**. Correlation is significant at the 0.01 level (2-tailed).

*. Correlation is significant at the 0.05 level (2-tailed).

The findings reveal several strong, moderate, and weak correlations between certain variables. Application of AI and Understanding AI ($r = .841$, $p < .01$) is the strongest observed correlation, indicating that a higher understanding of AI is significantly associated with the effective application of AI technologies in teaching practices. This underscores the importance of AI literacy among educators for successful integration of AI tools. A strong correlation is also found between Application of AI and Learning ($r = .732$, $p < .01$), which suggests that effective application of AI technologies can substantially enhance learning outcomes. The third strong correlation is between Understanding AI and Detecting AI ($r = .779$, $p < .01$). This high correlation suggests that educators who have a better understanding of AI are also more proficient in detecting AI applications, implying that a comprehensive grasp of AI concepts enhances the ability to recognize and evaluate AI tools effectively.

Moderate correlations are observed between the three pairs of categories. Application of AI and Detecting AI ($r = .618$, $p < .01$) moderate correlation indicates that the ability to detect AI applications is moderately associated with their effective application in teaching, reflecting that recognizing AI tools is a precursor to their successful use. A moderate positive correlation is also found between Learning and Understanding AI ($r = .660$, $p < .01$) which suggests that deeper knowledge of AI positively impacts educational outcomes, emphasizing the need for thorough AI education for teachers. Finally, a moderate positive correlation is observed between Learning and Application of AI in Emotion Regulation ($r = .486$, $p < .01$). This correlation signifies that applying AI for emotion regulation can moderately improve learning experiences, pointing to the emotional benefits AI can provide in educational settings.

A weak correlation is found between the categories of Application of AI and Potential Advantages ($r = .169$, $p = .087$): This weak correlation suggests a minor association between the application of AI and the perceived potential advantages of AI, indicating that while there is some connection, it is not particularly strong. Also, a weak correlation is observed between Understanding AI and Potential Advantage ($r = .163$, $p = .095$): Similar to the application of AI, understanding AI also shows a weak correlation with the perceived potential advantages, suggesting that other factors might influence these perceptions more strongly.

Regarding Training and Experimentation, one weak and one moderate correlations were observed; Formal Training and AI Application ($r = .203$, $p < .05$): There is a weak but significant correlation between receiving formal AI training and the application of AI technologies, indicating that professional development can enhance AI integration in teaching, though the effect size is modest. Experimentation with AI Tools ($r = .435$, $p < .01$) even without formal training, shows a moderate correlation with the Application of AI, highlighting the role of practical, hands-on experiences and peer recommendations in adopting AI technologies.

Moreover, the data highlights the significance of formal training and professional development in AI technologies for educators. The correlation between formal training in AI and various AI-related factors indicates that training plays a crucial role in enhancing educators' engagement with AI tools and technologies. Educators who have received formal training are more likely to perceive the potential benefits of AI in language teaching and learning, as evidenced by the positive correlations observed. Furthermore, the analysis reveals that educators who have experimented with AI-powered tools, even without formal training, show correlations with factors such as understanding AI, learning outcomes, and potential advantages. This suggests that hands-on experience with AI technologies, based on recommendations from colleagues or other sources, can influence educators' perceptions and practices in language education.

Overall, the correlations presented in the data underscore the complex interplay between AI technologies and language teaching and learning. Educators' understanding, training, and practical experience with AI tools are crucial factors that can shape the integration of AI in language education. By considering these correlations, educational stakeholders can make informed decisions about leveraging AI to enhance language teaching and learning practices.

CONCLUSION

This study provides valuable insights into the attitudes, experiences, and perceptions of English language educators regarding the integration of AI-powered tools in their teaching practices. The findings indicate a generally high level of self-reported AI literacy among educators, with most respondents demonstrating high competences in Detecting, Understanding, and Applying AI, and moderate competencies in AI Problem-solving and Learning. However, the ability to Create AI tools remains significantly low, emphasizing the need for more comprehensive training programs that equip educators with the skills required to innovate and develop AI technologies. Undoubtedly, we emphasize our belief that EL educators can effectively utilize AI technology in ELT without being able to Create AI themselves, as AI literacy encompasses, we argue, a vast range of related and more useful competences, such as an informed dialogue about AI in Education.

The findings further reveal that a remarkably small percentage of educators have received training in AI application, and among those who have, the perceived benefits were strikingly low. Whether they faced some self-imposed obstacles or encountered shortcomings in the existing training programs remains unclear. Yet, it must be emphasized, that educators who have received formal training in AI application are more likely to perceive the potential benefits of AI in language teaching and learning. What significantly helps, the findings suggest, is their openness to experiment with AI tools and their personal initiative to familiarize with the technology. The more they understand how AI functions, the more effective application of AI technologies in teaching practices is. Comprehensive formal training emerges as a crucial factor indicating that professional development and training in AI application can enhance AI integration in teaching.

We argue that EL educators are quite aware that the impact and the effectiveness of AI are two completely different concepts. Although these educators recognize the potential benefits of AI in ELT—such as time efficiency, accessibility, adaptive feedback, and enhanced language practice—their implementation of AI in everyday practice is not without concerns. These concerns include students' over-reliance on technology, the unreliability and inaccuracy of AI outputs, and issues of plagiarism and academic integrity. For EL educators with advanced AI proficiency, the additional "higher-order" concerns emerge, such as bias and cultural insensitivity, as well as teachers' well-being and vulnerability. The prevalence of concerns related to pedagogical impact, ethical considerations, and technological readiness highlights the complex landscape of AI integration in education.

To conclude, practical implications stemming from this research study suggest that, to effectively integrate AI in the English language education educators should start by defining clear learning objectives, whether improving proficiency, enhancing personalized learning, or fostering critical thinking. It is crucial to combine AI with traditional teaching methods as much/long as it does not jeopardize essential human interaction and prioritizes other goals rather than the development of communicative competence and language proficiency. Assuming that access to technology is assured to both students and learners, and educational institutions do implement their AI policies, educators should stay updated on AI advancements through continuous professional development.

REFERENCES

Alhalangy, A. G. I., & AbdAlgane, M. (2023). Exploring The Impact of AI on The EFL Context: A Case Study of Saudi Universities. *Journal of Intercultural Communication, 23*(2), 41–49. DOI: 10.36923/jicc.v23i2.125

Alharbi, W. (2023). AI in the Foreign Language Classroom: A Pedagogical Overview of Automated Writing Assistance Tools. *Hindawi Education Research International,* 2023, ID 4253331, https://doi.org/.DOI: 10.1155/2023/4253331

Ali, J. K. M., Shamsan, M. A. A., Hezam, T. A., & Mohammed, A. A. Q. (2023). Impact of chatgpt on learning motivation. *Journal of English Studies in Arabia Felix, 2*(1), 41–49. DOI: 10.56540/jesaf.v2i1.51

Almehmadi, W. (2024). Exploring the potential of ai techniques in teaching english as a foreign language: A systematic literature review. *Asian Journal of Social Sciences and Management Studies, 11*(2), 22–31. DOI: 10.20448/ajssms.v11i2.5576

Black, J. (2023). Past, present and tackling the future of artificial intelligence (ai) in education: Maintaining agency and establishing ai laws. *Open Journal of Social Sciences, 11*(07), 442–464. DOI: 10.4236/jss.2023.117031

Bozkurt, A. (2023). Generative AI, Synthetic Contents, Open Educational Resources (OER), and Open Educational Practices (OEP): A New Front in the Openness Landscape. *Open Praxis, 15*(3), 178–184. DOI: 10.55982/openpraxis.15.3.579

Cardona, M. A., Rodríguez, R. J., & Ishmael, K. (2023, May 25). Artificial Intelligence and the Future of Teaching and Learning: Insights and Recommendations. Policycommons.net; Office of Educational Technology. https://policycommons.net/artifacts/3854312/ai-report/4660267/

Carolus, A., Koch, M., Straka, S., Latoschik, M. E., & Wienrich, C. (2023). MAILS - Meta AI literacy scale: Development and testing of an AI literacy questionnaire based on well-founded competency models and psychological change- and meta-competencies. *Computers in Human Behaviour: Artificial Humans, 1*(2), 100014. Advance online publication. DOI: 10.1016/j.chbah.2023.100014

Chiu, T. K. F., & Chai, C. S. (2020). Sustainable curriculum planning for artificial intelligence education: A self-determination theory perspective. *Sustainability (Basel), 12*(14), 5568. DOI: 10.3390/su12145568

Choukaier, D. (2024). Integrating AI In English Language Pedagogy: Innovations And Outcomes In Teaching English As Second /Foreign Language *Educational Administration. Theory into Practice, 30*(5), 3811–3822. DOI: 10.53555/kuey.v30i5.3538

Dincer, N., & Bal, S. (2024). A Qualitative Journey on Instructors' Perceptions of Artificial Intelligence in EFL Education. In Fang, P. (Ed.), *AI in Language Learning, Teaching and Assessment* (pp. 78–100). IGI Global., DOI: 10.4018/979-8-3693-0872-1.ch005

Edmett, A., Ichaporia, N., Crompron, N., & Crichton, R. (2023). *Artificial intelligence and English language teaching: Preparing for the future.* British Council.

Gentile, M., Ottaviano, S., Perna, S., & Allegra, M. (2023). Do we still need teachers? navigating the paradigm shift of the teacher's role in the AI era. *Frontiers in Education, 8*, 1161777. Advance online publication. DOI: 10.3389/feduc.2023.1161777

Godwin-Jones, R. (2022). Partnering with AI: Intelligent writing assistance and instructed language learning. *Language Learning & Technology, 26*(2), 5–24. 10125/73474

Hieu, H. H., & Thao, L. T. (2024). Exploring the impact of AI in language education: Vietnamese EFL teachers' views on using chatgpt for fairy tale retelling tasks. *International Journal of Learning. Teaching and Educational Research, 23*(3), 486–503. DOI: 10.26803/ijlter.23.3.24

Holmes, W., Persson, J., Chounta, I., Wasson, B., & Dimitrova, V. (2022). *Artificial Intelligence and Education: A critical view through the lens of human rights, democracy and the rule of law*. Council of Europe.

Jiang, R. (2022). How does artificial intelligence empower EFL teaching and learning nowadays? a review of artificial intelligence in the EFL context. *Frontiers in Psychology, 13*, 1049401. Advance online publication. DOI: 10.3389/fpsyg.2022.1049401 PMID: 36467167

Koraishi, O. (2023). Teaching English in the Age of AI: Embracing ChatGPT to Optimize EFL Materials and Assessment. [LET Journal]. *Language Education & Technology, 3*(1), 55–72.

Long, D., & Magerko, B. (2020). What is AI Literacy? Competencies and Design Considerations. *Proceedings of the 2020 CHI Conference on Human Factors in Computing Systems*. https://doi.org/DOI: 10.1145/3313831.3376727

Mabuan, R. A. (2024). ChatGPT and ELT: Exploring teachers' voices. [IJTE]. *International Journal of Technology in Education, 7*(1), 128–153. DOI: 10.46328/ijte.523

Moybeka, A. (2023). Artificial intelligence and english classroom: the implications of ai toward efl students' motivation. *Edumaspul - Jurnal Pendidikan,* 7(2), 2444-2454. https://doi.org/.DOI: 10.33487/edumaspul.v7i2.6669

Mukhallafi, T. (2020). Using artificial intelligence for developing English language teaching/learning: An analytical study from university students' perspective. *International Journal of English Linguistics, 10*(6), 40. DOI: 10.5539/ijel.v10n6p40

Ng, D. T. K., Leung, J. K. L., Chu, K. W. S., & Qiao, M. S. (2021). AI literacy: Definition, teaching, evaluation and ethical issues. *Proceedings of the Association for Information Science and Technology, 58*(1), 504–509. DOI: 10.1002/pra2.487

Ng, D. T. K., Leung, J. K. L., Su, J., Ng, R. C. W., & Chu, S. K. W. (2023). Teachers' AI digital competencies and twenty-first century skills in the post-pandemic world. *Educational Technology Research and Development*, *71*(1), 137–161. DOI: 10.1007/s11423-023-10203-6 PMID: 36844361

Popenici, S., & Kerr, S. (2017). Exploring the impact of artificial intelligence on teaching and learning in higher education. *Research and Practice in Technology Enhanced Learning*, *12*(1), 22. Advance online publication. DOI: 10.1186/s41039-017-0062-8 PMID: 30595727

Sharadgah, T., & Sa'di, R. (2022). A systematic review of research on the use of artificial intelligence in English language teaching and learning (2015-2021): What are the current effects? *Journal of Information Technology Education*, *21*, 337–377. DOI: 10.28945/4999

Sharma, R. C., & Bozkurt, A. (2024). Transforming Education With Generative AI: Prompt Engineering and Synthetic Content Creation. In www.igi-global.com. IGI Global. https://www.igi-global.com/book/transforming-education-generative/327460

Sumakul, D. T., Hamied, F. A., & Sukyadi, D. (2022). Artificial intelligence in EFL classrooms: Friend or foe? *LEARN Journal: Language Education and Acquisition Research Network*, *15*(1), 232–256.

Tica, L., & Krsmanović, I. (2024). Overcoming the Writer's Block? Exploring Students' Motivation and Perspectives on Using Chat GPT as a Writing Assistance Tool in ESP. *ELOPE: English Language Overseas Perspectives and Enquiries,* 21 (1), 129- 149 (316). https://doi.org/.DOI: 10.4312/elope.21.1.129-149

Vera, F. (2023). Integrating Artificial Intelligence (AI) in the EFL Classroom: Benefits and Challenges. *Transformar,* 4(2), 66–77. Recuperado a partir de https://revistatransformar.cl/index.php/transformar/article/view/93

Wang, B., Rau, P.-L. P., & Yuan, T. (2023). Measuring user competence in using artificial intelligence: Validity and reliability of artificial intelligence literacy scale. *Behaviour & Information Technology*, *42*(9), 1324–1337. https://ideas.repec.org/a/taf/tbitxx/v42y2023i9p1324-1337.html. DOI: 10.1080/0144929X.2022.2072768

Yang, C., Shu-liang, H., & Yong, Y. (2020). A practical teaching mode for colleges supported by artificial intelligence. *International Journal of Emerging Technologies in Learning*, *15*(17), 195. DOI: 10.3991/ijet.v15i17.16737

Zhai, X. (2022, December 27). ChatGPT User Experience: Implications for Education. Papers.*ssrn*.com. https://papers.ssrn.com/sol3/papers.cfm?abstract_id=4312418 DOI: 10.2139/ssrn.4312418

Zhao, L., Wu, X., & Luo, H. (2022). Developing ai literacy for primary and middle school teachers in china: Based on a structural equation modeling analysis. *Sustainability (Basel)*, *14*(21), 14549. DOI: 10.3390/su142114549

KEY TERMS AND DEFINITIONS

AI Literacy: The ability to recognize AI and explain how AI technology works, as well as the ability to apply AI for a particular purpose, taking into account ethical considerations. It may also include the ability to create and improve AI applications. Also includes participating in informed interdisciplinary dialogues on AI and education at a broader educational level.

AI in Higher Education (AIED): refers to the use of AI in higher education institutions by teachers, administrators and students to improve processes and learning and teaching experiences.

AI Enhanced Learning: Learning supported by the use of AI applications such as Large Language Models and the like. This can contribute to the individualization of learning processes.

Self-Reported AI Literacy: AI literacy is measured using a survey that includes 'can do' statements, i.e. respondents assess their skills by answering questions about what they can/cannot do in relation to AI.

Digital Divide: The assumption that not all people have equal access to digital technologies.

Lingua Franca: A language used by native speakers from different countries and with different mother tongues to fulfil a specific purpose (here: to develop, use and improve AI technologies).

Bias: In an AI context, bias describes AI output that is based on certain preconceptions and is therefore not correct/objective. Bias can be caused by distorted training data/algorithms.

Chapter 7
The Role of Artificial Intelligence in Linguistic Corpus Analysis

Hélder Fanha Martins
https://orcid.org/0000-0003-3544-0703
Polytechnic University of Lisbon, Portugal & CETAPS - Centre for English, Translation and Anglo-Portuguese Studies, NOVA University of Lisbon, Portugal

ABSTRACT

This chapter explores the transformative role of artificial intelligence (AI) in linguistic corpus analysis within applied linguistics. It begins with an overview of applied linguistics and the significant methodological development of corpus analysis, emphasizing its applications in teaching, language use analysis, and lexicography. The integration of AI in linguistic research is examined, focusing on advancements in natural language processing (NLP) and machine learning, which enhance the depth and accuracy of language analysis. The chapter highlights how AI-driven tools, such as deep learning models and neural networks, facilitate complex tasks like speech recognition, sentiment analysis, and text classification. It also discusses the evolution of corpus analysis tools and the impact of AI innovations on language teaching and translation research. The chapter concludes by addressing the challenges and future trends in AI and corpus analysis, underscoring the potential for interdisciplinary collaboration

DOI: 10.4018/979-8-3693-5477-3.ch007

and the ethical considerations involved in AI applications in linguistics.

1. INTRODUCTION

1.1 Overview of Applied Linguistics and Corpora Analysis

Applied linguistics, a multidisciplinary field of study, encompasses a broad range of activities that involve the analysis and application of language-related research. It is an area primarily concerned with solving or addressing real-world language problems, often through the use of empirical methods. A significant methodological development in this field has been corpus analysis, which involves the study of language as expressed in corpora, or large collections of natural texts. Corpus analysis in applied linguistics has proven to be a flexible and powerful tool. It provides researchers with rich contextual data, enabling the analysis of discourse in various contexts and the examination of language use across different domains (Viana, Menezes, & Mendes, 2011). This methodology has been instrumental in teaching foreign languages, enhancing leisure reading, and forming essential linguistic skills among students (Tolmasova, 2022; Healey, 2019).

Qualitative corpus analysis, particularly, allows for in-depth investigations of linguistic phenomena, grounded in authentic, communicative situations. This approach is invaluable in understanding how language is used in real-life contexts and how it evolves over time (Baksa-Haskó, 2020). Moreover, corpus linguistics acknowledges the importance of considering register differences in language patterns, as the use of language in speech and writing varies dramatically, influencing how language is understood and taught (Biber, 2012).

Corpus linguistics plays a critical role in various fields of linguistic research, such as lexicography, syntax, and foreign language education. It provides a unique perspective on linguistic issues, allowing linguists to quickly find examples and explore text based on actual usage patterns of the language (Irfan, 2015). This methodology has also been extended to other disciplines, such as clinical psychology, where it contributes to therapeutic interventions by providing linguistic evidence supporting qualitative findings.

In summary, corpus analysis in applied linguistics has evolved to become a pivotal methodology, fostering a deeper understanding of language patterns, usage, and evolution. Its application across various linguistic domains underscores its versatility and effectiveness in addressing real-world language issues.

1.2 The Role of AI in Linguistic Research

The integration of artificial intelligence (AI) in linguistic research has brought about transformative changes in recent years. AI's application in this field has expanded the scope and depth of linguistic analysis, offering sophisticated tools and methods for understanding language in unprecedented ways. Recent advancements in AI have focused on enhancing natural language processing (NLP) capabilities, such as dependency parsing, domain adaptation, and deep parsing. These advancements are crucial for applications like question answering, speech recognition, and machine translation, offering more accurate and nuanced understanding of language structures and meanings (Bunt et al., 2010).

The use of deep learning, big data, and social computing in AI has significantly advanced pattern recognition, a fundamental aspect of linguistic research. These developments have paved the way for more complex and comprehensive analyses of linguistic data, facilitating greater insights into language patterns and usage. Moreover, AI has made significant strides in the field of mental health and substance use research, particularly through social media data analysis. Lexicon-based methods, which are popular in this area, benefit greatly from AI's ability to process large datasets and uncover patterns that might be missed by human analysts (Conway et al., 2019).

Additionally, AI has introduced differentiable data-structures and end-to-end learning paradigms, such as external memory and reinforcement learning, to linguistic research. These innovations have opened new avenues in exploring how language is processed and understood by machines, thus enhancing our understanding of human language processing (Xu, 2016).

AI has specifically reshaped corpus linguistics by automating tasks that were traditionally labour-intensive. Tasks like tagging, parsing, and annotation of large corpora, which once required extensive manual effort, can now be performed automatically using AI-driven tools. These tools enable more efficient data handling, allowing researchers to work with much larger corpora than was previously possible. Machine learning algorithms can classify parts of speech, identify syntactic patterns, and even extract semantic relationships, thereby enhancing the precision and scale of linguistic analysis.

The role of AI in linguistic research is increasingly prominent, driven by technological advancements that have expanded our capabilities in analysing and understanding language. AI's contribution to linguistics not only enhances existing methodologies but also introduces new possibilities for exploring the complexities of human language. AI and corpus linguistics are increasingly intertwined, with AI providing new levels of efficiency, depth, and insight into language analysis. AI-driven corpus analysis not only augments traditional methods but also opens new avenues for exploring language complexities, thereby transforming linguistic research into a more data-driven, scalable, and nuanced discipline.

1.3 Purpose and Scope of the Chapter

The primary purpose of this chapter is to investigate the evolving interplay between artificial intelligence and corpus analysis in the field of applied linguistics. In an era where AI is rapidly advancing, its impact on linguistic research is increasingly significant, introducing new tools and methodologies that redefine our understanding of language. This chapter not only explores these developments but also explicitly focuses on how they can be harnessed by educators to improve language instruction. By connecting AI and corpus linguistics to practical teaching practices, this chapter aims to offer educators innovative tools and methods to enrich language learning in the classroom.

To provide a comprehensive exploration, the chapter will include practical examples of how these advancements can be applied in a teaching context. For instance, AI can be used by teachers to create tailored vocabulary lists based on authentic corpus data, enabling them to address the specific needs of students at different proficiency levels. Lesson plans might involve students using corpus tools to analyse the frequency of key vocabulary items in different genres, helping them understand contextual usage. Activities such as using concordancers to investigate collocations or examining authentic examples of grammatical structures will also be highlighted, demonstrating how corpus analysis can be directly integrated into the language classroom to enhance learners' understanding of real-world language use. The chapter will also explore the impact of AI-driven corpus analysis across various domains of linguistic research. This involves a review of how such integration has influenced key areas like language teaching, translation studies, lexicography, and more, providing practical implications of AI in applied linguistics. A significant portion of the chapter will be dedicated to presenting case studies and real-world examples where AI and corpus analysis have converged successfully. These examples will demonstrate the practical applications and benefits of this integration, offering a clear view of its potential in real-world scenarios.

In addition, the chapter will address the challenges and considerations involved in merging AI with corpus analysis, such as data quality, ethical concerns, and the necessity for interdisciplinary collaboration. It will also speculate on the future of AI in linguistic studies, pondering how ongoing technological advancements might continue to shape and transform the field.

In essence, this chapter seeks to provide a detailed overview of the current landscape of AI in applied linguistics, with a particular focus on corpus analysis. It aims to shed light on future trends and potential research areas, ultimately contributing to the growing body of knowledge at the intersection of AI and linguistics.

2. ADVANCEMENTS IN AI-DRIVEN TOOLS FOR CORPUS ANALYSIS

2.1 Evolution of Tools like 'Linguist's Workbench' and 'Linguistic Database'

Recent advancements in AI-driven tools for corpus analysis have significantly enhanced the capabilities of linguistics research. The evolution of tools like 'Linguist's Workbench' and 'Linguistic Database' reflects this progress, integrating cutting-edge technologies to facilitate more sophisticated and comprehensive linguistic analyses. One notable development is the integration of linguistics with translation, which has been instrumental in enhancing the relationship between corpus linguistics and translation studies. This convergence has led to more nuanced and accurate translation processes, drawing upon the rich linguistic data available in modern corpora (Leng, 2019).

Corpus linguistics approaches and corpus analysis software have been refined to reveal thematic developments, changes in discourse, and highlight key lexical items in both literary and non-literary texts. These advancements allow researchers to delve deeper into the evolution of language use across various texts and contexts. Current progress in tools like BNCweb and CQPWeb have included capabilities to code individual concordance lines for structural, functional, and discoursal features. This advancement allows for more rigorous descriptions and theories about language in use, providing a finer-grained analysis of linguistic data (Smith, Hoffmann, & Rayson, 2007). The SWS-AL Workbench, for instance, offers an accessible and streamlined interface with a wide range of analysis options. It combines classic corpus linguistic analysis with recent NLP approaches, making it an invaluable tool for modern linguistic research (Krasselt et al., 2023).

These tools support an incremental process of corpus analysis, employing methods from computational linguistics, information retrieval, and knowledge engineering. This approach facilitates the acquisition of domain knowledge from natural language, enhancing the efficiency and accuracy of linguistic research (Mikheev & Finch, 1997). In essence, the evolution of AI-driven tools for corpus analysis, such as 'Linguist's Workbench' and 'Linguistic Database', has significantly expanded the capabilities of linguistic researchers. These tools have not only automated and streamlined the analysis process but have also opened new horizons for in-depth linguistic exploration and interpretation, marking a significant leap in the field of applied linguistics.

Teachers can use tools like BNCweb or CQPWeb to engage students in analysing authentic language use across various contexts. For example, instructors can introduce frequency analysis exercises where students explore how word usage changes depending on the genre, audience, or register. By using these tools, students can compare the frequency of specific words or phrases in different types of texts, such as academic articles, fiction, and spoken dialogue. This helps them gain insights into how language use varies across different communicative settings, enhancing their understanding of register and appropriateness.

Teachers can also leverage these tools to provide students with exposure to authentic texts, which is crucial for developing language proficiency. For instance, students could use BNCweb to identify common collocations of high-frequency words, or to analyse the use of modals in spoken vs. written contexts. These activities not only help students see how language is used naturally but also build their analytical skills by encouraging them to notice patterns and make inferences based on real data. Such hands-on experience with corpus tools makes learning more interactive and empowers students to become more autonomous learners.

2.2 Next-Generation Software Tools in Corpus Linguistics

The field of corpus linguistics has seen significant advancements with the development of next-generation software tools. These tools represent a leap forward in terms of functionality, user-friendliness, and analytical depth, offering linguists unprecedented capabilities for linguistic analysis. Recent improvements have seen software like WordSmith Tools and TextStat being used to develop writing skills by revealing patterns of authentic language use. These tools allow for a detailed analysis of language patterns, contributing significantly to the development of writing and language skills (Klimova, 2014). These tools offer a window into authentic language use by revealing intricate patterns in large corpora, which are collections of written or spoken texts. This capability is pivotal for understanding how language is used in real-life contexts, thereby providing valuable insights for those looking to improve their writing skills.

WordSmith Tools, for example, is a comprehensive suite that includes features for conducting detailed lexical analysis, concordancing, and word frequency counts. This allows users to delve into specific aspects of language, such as the most commonly used words in a given corpus, the context in which certain words are used, and patterns of syntax and grammar. Such analysis is incredibly useful for writers looking to adapt their style to fit certain genres or registers. TextStat, on the other hand, provides a user-friendly interface for textual analysis, enabling users to conduct simple yet powerful investigations into texts. It can analyse documents for readability, complexity, and word frequency, among other features. This is particularly beneficial for writers seeking to tailor their language for specific audiences, ensuring that their writing is accessible and engaging.

The use of these tools in educational settings has been transformative. By exposing students and writers to authentic examples of language use, they can develop a more nuanced understanding of language, beyond the confines of traditional rule-based learning. This exposure is crucial for the development of writing skills, as it provides learners with a richer, more varied linguistic palette to draw from for their own writing. By leveraging these tools to uncover patterns of authentic language use, learners and educators can access a wealth of linguistic insights, aiding in the development of more refined and effective writing skills (Klimova, 2014). Specialized software for corpus analysis now includes features for primary text processing and automated markup. These advancements achieve maximum effectiveness in research and teaching in areas such as foreign languages and translation (Gorozhanov & Guseynova, 2020). The Corpus Analysis Toolkit represents another step forward, providing a bespoke suite of software for processing and analysing multilevel annotations of time-aligned linguistic data (Wilson & Carson-Berndsen, 2009).

The landscape of corpus linguistics has been revolutionized by specialized software that now incorporates advanced features for primary text processing and automated markup. These features have significantly increased the effectiveness of linguistic research and teaching, especially in areas such as foreign languages and translation. With tools that can automatically process and markup texts, researchers and educators are able to analyse language data more efficiently and accurately. This automation is particularly valuable in translation studies, where understanding the nuances of language use and structure is crucial. It allows for a more detailed examination of linguistic phenomena, leading to more informed and nuanced translations (Gorozhanov & Guseynova, 2020).

The Corpus Analysis Toolkit represents a significant advancement in the field. This bespoke suite of software is designed to process and analyse multilevel annotations of time-aligned linguistic data, making it an invaluable resource for linguists working with complex datasets. Its ability to handle multilevel annotations means that researchers can delve into various layers of linguistic information – from phonetics to discourse level – within the same dataset. This is particularly useful in studies where the timing and sequencing of linguistic events are critical, such as in conversational analysis or in the study of language acquisition. The toolkit's capacity for handling time-aligned data adds a temporal dimension to corpus analysis, allowing for a more dynamic and comprehensive exploration of language use over time (Wilson & Carson-Berndsen, 2009).

The Glozz platform has emerged as a highly versatile corpus annotation tool, offering advanced visualization, querying, and evaluation possibilities. This represents a significant enhancement in the field of corpus linguistics tools, providing linguists with robust tools for detailed linguistic analysis (Widlöcher & Mathet, 2012). One of the key features of the Glozz platform is its highly versatile corpus annotation tool. This tool facilitates detailed and nuanced annotation of linguistic data, allowing researchers to mark and categorize various linguistic elements within a corpus. This level of detail is essential for in-depth linguistic analyses, such as studying syntactic structures, discourse patterns, or semantic nuances. Another notable aspect of the Glozz platform is its advanced visualization capabilities. These features enable researchers to not only annotate but also visually explore complex linguistic data. This is particularly useful for identifying patterns and relationships that may not be immediately apparent through traditional textual analysis. The querying and evaluation possibilities further enhance the platform's utility, allowing for sophisticated searches and analyses of the annotated data.

Also, the Glozz platform supports multilingualism and offers diverse text types, making it suitable for a wide range of linguistic research endeavours. Its ability to handle multiple languages and various text genres broadens its applicability, catering to researchers working in different linguistic domains. The platform also ensures sorted results, relevance, and accessibility on the internet, making it a convenient tool for linguists worldwide. In summary, the Glozz platform represents a significant advancement in corpus linguistics tools, offering a combination of annotation, visualization, and analysis capabilities. Its versatility and range of features make it an invaluable resource for linguists looking to conduct detailed and comprehensive analyses of linguistic data.

Software-based tools for semi-automated analysis of large text volumes, such as topic modelling and corpus linguistics, offer quick insights but require careful linguistic considerations for valid results. These tools are particularly useful in domains like climate change discourse analysis, where they help parse vast amounts of data to extract meaningful patterns and trends (Grundmann, 2022). Rainer Grundmann's paper on the use of large text news archives for the analysis of climate change discourse brings forward several methodological insights and observations. The paper focuses on how software-based tools for semi-automated analysis of large volumes of text, such as topic modelling and corpus linguistics, can offer new and interesting insights into climate change discourse. These tools provide a means to quickly analyse vast amounts of text data from news archives, revealing patterns and trends in how climate change is discussed and reported.

Grundmann emphasizes that while these tools can generate intriguing results swiftly, they require careful consideration of linguistic aspects to ensure validity. This consideration is crucial when interpreting results, as linguistic nuances and context play a significant role in understanding climate change discourse. The paper highlights the potential of these tools to provide novel insights into the framing and evolution of climate change narratives over time, shedding light on how different aspects of climate change are emphasized or downplayed in media reporting. Moreover, Grundmann's paper underscores the importance of understanding the methodological limitations and biases that may arise from using digitalized text archives. This includes considerations around the selection of sources, the representativeness of the data, and the potential impact of the digitalization process on the integrity of the textual data.

Grundmann's work provides a critical perspective on the use of advanced text analysis tools in environmental communication research. It suggests that while these tools open new avenues for exploring large-scale textual data, researchers must be mindful of linguistic intricacies and methodological challenges to fully leverage their potential in understanding complex discourses such as those surrounding climate change (Grundmann, 2021).

These next-generation tools in corpus linguistics mark a significant advancement in the field, equipping researchers with more powerful and versatile resources for linguistic analysis. They have broadened the scope of corpus linguistics, enabling more comprehensive and nuanced investigations into language use and evolution.

The educational applications of next-generation corpus tools like WordSmith Tools and TextStat are immense, offering teachers practical ways to enhance their language lessons. For instance, teachers can use WordSmith to help students understand collocations by showing concordance lines of a particular word. This allows learners to observe the typical contexts in which a word appears and the most common words that accompany it, which is essential for developing more natural and fluent language use. For example, a teacher could use WordSmith to explore the word "make" with students, revealing collocations like "make a decision" or "make an effort," which would help learners better grasp how these phrases are used in everyday communication.

TextStat is another powerful tool that can be effectively employed in the classroom to make learning more data-driven. Teachers can use TextStat to help students assess their own writing by measuring word frequency and text complexity, and then comparing these metrics to those found in a target corpus. For example, in a classroom scenario, students might be asked to write a short essay and then use TextStat to analyse it, focusing on word frequency, sentence length, and overall readability. By comparing their own results to a corpus of proficient-level texts, students can identify areas where their vocabulary might be too simplistic or where their sentences could be made clearer and more effective. This type of self-assessment encourages students to reflect on their writing and make improvements based on objective data, thereby fostering more independent and informed learning.

2.3 Impact of AI Innovations on Language Analysis

Research by Xue et al. (2023) discusses the significant achievements of AI, particularly emphasizing its impact on language analysis, including NLP, image analysis, and computer vision. This research illustrates how AI innovations have contributed to the advancement of linguistic analysis, offering new methodologies and insights. NLP techniques, enhanced by AI, have become more sophisticated, enabling more accurate and nuanced analysis of language. This includes better syntax parsing, semantic analysis, and sentiment analysis, which are crucial for understanding the complexities of human language in various contexts, such as social media, literature, and technical documents.

AI's role in image analysis and computer vision also intersects with linguistic research, especially in areas like multimodal communication and language learning. The integration of visual data with textual analysis allows for a more holistic understanding of communication, considering both verbal and non-verbal elements. This is particularly relevant in fields such as discourse analysis, where the combination of text and image can provide deeper insights into the intended message and its reception.

Moreover, these advancements have facilitated the processing of large datasets, enabling researchers to handle and analyse vast amounts of linguistic data efficiently. This has implications for corpus linguistics, where large collections of texts can be analysed to uncover language trends, patterns, and usage in real-world settings. In essence, the impact of AI innovations, as discussed by Xue et al. (2023) showcases the growing intersection of AI and linguistic analysis. These advancements have not only enhanced traditional methods of language study but have also opened new avenues for exploration in understanding the dynamics of language and communication.

2.4 Teaching Applications of AI-Driven Corpus Tools

The integration of AI-driven corpus tools into language teaching offers educators powerful resources to make language learning more engaging, authentic, and data-driven. This section explores several ways teachers can utilize these tools in their classrooms to support vocabulary learning, grammar practice, and writing improvement.

Using corpora to teach vocabulary is an effective way to help students understand words in their real-life context. Teachers can guide students in using corpus tools to explore examples of vocabulary in different genres and registers. By doing this, students can observe how the meaning and use of a word may change depending on the context. For instance, teachers can use a corpus tool like Sketch Engine to find authentic examples of the word "run" used in different ways, such as "run a business" versus "go for a run," to illustrate the concept of polysemy. This approach not only helps students expand their vocabulary but also develops their understanding of nuances and collocations, ultimately enabling them to use words more appropriately and naturally.

AI-driven corpus tools can provide learners with a unique opportunity to explore grammatical structures in a more interactive and exploratory way. Teachers can employ concordance lines from corpora to show students how specific grammatical structures are used in authentic texts. For example, students can use tools like CQPWeb to analyse how different tenses of a verb are used across spoken and written corpora, helping them understand the differences between formal and informal language usage. By examining these concordance lines, students can better grasp grammar rules in real-world contexts rather than just learning prescriptive rules. This helps to demystify grammar, making it less abstract and more directly relevant to students' own language use.

AI-based corpus tools can also play an essential role in improving students' writing skills. By using corpus tools to compare their writing to authentic texts, students can gain insight into aspects of their writing that need refinement. For instance, teachers can have students use TextStat to analyse their essays, focusing on metrics such as word frequency, sentence length, and lexical diversity. By comparing these statistics to those found in a target corpus of proficient-level writing, students can identify areas where their vocabulary might need expansion or where their sentence structures might be overly simple. Teachers can also encourage students to use concordancers to see how certain phrases or sentence structures are used by native speakers, providing a model for them to emulate. This practice not only helps students develop better writing habits but also empowers them to become more independent learners who can self-assess and improve their work using data-driven approaches.

Incorporating AI-driven corpus tools into lesson plans can make language teaching more dynamic and engaging. For example, teachers can design a lesson around exploring idiomatic expressions using a corpus, asking students to find examples of idioms in use and then create their own sentences using those idioms. Alternatively, a lesson could focus on discourse markers, where students use corpus tools to identify and analyze how native speakers use phrases like "on the other hand" or "in contrast" to structure their arguments. By involving students in hands-on corpus analysis, teachers can foster a more active learning environment where students take an investigative approach to language, discovering patterns and rules for themselves.

3. DEEP LEARNING AND NEURAL NETWORKS IN CORPUS LINGUISTICS

3.1 Application of Deep Learning Models for Text Analysis

Deep learning models have significantly advanced the field of text analysis in corpus linguistics, offering a range of applications that enhance our understanding of language patterns and structures. These models apply complex algorithms and neural network architectures to analyse textual data, providing insights that were previously unattainable with traditional linguistic methods.

One of the notable applications of deep learning in corpus linguistics is in tasks such as dialogue policy formulation, zero pronoun resolution, and noun phrase coreference resolution. These tasks are fundamental in understanding the nuances of conversational language and textual coherence, which are critical in areas like discourse analysis and natural language understanding (Linzen, 2021).

In dialogue policy formulation, deep learning models analyse large datasets of human conversations, enabling the development of algorithms that guide AI-based dialogue systems. These models are crucial in creating natural and contextually relevant responses in chatbots or virtual assistants, significantly improving interactions in applications such as customer service. By learning from various dialogue scenarios, these algorithms make AI interactions more coherent and context-aware, which is essential for maintaining effective communication in customer service and other interactive applications.

Zero pronoun resolution, another critical area, involves identifying implicit subjects or objects in sentences, a feature prevalent in languages like Japanese and Chinese. Deep learning models excel in predicting these missing entities by understanding the patterns and contexts in which zero pronouns occur. This capability is vital for tasks such as machine translation and cross-language information retrieval, where comprehending these implicit linguistic elements is necessary to preserve the coherence and meaning of translated texts.

Furthermore, in noun phrase coreference resolution, deep learning models demonstrate their proficiency by identifying when different noun phrases in a text refer to the same entity. This task requires parsing through large texts to determine the relationships between various noun phrases and resolving ambiguities in reference. Accurate coreference resolution is essential for information extraction, summarization, and question-answering systems, where understanding the linkages between different text parts is crucial for coherent and accurate information extraction or generation.

These applications of deep learning in corpus linguistics significantly enhance the processing and understanding of natural language, especially in complex conversational contexts. Leveraging large corpora for training, these models offer substantial improvements in the accuracy and efficiency of dialogue policy formulation, zero pronoun resolution, and noun phrase coreference resolution, contributing to advancements in various natural language processing and computational linguistics applications.

Deep learning models have also been employed in sentiment analysis, opinion extraction, and knowledge discovery in large datasets. For instance, the MATT-CNN-BILSTM model improves sentiment analysis performance by learning local and global semantic features, especially in corpora with weak label characteristics. This application is crucial in fields like market research and social media analysis, where understanding public sentiment and opinion trends is vital (Zhang et al., 2022; Medrouk, 2017).

In sentiment analysis, deep learning models like the MATT-CNN-BILSTM have revolutionized the way we analyse text data (Zhou et al., 2022). This model, in particular, stands out for its ability to effectively interpret and classify sentiments by learning both local and global semantic features within text corpora. This is especially beneficial in corpora where labelling is weak or inconsistent, a common challenge in natural language datasets. By accurately identifying sentiments, these models facilitate a deeper understanding of public opinions and emotional tones expressed in various texts, making them indispensable tools in market research and social media analysis. In these fields, accurately gauging public sentiment can provide critical insights for brand management, political campaigning, and understanding consumer behaviour.

Opinion extraction is another area where deep learning models excel. They can sift through vast amounts of unstructured data to identify and extract subjective information. This capability is vital for businesses and researchers who seek to understand public opinions on products, services, or various issues. By automating the extraction of opinions from large datasets, deep learning models save time and increase the accuracy of market and social research.

Additionally, in the field of knowledge discovery, deep learning models can uncover patterns and insights from extensive text datasets that would be impossible to discern manually. They can identify trends, predict outcomes, and provide recommendations based on the analysis of text data. This application is incredibly valuable in fields such as academic research, where understanding the evolution of ideas and discourse can provide new perspectives on a subject.

The application of deep learning models in sentiment analysis, opinion extraction, and knowledge discovery has become a cornerstone in modern corpus linguistics. Their ability to process and analyse large volumes of text data with high accuracy and efficiency makes them invaluable in various domains, including market research and social media analysis, where understanding and interpreting public sentiment and opinions are crucial (Zhou et al., 2022).

Deep learning-based text classification has also been applied in various areas such as news categorization, question answering, and natural language inference. These models can classify text based on content, sentiment, or other linguistic features, aiding in the organization and interpretation of large textual corpora (Minaee et al., 2020). Deep learning-based text classification has revolutionized the way we interact with and understand large volumes of text, with applications extending to news categorization, question answering, and natural language inference.

In the context of news categorization, deep learning models have shown exceptional proficiency. By analysing textual content, these models can automatically categorize news articles into predefined topics such as politics, sports, or entertainment. This categorization not only aids in the efficient organization of news content for media outlets but also enhances the user experience by enabling personalized news feeds and recommendations. For publishers and media analysts, this automated categorization provides valuable insights into news trends and public interests.

Question answering systems have also been greatly enhanced by deep learning models. These systems can understand and process natural language queries, retrieving relevant information or specific answers from large datasets. By employing techniques like semantic analysis and context understanding, deep learning models can provide accurate and contextually appropriate responses to a wide range of questions. This capability is crucial in applications such as virtual assistants, customer service bots, and educational tools, where providing precise information in response to user queries is essential.

Natural language inference, another area benefiting from deep learning, involves determining the logical relationships between sentences or phrases, such as entailment, contradiction, or neutrality. Deep learning models excel in identifying these relationships, enabling a deeper understanding of textual coherence and logical structure. This is particularly important in tasks like text summarization, where the model must understand the underlying narrative to generate coherent and concise summaries. Furthermore, in legal and academic research, natural language inference helps in analysing documents to deduce logical connections and inconsistencies within the text.

Overall, the application of deep learning in text classification extends well beyond mere categorization. By enabling more sophisticated approaches to question answering and natural language inference, deep learning models facilitate a more nuanced and comprehensive understanding of textual data. These advancements not only aid in the practical organization and retrieval of information but also contribute significantly to the field of computational linguistics, offering deeper insights into the complexities of human language (Minaee et al., 2020).

Additionally, deep learning models have been instrumental in legal analytics for text classification, information extraction, and information retrieval, focusing on semantic feature representations. This application is particularly important in legal studies where understanding the semantic nuances and extracting relevant information from legal texts is essential (Chalkidis & Kampas, 2018). These models excel in understanding and representing semantic features of legal texts, which is crucial given the complex and nuanced nature of legal language.

In the area of text classification, deep learning models are adept at categorizing legal documents into various types, such as contracts, court opinions, or statutes. This classification is based on the semantic content of the texts, enabling legal professionals and researchers to quickly sort and access relevant documents. This capability not only streamlines legal research but also aids in organizing large legal databases, making them more accessible and manageable.

Information extraction in legal texts is another area where deep learning models shine. These models can identify and extract key pieces of information from legal documents, such as party names, dates, legal references, and case facts. This automated extraction is particularly beneficial in tasks like legal research and case preparation, where sifting through vast amounts of legal texts can be time-consuming and labour-intensive. By automating this process, deep learning models significantly enhance efficiency and accuracy in legal work.

In the context of information retrieval, deep learning models facilitate the retrieval of specific legal information from large corpora. Utilizing semantic feature representations, these models can comprehend the context and relevance of legal queries, returning the most pertinent documents or information. This is invaluable in legal practice and research, where finding precise legal precedents, statutes, or case law is essential for effective argumentation and decision-making.

Overall, deep learning models have become integral tools in legal analytics, offering innovative solutions for handling and interpreting complex legal texts. By focusing on semantic feature representations, these models provide legal professionals with powerful tools for classification, information extraction, and retrieval, significantly enhancing their ability to engage with legal texts in an effective and informed manner (Chalkidis & Kampas, 2018). The application of deep learning models for text analysis in corpus linguistics has opened new avenues for linguistic research. These models provide the ability to extract, process, and analyse linguistic data with greater depth and accuracy, leading to more profound insights into language use and structure.

3.2 Neural Networks in Analysing Spoken and Written Texts

Neural networks have been increasingly applied to analyse both spoken and written texts, offering a range of innovative approaches to linguistics and language processing.

In spoken language analysis, neural networks are instrumental in tasks such as speech recognition and text-to-speech synthesis. These networks can detect signals using advanced techniques like angular modulation, ensuring correct spelling and pronunciation of words. This is crucial in developing efficient and accurate speech recognition systems, which are increasingly used in applications ranging from virtual assistants to automated transcription services (Al Smadi et al., 2015).

Neural networks also play a key role in text normalization for speech applications. By converting written text into a form suitable for speech synthesis, neural networks improve the accuracy and efficiency of text-to-speech systems. This is especially valuable for creating natural and adaptable speech in systems ranging from navigational aids to educational tools (Zhang et al., 2019).

In the field of written text analysis, neural networks are used to perform complex tasks such as text classification, sentiment analysis, and information extraction. By modelling linguistic features and learning from large corpora, neural networks can classify subjects, detect sentiment, and extract relevant information from vast amounts of text. This capability is crucial in areas such as content analysis, decision support systems, and expert systems, where accurate and efficient text analysis is essential (Zhaxybayev et al., 2022). The work of Zhaxybayev highlights the diverse applications of neural networks in analysing both spoken and written texts, showcasing their versatility and effectiveness in various linguistic tasks.

For spoken language, neural networks are employed in critical stages of speech synthesis, including syllable and stress recognition, text-to-phonemes translation, and control parameters generation. This comprehensive approach allows for the production of natural and accurate speech synthesis, enhancing applications such as automated voice response systems and virtual assistants. The ability of neural networks to handle complex linguistic elements like stress and intonation patterns in speech synthesis significantly contributes to the naturalness and clarity of the synthesized speech (Moisa et al., 2001).

In the context of written texts, neural networks have been applied to solve morphological text analysis. This involves identifying each word's part of speech and effectively comparing their performance with dictionary methods. Such analysis is crucial in understanding the grammatical structure of texts and is instrumental in applications ranging from automated text translation to educational software for language learning (Zhdanova et al., 2022).

Furthermore, neural networks enhance text normalization in speech applications, such as text-to-speech synthesis (TTS). By improving the accuracy and efficiency of converting written text into a form suitable for speech, neural networks contribute to the development of more seamless and effective TTS systems. This application is vital in creating user-friendly and accessible technologies, especially for individuals with visual impairments or reading difficulties (Zhang et al., 2019).

Zhaxybayev's research (2022) underscores the significant role of neural networks in enhancing our ability to process and understand both spoken and written forms of language. Through applications in speech synthesis, morphological analysis, and text normalization, neural networks demonstrate their ability to handle complex linguistic tasks, thereby contributing greatly to the advancement of language processing technologies.

Neural networks have been successfully applied in language modelling, significantly reducing word error rates in continuous speech recognition systems. This application is particularly beneficial in fields like broadcast news, where accurate and real-time transcription of spoken language is required (Schwenk & Gauvain, 2005).

In summary, neural networks have become a cornerstone in the analysis of both spoken and written texts. Their ability to handle complex linguistic tasks with high accuracy and efficiency has made them invaluable in a wide range of applications, from speech recognition and synthesis to comprehensive text analysis and language modelling.

3.3 Case Study: XTest's Contribution to Multilingual Corpus Analysis

The contribution of XTest to multilingual corpus analysis, as discussed by Rithy et al. (2022), represents a significant advancement in the field of computational linguistics. XTest is a parallel multilingual corpus that includes test cases for code translation, providing a comprehensive dataset covering nine languages and thirty systems. This resource is pivotal for translating code between high-resource and low-resource programming languages. XTest's contribution is particularly noteworthy in the field of code translation, a growing area of interest in linguistic research. By covering a diverse range of languages, XTest addresses the challenge of translating programming code across languages that have varying levels of resources available. This is crucial for the development of inclusive and accessible technology, as it allows for the creation of software and applications that are usable in a wider range of linguistic contexts.

Moreover, XTest's dataset facilitates research in the intersection of computational linguistics and software engineering. Researchers and developers can use it to evaluate and improve the performance of code translation systems, ensuring that they are effective across different languages. This is particularly important for the development of multilingual programming environments and tools, which are essential in a globalized technology landscape.

The inclusion of both high-resourced and low-resourced languages in XTest also contributes to the field of machine translation, particularly in contexts where computational resources are limited. By providing a dataset that includes less commonly represented languages, XTest enables researchers to develop more robust and versatile translation models that can cater to a broader audience.

XTest's contribution to multilingual corpus analysis extends beyond traditional linguistic boundaries, intersecting with the domain of software engineering and machine translation. Its comprehensive dataset covering a diverse range of languages serves as a valuable resource for advancing research and development in code translation, particularly in multilingual and multicultural contexts (Rithy et al., 2022).

4. AI IN AUTOMATED ANNOTATION AND ANALYSIS

4.1 Large Text Corpora for Shallow and Deep Linguistic Levels

Large text corpora play a crucial role in analysing both shallow and deep linguistic levels, offering extensive data resources that are fundamental for linguistic research and natural language processing. At the shallow linguistic level, large text corpora provide the necessary breadth and diversity of language use for tasks such as part-of-speech tagging, chunking, and syntactic parsing. These tasks require extensive data to accurately capture the variability and complexity of language. Large corpora allow for the training of models that can recognize and categorize basic linguistic units with high accuracy, which is essential for any further linguistic analysis or language technology application (Aregbesola et al., 2020).

In terms of deep linguistic analysis, large text corpora provide the depth and quality of data required for more complex tasks such as semantic role labelling, discourse analysis, and pragmatics. These tasks delve into the deeper structures and meanings of language, necessitating a large and diverse dataset that can capture the nuances of human language. Large corpora facilitate the development of sophisticated models that can understand and interpret language at a level that is closer to human understanding, which is particularly important for applications in areas such as machine translation and automated content generation (Lu, 2014).

Additionally, large text corpora have been instrumental in the advancement of language modelling, especially in the development of context-aware language models that can predict linguistic elements based on their usage in real-world contexts. These models, trained on extensive text data, have significantly improved the performance of language processing systems in tasks such as speech recognition, text generation, and sentiment analysis. The use of large text corpora is indispensable for both shallow and deep linguistic analysis. They provide the foundation for developing robust and accurate language processing tools and contribute significantly to the understanding of both the structure and function of language across various contexts and applications.

At the shallow linguistic level, AI, particularly through advancements in machine learning and neural networks, has greatly enhanced the efficiency and accuracy of processing vast amounts of text. Essential tasks such as part-of-speech tagging, syntactic parsing, and named entity recognition have become more precise and faster, thanks to these AI models. This efficiency is critical for foundational linguistic analysis and preparing data for more complex processing.

Deep linguistic analysis has also seen significant improvements with AI advancements. Modern techniques like deep learning and transformer models offer a nuanced understanding of complex linguistic structures and meanings. These AI models excel in analysing context, inferring sentiment, and even recognizing subtle linguistic elements like irony or metaphor. This depth of analysis is vital for applications that require a sophisticated understanding of language, such as machine translation and content generation.

The development of large-scale language models like BERT and GPT represents a major leap forward. Trained on extensive text corpora, these models capture a wide range of linguistic nuances and contextual information, making them adept at language generation, question answering, and text summarization. Their ability to understand context and semantics has been a game-changer in natural language processing.

AI has also broadened the scope of linguistic analysis to include cross-linguistic and multimodal data. This expansion allows for the analysis of language patterns across different languages and the integration of text with other data forms, such as audio or visuals. Such capabilities are crucial for developing comprehensive NLP systems that function effectively in diverse linguistic and cultural environments.

AI's proficiency in handling big data has also enabled linguists to work with larger and more diverse datasets. This includes unstructured text from sources like social media, online forums, and digital publications, providing a more comprehensive and representative sample of language usage in various contexts.

These recent AI developments offer transformative capabilities for analysing large text corpora. These advancements not only enhance the efficiency and accuracy of linguistic analysis but also open new avenues for exploring the complexities of human language, making them indispensable in the modern linguistic landscape.

Two notable and recent contributions exemplify these advancements.

The first contribution is by Chen et al. (2023), who developed the MQTTS system. This system, trained on real-world speech from sources like YouTube and podcasts, outperforms existing text-to-speech (TTS) systems in several objective and subjective measures. The MQTTS system's ability to handle spontaneous speech marks a significant advancement in natural language processing, particularly in speech synthesis. It showcases how AI can be trained on large, diverse datasets to produce more natural and accurate spoken language outputs, an essential aspect of deep linguistic processing (Chen et al., 2023).

Another significant advancement comes from Kudugunta et al. (2024), who conducted a quality audit of web-crawled multilingual datasets. Their work highlights the systematic issues often present in lower-resource corpora, making them difficult to use for linguistic analysis. The study recommends techniques to evaluate and improve the quality of multilingual corpora. This research is crucial for both shallow and deep linguistic levels as it addresses the challenges of working with large text corpora in multiple languages. By improving the quality of these datasets, researchers can ensure more reliable and accurate linguistic analysis, which is vital for a range of applications, from machine translation to sentiment analysis (Kudugunta et al., 2024).

These studies demonstrate how recent AI advancements are crucial for enhancing the analysis capabilities at both shallow and deep linguistic levels, especially when dealing with large and diverse text corpora.

5. TECHNICAL APPLICATION: AI IN LANGUAGE DATA ANALYTICS

5.1 Machine Learning Algorithms and NLP Techniques in Corpus Analysis

New findings in machine learning algorithms and NLP techniques have significantly enhanced the capabilities for corpus analysis, particularly in language data analytics.

Samuel et al. (2022) introduced a domain-specific NLP corpus aimed at training conversational agents to provide mental health support for bi-national couples in long-term relationships. This innovative use of NLP corpus analysis highlights the potential for specialized, targeted applications of AI in addressing specific social and interpersonal issues. The creation of such a corpus demonstrates the evolving role of NLP in addressing diverse and nuanced communication needs, leveraging AI to develop more empathetic and context-aware conversational agents.

Another significant development is from Sougandh et al. (2022), who worked on CV parsing using NLP processing. Their approach to creating candidate profiles based on talents mentioned in resumes showcases how NLP can be used for extracting specific information from large text datasets in a structured manner. This application is particularly relevant in the recruitment and human resources sector, where sorting and analysing large volumes of resumes efficiently can significantly improve the hiring process. The implementation of such NLP techniques in CV parsing reflects the growing trend of applying AI for practical, real-world problems in various industries.

These studies exemplify the breadth of machine learning and NLP applications in corpus analysis, highlighting the versatility of AI in addressing both specialized and broad-scale linguistic challenges. The continued evolution of these technologies is pivotal in advancing our understanding and utilization of language data across various domains.

5.2 The Role of AI in Data-Driven Language Learning

The role of AI in data-driven language learning, particularly through machine learning algorithms and NLP techniques, has seen significant developments in recent years, enhancing the efficiency and effectiveness of corpus analysis.

Crosthwaite et al. (2023) discusses the benefits and limitations of using corpora and generative artificial intelligence (GenAI) for understanding language patterns and usage. Corpora have the advantage of being a known quantity; we can identify the specific texts they comprise, such as the BNC2014 and BAWE, which allows for detailed analysis of language patterns, including multi-word units and collocations. This level of detail and transparency is something current large language models like ChatGPT lack, as it's not possible to trace back to the specific texts they have been trained on. However, GenAI also offers unique strengths in exploring language use that corpora have not fully addressed. The article suggests that integrating both corpus and GenAI methodologies could offer language learners a more comprehensive insight into language function across various contexts than relying on a single approach.

Samuel et al. (2022) also introduced a domain-specific NLP corpus aimed at training conversational agents in mental health support for bi-national couples. This innovative application demonstrates how AI can be tailored to address specific communicative needs and scenarios in language learning. By leveraging NLP, AI systems can better understand and respond to the linguistic and emotional nuances of learners, making them more effective in facilitating language learning in specific contexts.

These advancements in AI for language learning reflect a broader trend towards more personalized, intuitive, and context-aware language education tools. By harnessing the power of AI, language learning can be transformed into a more adaptive, responsive, and effective process.

6. AI IN LEXICAL ANALYSIS AND PROFILING

6.1 Creation of Word Frequency Lists and Distribution Profiling

Current advancements in AI, particularly in machine learning and natural language processing (NLP), have significantly enhanced the creation of word frequency lists and distribution profiling in lexical analysis.

Ulugbek Nurmukhamedov and Stuart Webb (2019) focused on lexical coverage and profiling, demonstrating how AI advancements facilitate the creation of word frequency lists and the profiling of word distributions at different frequency levels within texts. Their work underscores the utility of AI in identifying common usage patterns and variances in word frequency, which is crucial for understanding language use in various contexts. Such analyses are vital for language teaching, linguistics research, and automated text processing, offering insights into the frequency and distribution of words across large corpora (Nurmukhamedov & Webb, 2019).

Additionally, Peter Hendrix and Ching Sun's 2020 study on nonword frequency and semantic neighbourhood density in lexical processing highlights how AI techniques enhance our understanding of word recognition. Their research reveals the impact of word frequency and semantic context on language processing, both critical for natural language understanding and AI systems' development for language analysis. This study contributes to our knowledge of how AI can be used to analyse and interpret linguistic patterns, particularly in understanding the complexities of word recognition and decision processes (Hendrix & Sun, 2020).

These studies illustrate how recent AI advancements contribute to lexical analysis, particularly in the creation of word frequency lists and distribution profiling. They underscore the importance of AI in enhancing language models used for various applications, including text analysis, language learning tools, and linguistic research.

7. AI IN LANGUAGE ASSESSMENT AND EDUCATIONAL APPLICATIONS

7.1 Automated Essay Scoring and Learner Language Analysis

The fields of language assessment and educational applications have been significantly enhanced by recent advancements in AI, particularly in automated essay scoring and learner language analysis.

In 2020, Yang et al. introduced a novel approach to enhancing automated essay scoring performance. They utilized fine-tuning pre-trained language models with a combination of regression and ranking, outperforming state-of-the-art neural and statistical models. This advancement showcases how sophisticated AI models can improve the accuracy and reliability of essay scoring systems, providing a more nuanced understanding of written language and student writing abilities (Yang et al., 2020).

An Automated Essay Scoring model based on the stacking method was developed and it significantly improved average Quadratic Weighted Kappa (QWK) values, showing an enhancement of 1.0% to 2.8% compared to baseline models like neural networks and feature-engineered systems. This research indicates the potential of combining different AI approaches to create more effective automated scoring systems, which can accurately evaluate and provide feedback on student essays (Li et al., 2022).

The study by Li et al. (2022) represents a significant advancement in the field of automated essay scoring (AES) through the application of AI. Their development of an AES model based on the stacking method has marked a notable improvement in the accuracy and reliability of scoring student essays. The stacking method utilized in their model involves layering different machine learning algorithms, enabling the system to leverage the strengths of each to achieve a more refined and accurate assessment. This approach contrasts with traditional AES systems that often rely on a single algorithm or a linear combination of features. By stacking different models, Li and colleagues' system can capture a wider range of linguistic features and nuances present in student essays, leading to a more comprehensive evaluation.

Their model showed significant improvements in scoring accuracy, as evidenced by the enhanced average QWK values. The QWK metric is commonly used in AES to measure the agreement between the automated scores and those given by human raters. An improvement of 1.0% to 2.8% in QWK values compared to baseline models indicates that the stacked model is more aligned with human judgment, thus enhancing the reliability and validity of the scoring.

This study's approach also highlights the potential of AI to provide nuanced feedback on student writing. Rather than simply assigning a grade, the model's ability to analyse various aspects of writing can offer students detailed insights into areas such as argument strength, coherence, grammatical accuracy, and stylistic elements. This kind of feedback is invaluable for educational purposes, as it guides students in refining their writing skills more effectively. In summary, the model demonstrates a significant step forward in AES. Their innovative use of the stacking method in AI models not only improves the accuracy of essay scoring but also opens up new possibilities for detailed and constructive feedback in educational settings, contributing to more effective and personalized learning experiences (Li et al., 2022).

These studies demonstrate the ongoing evolution of AI in the field of educational technology, particularly in assessing and enhancing language learning. The application of advanced AI techniques in automated essay scoring and learner language analysis not only streamlines the assessment process but also provides more detailed and insightful feedback to learners, contributing to more effective and personalized educational experiences.

7.2 Ontologies in NLP for Educational Applications

Current progress in natural language processing and machine learning, have greatly influenced the development of ontologies for educational applications. These advancements have enhanced the capabilities of ontologies in capturing and representing knowledge, making them more effective for a variety of educational purposes.

Leveraging ontologies for rapid customization of NLP pipelines were discussed by Erekhinskaya et al. (2020) that highlights how ontologies can power rule engines and provide standard output formats across various domains, including education. This rapid customization capability is essential for developing educational applications that can adapt to different learning contents and styles, thereby enhancing the learning experience.

Ontologies significantly enhance NLP applications in education, providing a structured way to categorize and organize knowledge that makes computer understanding of human language more effective. This advancement allows for personalized and interactive educational experiences. For instance, ontologies enable intelligent tutoring systems to understand student queries and provide tailored responses, significantly improving learning outcomes (Fernández et al., 2020). Additionally, they support the organization of educational content, making it more accessible to students and facilitating automated assessment processes that offer personalized feedback, crucial for effective learning (Smith & Patel, 2019).

However, creating and implementing ontologies comes with challenges, including the complexity of development and the need for ongoing maintenance to reflect new knowledge. Ensuring interoperability across different systems also remains a significant hurdle (Jones et al., 2021).

Despite these challenges, the integration of ontologies into educational NLP applications offers promising future directions, such as enhancing semantic web technologies for better resource discoverability and creating adaptive learning environments that respond to student needs in real-time (Liu et al., 2022). These developments indicate a bright future for the role of ontologies in transforming educational experiences, making learning more personalized, interactive, and effective (Kumar & Singh, 2020).

These studies demonstrate the growing importance of ontologies in NLP for educational applications. By enhancing the representation and management of knowledge, ontologies facilitate the development of more sophisticated and effective educational tools. This aligns with the overall trend of AI advancements, where the focus is not only on processing information but also on making it more accessible and understandable for educational purposes.

8. CONCLUSION AND FUTURE DIRECTIONS

8.1 Summary of AI's Impact on Corpus Analysis in Applied Linguistics

Overall, the exploration of technology-enhanced tools and the impact of artificial intelligence on corpus analysis in applied linguistics has revealed a dynamic and rapidly evolving landscape. From the development of advanced AI-driven tools for corpus analysis, such as 'Linguist's Workbench' and 'Linguistic Database', to the integration of deep learning and neural networks for analysing spoken and written texts, AI has significantly broadened the scope and depth of linguistic research.

The advancements in methodologies for constructing Artificial Intelligence Markup Language knowledge bases and the use of ontologies in NLP have further enriched our understanding and utilization of language data, particularly in educational settings. Automated essay scoring and learner language analysis have demonstrated how AI can streamline assessment processes while providing detailed and insightful feedback, contributing to more effective and personalized educational experiences.

Moreover, the creation of word frequency lists and distribution profiling has been revolutionized by AI, offering nuanced insights into language use and evolution. This is crucial not only for linguistics research but also for practical applications in various domains such as market research, social media analysis, and educational technology.

Throughout the corpus of research analysed, it is evident that AI has become an indispensable tool in the field of applied linguistics. Its ability to handle complex linguistic tasks with high accuracy and efficiency has made it invaluable in a wide range of applications. AI's contributions to linguistic research not only enhance traditional methodologies but also introduce new possibilities for exploring the complexities and subtleties of human language. In essence, the integration of AI in corpus analysis marks a significant shift towards more sophisticated, data-driven, and computationally advanced approaches in linguistics. As AI continues to evolve, its role in enhancing our understanding of language, its structure, and its function, is likely to become even more pronounced, paving the way for new discoveries and innovations in the field of applied linguistics.

8.2 Implications for Future Research and Practice

The integration of artificial intelligence in corpus analysis within applied linguistics not only marks a significant advancement in current research methodologies but also opens up a myriad of possibilities for future research and practice. In terms of future research, the continuous evolution of AI and its applications in linguistics promises deeper insights into language processing and usage. Researchers can anticipate more sophisticated tools for analysing large and diverse language datasets, enabling them to uncover patterns and relationships that were previously inaccessible. This will likely lead to new theoretical understandings in linguistics, as well as practical applications in language teaching, translation, and computational linguistics.

Additionally, the intersection of AI with corpus analysis offers potential for interdisciplinary research, bridging linguistics with fields such as cognitive science, psychology, and computer science. This interdisciplinary approach can provide a more holistic understanding of language as a complex human faculty, involving not just linguistic but also cognitive and social dimensions.

In practice, the advancements in AI-driven corpus analysis will continue to enhance language education and assessment. Personalized learning experiences powered by AI can cater to individual learning styles and needs, thereby improving language acquisition and proficiency. Similarly, in language assessment, AI-driven tools can provide more accurate, efficient, and fair evaluations of language skills.

The advancements in AI will have significant implications in areas such as natural language processing, automated translation, and voice recognition technology. These technologies are becoming increasingly important in our globalized world, and improvements in these areas can lead to more effective communication and accessibility across language barriers.

Finally, as AI continues to evolve, it is crucial to consider the ethical implications of its use in applied linguistics. This includes ensuring fairness and bias mitigation in language processing tools, protecting user data privacy, and maintaining transparency in AI algorithms. The implications of AI in corpus analysis for future research and practice in applied linguistics are profound and far-reaching. As AI technologies become more advanced and integrated, they will undoubtedly continue to transform the landscape of language research and its practical applications, offering exciting possibilities and new challenges.

REFERENCES

Al Smadi, T., Al Issa, H. A., Trad, E., & Al Smadi, K. A. (2015). Artificial intelligence for speech recognition based on neural networks. *Journal of Signal and Information Processing*, *6*(02), 66–72. DOI: 10.4236/jsip.2015.62006

Aregbesola, M. K., Ganiyu, R. A., Olabiyisi, S. O., & Omidiora, E. O. (2020). A Comparative Study of Deep and Shallow Parsing Approaches to Automated Grammaticality Evaluation. *Journal of Computer Science and Its Application*, *27*(1). Advance online publication. DOI: 10.4314/jcsia.v27i1.2

Baksa-Haskó, G. (2020). Possibilities for Correcting SQL Exercises Automatically. In The Impact of the 4th Industrial Revolution on Engineering Education: Proceedings of the 22nd International Conference on Interactive Collaborative Learning (ICL2019)–Volume 2 22, 588-597. Springer International Publishing.

Biber, D. (2012). Register as a predictor of linguistic variation. *Corpus Linguistics and Linguistic Theory*, *8*(1), 9–37. DOI: 10.1515/cllt-2012-0002

Bunt, H., Merlo, P., & Nivre, J. (Eds.). (2010). *Trends in parsing technology: Dependency parsing, domain adaptation, and deep parsing* (Vol. 43). Springer Science & Business Media. DOI: 10.1007/978-90-481-9352-3

Chalkidis, I., & Kampas, D. (2019). Deep learning in law: Early adaptation and legal word embeddings trained on large corpora. *Artificial Intelligence and Law*, *27*(2), 171–198. DOI: 10.1007/s10506-018-9238-9

Chen, L. W., Watanabe, S., & Rudnicky, A. (2023). A vector quantized approach for text to speech synthesis on real-world spontaneous speech. arXiv preprint arXiv:2302.04215.

Conway M, Hu M, Chapman W. (2019). Recent Advances in Using Natural Language Processing to Address Public Health Research Questions Using Social Media and Consumer-Generated Data. Aug;28(1):208-217. . Epub 2019 Aug 16. PMID: 31419834; PMCID: PMC6697505.DOI: 10.1055/s-0039-1677918

Crosthwaite, P., & Baisa, V. (2023). Generative AI and the end of corpus-assisted data-driven learning? Not so fast! *Applied Corpus Linguistics, 3*(3), 100066. DOI: 10.1016/j.acorp.2023.100066

Diefenbach, D., López, V., Singh, K., & Maret, P. (2018). Core techniques of question answering systems over knowledge bases: A survey. *Knowledge and Information Systems, 7*(3), 33–51. DOI: 10.1007/s10115-017-1100-y

Erekhinskaya, T., Tatu, M., Balakrishna, M., Patel, S., Strebkov, D., & Moldovan, D. (2020). Ten ways of leveraging ontologies for rapid natural language processing customization for multiple use cases in disjoint domains. *Open Journal of Semantic Web, 7*, 33–51.

Fernández, S., Gómez-Pérez, J. M., & Juristo, N. (2020). Ontologies in educational NLP applications: A systematic review. *Computers & Education, 143*, 103682.

Gorozhanov, A. I., & Guseynova, I. A. (2020). Corpus analysis of the grammatical categories' constituents in fiction texts considering the linguo-regional component, Siberian Federal University. Humanities & Social Sciences, 13 (12).

Grundmann, R. (2022). Using large text news archives for the analysis of climate change discourse: Some methodological observations. *Journal of Risk Research, 25*(3), 395–406. DOI: 10.1080/13669877.2021.1894471

Healey, B. (2019). How children experience creative writing in the classroom. *Australian Journal of Language and Literacy, 42*(3), 184–194. DOI: 10.1007/BF03652037

Hendrix, P., & Sun, C. C. (2020). A word or two about nonwords: Frequency, semantic neighborhood density, and orthography-to-semantics consistency effects for nonwords in the lexical decision task. *Journal of Experimental Psychology. Learning, Memory, and Cognition, 47*(1), 157–183. DOI: 10.1037/xlm0000819 PMID: 31999159

Irfan, R., King, C. K., Grages, D., Ewen, S., Khan, S. U., Madani, S. A., Kolodziej, J., Wang, L., Chen, D., Rayes, A., Tziritas, N., Xu, C.-Z., Zomaya, A. Y., Alzahrani, A. S., & Li, H. (2015). A survey on text mining in social networks. *The Knowledge Engineering Review*, *30*(2), 157–170. DOI: 10.1017/S0269888914000277

Jones, R., Zhang, X., & Jacobsen, K. (2021). Challenges in ontology development and integration for educational applications. *Journal of the Association for Information Science and Technology*, *72*(10), 1245–1260.

Klimova, B. F. (2014). Approaches to the teaching of writing skills. *Procedia: Social and Behavioral Sciences*, *112*, 147–151. DOI: 10.1016/j.sbspro.2014.01.1149

Krasselt, J., Dreesen, P., Stücheli-Herlach, P., Lemmenmeier, D., Cho, S., Rothenhäusler, K., & Fluor, M. (2023). Swiss-AL: platform for language data in applied sciences: on challenges in the field of language open research data. In 1st Conference on Research Data Infrastructure (CoRDI)-Connecting Communities, Karlsruhe, Germany, 12-14 September 2023 (Vol. 1). TIB Open Publishing. DOI: 10.52825/cordi.v1i.249

Kudugunta, S., Caswell, I., Zhang, B., Garcia, X., Xin, D., Kusupati, A., & Firat, O. (2024). Madlad-400: A multilingual and document-level large audited dataset. *Advances in Neural Information Processing Systems*, **•••**, 36.

Kumar, A., & Singh, M. (2020). Adaptive learning environments with ontologies: Towards a better understanding of learning styles. *Learning and Individual Differences*, *78*, 101832.

Leng, L., & Shan, G. (2019). Analysis and research on lexical errors in machine translation in Chinese and Korean translation. *International Journal of Frontiers in Engineering Technology*, *1*(1), 30–37.

Li, C., Lin, L., Mao, W., Xiong, L., & Lin, Y. (2022). An automated essay scoring model based on stacking method. In 2022 IEEE 2nd International Conference on Software Engineering and Artificial Intelligence (SEAI), 248-252. IEEE. DOI: 10.1109/SEAI55746.2022.9832246

Linzen, T., & Baroni, M. (2021). Syntactic structure from deep learning. *Annual Review of Linguistics*, *7*(1), 195–212. DOI: 10.1146/annurev-linguistics-032020-051035

Liu, H., Lai, C., & Xu, W. (2022). Leveraging ontologies for semantic web-enabled educational resources. *Educational Technology Research and Development*, *70*(1), 371–390. PMID: 35125846

Lu, X. (2014). *Computational methods for corpus annotation and analysis*. Springer. DOI: 10.1007/978-94-017-8645-4

Medrouk, L., & Pappa, A. (2017). Deep learning model for sentiment analysis in multi-lingual corpus. In Neural Information Processing: 24th International Conference, ICONIP 2017, Guangzhou, China, November 14-18, 2017 [Springer International Publishing.]. *Proceedings*, *24*(Part I), 205–212.

Mikheev, A., & Finch, S. (1997). A workbench for finding structure in texts. In *Fifth Conference on Applied Natural Language Processing*, 372-379. DOI: 10.3115/974557.974611

Minaee, S., Kalchbrenner, N., Cambria, E., Nikzad, N., Chenaghlu, M., & Gao, J. (2021). Deep learning—based text classification: A comprehensive review. *ACM Computing Surveys*, *54*(3), 1–40. DOI: 10.1145/3439726

Moisa, T., Ontanu, D., & Dediu, A. H. (2001). Speech synthesis using neural networks trained by an evolutionary algorithm. In Computational Science-ICCS 2001: International Conference San Francisco, CA, USA, May 28—30, 2001 Proceedings, Part II 1, 419-428. Springer Berlin Heidelberg. DOI: 10.1007/3-540-45718-6_46

Nurmukhamedov, U., & Webb, S. (2019). Coverage and profiling: Lexical coverage in L2 reading and speed of lexical access during reading. *Applied Linguistics*, *40*(5), 841–865.

Ratner, A., & Ré, C. (2018). Knowledge base construction in the machine-learning era: three critical design points: joint-learning, weak supervision, and new representations. *ACM Queue; Tomorrow's Computing Today*, *16*(3), 79–90. DOI: 10.1145/3236386.3243045

Rithy, I. J., Shakil, H. H., Mondal, N., Sultana, F., & Shah, F. M. (2022). XTest: A Parallel Multilingual Corpus with Test Cases for Code Translation and Its Evaluation. In 2022 25th International Conference on Computer and Information Technology (ICCIT), 623-628. IEEE. DOI: 10.1109/ICCIT57492.2022.10055851

Samuel, N., Caporusso, N. & Ferman, D. (2022). A Peer-to-Peer Corpus for Conversational Agents for Long-Distance Relationships. Intelligent Human Systems Integration (IHSI 2022): Integrating People and Intelligent Systems, 22(22).

Schwenk, H., & Gauvain, J. L. (2005). Training neural network language models on very large corpora. In *Proceedings of human language technology conference and conference on empirical methods in natural language processing*, 201-208. DOI: 10.3115/1220575.1220601

Smith, L., & Patel, V. (2019). Enhancing education through ontologies and NLP. *Journal of Educational Technology & Society*, *22*(3), 28–40.

Smith, N., Hoffmann, S., & Rayson, P. (2007). Corpus tools and methods today and tomorrow: Incorporating user-defined annotations. In *Corpus Linguistics Conference (CL2007).*

Sougandh, T. G., Reddy, N. S., & Belwal, M. (2023). Automated Resume Parsing: A Natural Language Processing Approach. In 2023 7th International Conference on Computation System and Information Technology for Sustainable Solutions (CSITSS), 1-6. IEEE. DOI: 10.1109/CSITSS60515.2023.10334236

Tolmasova, K. A. (2022). Using corpus linguistics in teaching leisure reading. *The American Journal of Social Science and Education Innovations*, *4*(04), 34–39. DOI: 10.37547/tajssei/Volume04Issue04-05

Viana, V., Menezes, D., & Mendes, M. (2011). Revelando sentidos na prática docente: A abordagem de corpus na análise do discurso. *DELTA. Documentação de Estudos em Lingüística Teórica e Aplicada*, *27*(2), 175–217. DOI: 10.1590/S0102-44502011000200001

Widlöcher, A., & Mathet, Y. (2012). The glozz platform: A corpus annotation and mining tool. In *Proceedings of the 2012 ACM symposium on Document engineering*, 171-180. DOI: 10.1145/2361354.2361394

Wilson, S., & Carson-Berndsen, J. (2011). The corpus analysis toolkit-analysing multilevel annotations. In Human Language Technology. Challenges for Computer Science and Linguistics: 4th Language and Technology Conference, LTC 2009, Poznan, Poland, November 6-8, 2009, Revised Selected Papers 4, 94-104. Springer Berlin Heidelberg.

Xu, Y., Jia, R., Mou, L., Li, G., Chen, Y., Lu, Y., & Jin, Z. (2016). Improved relation classification by deep recurrent neural networks with data augmentation. arXiv preprint arXiv:1601.03651.

Xue, B., Green, R., & Zhang, M. (2023). Artificial Intelligence in New Zealand: Applications and innovation. *Journal of the Royal Society of New Zealand, 53*(1), 1–5. DOI: 10.1080/03036758.2023.2170165 PMID: 39439988

Yang, R., Cao, J., Wen, Z., Wu, Y., & He, X. (2020). Enhancing automated essay scoring performance via fine-tuning pre-trained language models with combination of regression and ranking. In *Findings of the Association for Computational Linguistics* (pp. 1560–1569). EMNLP. DOI: 10.18653/v1/2020.findings-emnlp.141

Zhang, H., Sproat, R., Ng, A. H., Stahlberg, F., Peng, X., Gorman, K., & Roark, B. (2019). Neural models of text normalization for speech applications. *Computational Linguistics*, *45*(2), 293–337. DOI: 10.1162/coli_a_00349

Zhang, K., Zhang, K., Zhang, M., Zhao, H., Liu, Q., Wu, W., & Chen, E. (2022). Incorporating dynamic semantics into pre-trained language model for aspect-based sentiment analysis. arXiv preprint arXiv:2203.16369. DOI: 10.18653/v1/2022.findings-acl.285

Zhaxybayev, D. O., & Barakhnin, V. B. (2022). Coordinate Indexing Algorithms Taking Into Account the Classification Signs-terms in the Subject Area. Computational nanotechnology, 9(1), 21-31.

Zhdanova, A. N., Kupriyanov, A. V., & Sherenkov, D. S. (2022). Morphological text analysis using neural networks. In *2022 VIII International Conference on Information Technology and Nanotechnology (ITNT)*, 1-4. IEEE.

Zhou, Z., Chen, J., Wu, J., & Wang, R. (2022). Sentiment Analysis Method for Agricultural Product Review Based on Corpus Characteristics and Deep Learning Model. In *2022 International Conference on Machine Learning and Intelligent Systems Engineering (MLISE)*, 423-430. IEEE. DOI: 10.1109/MLISE57402.2022.00091

Compilation of References

Akgun, S., & Greenhow, C. (2022). Artificial intelligence in education: Addressing ethical challenges in K-12 settings. *AI and Ethics*, *2*(3), 431–440. DOI: 10.1007/s43681-021-00096-7 PMID: 34790956

Al Smadi, T., Al Issa, H. A., Trad, E., & Al Smadi, K. A. (2015). Artificial intelligence for speech recognition based on neural networks. *Journal of Signal and Information Processing*, *6*(02), 66–72. DOI: 10.4236/jsip.2015.62006

Alam, A. (2023). Harnessing the power of AI to create intelligent tutoring systems for enhanced classroom experience and improved learning outcomes. In G. Rajakumar, Ke-Lin Du, & Álvaro Rocha (Eds.), *Intelligent Communication Technologies and Virtual Mobile Networks* (pp. 571–591). Springer Nature Singapore. DOI: 10.1007/978-981-99-1767-9_42

Al-Badi, A., Khan, A., & Eid-Alotaibi, . (2022). Perceptions of learners and instructors towards artificial intelligence in personalized learning. *Procedia Computer Science*, *201*, 445–451. DOI: 10.1016/j.procs.2022.03.058

Al-Dosakee, K., & Ozdamli, F. (2021). Gamification in teaching and learning languages: A systematic literature review. *Revista Românească Pentru Educaţie Multidimensională, 13*(2), 559–577. Researchgate. https://doi.org/DOI: 10.18662/rrem/13.2/436

Alfadil, M. (2020). Effectiveness of virtual reality game in foreign language vocabulary acquisition. *Computers & Education*, *153*, 103893. Advance online publication. DOI: 10.1016/j.compedu.2020.103893

Alhalangy, A. G. I., & AbdAlgane, M. (2023). Exploring The Impact of AI on The EFL Context: A Case Study of Saudi Universities. *Journal of Intercultural Communication*, *23*(2), 41–49. DOI: 10.36923/jicc.v23i2.125

Alharbi, W. (2023). AI in the Foreign Language Classroom: A Pedagogical Overview of Automated Writing Assistance Tools. *Hindawi Education Research International,* 2023, ID 4253331, https://doi.org/.DOI: 10.1155/2023/4253331

Ali, J. K. M., Shamsan, M. A. A., Hezam, T. A., & Mohammed, A. A. Q. (2023). Impact of chatgpt on learning motivation. *Journal of English Studies in Arabia Felix*, *2*(1), 41–49. DOI: 10.56540/jesaf.v2i1.51

Al-Jarf, R. (2024). Students' assignments and research papers generated by AI: Arab instructors' views. *Journal of Computer Science and Technology Studies*, *6*(2), 92–98. DOI: 10.32996/jcsts.2024.6.2.11

Alkaissi, H., & McFarlane, S. I. (2023). Artificial hallucinations in ChatGPT: Implications in scientific writing. *Cureus*, *15*(2). Advance online publication. DOI: 10.7759/cureus.35179 PMID: 36811129

Alm, A., & Ohashi, L. (2024). A worldwide study on language educators' initial response to ChatGPT. *Technology in Language Teaching & Learning*, *6*(1), 1–23. DOI: 10.29140/tltl.v6n1.1141

Almehmadi, W. (2024). Exploring the potential of ai techniques in teaching english as a foreign language: A systematic literature review. *Asian Journal of Social Sciences and Management Studies*, *11*(2), 22–31. DOI: 10.20448/ajssms.v11i2.5576

Alrawashdeh, G. S., Fyffe, S., Azevedo, R. F. L., & Castillo, N. M. (2024). Exploring the impact of personalized and adaptive learning technologies on reading literacy: A global meta-analysis. *Educational Research Review*, *42*, 100587. Advance online publication. DOI: 10.1016/j.edurev.2023.100587

Al-Zahrani, A. M., & Alasmari, T. M. (2024). Exploring the impact of artificial intelligence on higher education: The dynamics of ethical, social, and educational implications. *Humanities & Social Sciences Communications*, *11*(1), 1–12. DOI: 10.1057/s41599-024-03432-4

Aregbesola, M. K., Ganiyu, R. A., Olabiyisi, S. O., & Omidiora, E. O. (2020). A Comparative Study of Deep and Shallow Parsing Approaches to Automated Grammaticality Evaluation. *Journal of Computer Science and Its Application*, *27*(1). Advance online publication. DOI: 10.4314/jcsia.v27i1.2

Arroyo, I., Woolf, B. P., Burelson, W., Muldner, K., Rai, D., & Tai, M. (2014). A multimedia adaptive tutoring system for mathematics that addresses cognition, metacognition and affect. *International Journal of Artificial Intelligence in Education*, *24*(4), 387–426. DOI: 10.1007/s40593-014-0023-y

Atkinson, D. (2002). Toward a sociocognitive approach to second language acquisition. *Modern Language Journal*, *86*(4), 525–545. DOI: 10.1111/1540-4781.00159

Bai, S., Hew, K. F., & Huang, B. (2020). Does gamification improve student learning outcome? Evidence from a meta-analysis and synthesis of qualitative data in educational contexts. *Educational Research Review*, *30*, 100322. DOI: 10.1016/j.edurev.2020.100322

Baksa-Haskó, G. (2020). Possibilities for Correcting SQL Exercises Automatically. In The Impact of the 4th Industrial Revolution on Engineering Education: Proceedings of the 22nd International Conference on Interactive Collaborative Learning (ICL2019)–Volume 2 22, 588-597. Springer International Publishing.

Balci, S., Secaur, J. M., & Morris, B. J. (2022). Comparing the effectiveness of badges and leaderboards on academic performance and motivation of students in fully versus partially gamified online physics classes. *Education and Information Technologies*, *27*(6), 8669–8704. DOI: 10.1007/s10639-022-10983-z PMID: 35308640

Barrot, J. S. (2023). Using automated written corrective feedback in the writing classrooms: Effects on L2 writing accuracy. *Computer Assisted Language Learning*, *36*(4), 584–607. DOI: 10.1080/09588221.2021.1936071

Becker, S. A., Brown, M., Dahlstrom, E., Davis, A., DePaul, K., Diaz, V., & Pomerantz, J. (2018). *NMC horizon report: 2018 higher education edition*. EDUCAUSE Publications., https://library.educause.edu/resources/2018/8/2018-nmc-horizon-report

Bergert, C., Köster, A., Krasnova, H., & Turel, O. (2020). Missing Out on Life: Parental Perceptions of Children's Mobile Technology Use. [Zentrale Tracks]. *Wirtschaftsinformatik*, •••, 568–583.

Bernard, R. M., Borokhovski, E., Schmid, R. F., Waddington, D. I., & Pickup, D. I. (2019). Twenty-first century adaptive teaching and individualized learning operationalized as specific blends of student-centered instructional events: A systematic review and meta-analysis. *Campbell Systematic Reviews*, *15*(1–2), e1017. Advance online publication. DOI: 10.1002/cl2.1017 PMID: 37131463

Bezzina, S., Dingli, A., & Pfeiffer, A. (2022). Leveraging gamification in education through artificial intelligence. In *Proceedings of the 16th International Technology, Education and Development Conference (INTED2022)*, DOI:DOI: 10.21125/inted.2022.2206

Bialystok, E. (1978). A Theoretical Model of Second Language Learning. *Modern Language Journal*, *28*, 69–83.

Biber, D. (2012). Register as a predictor of linguistic variation. *Corpus Linguistics and Linguistic Theory*, *8*(1), 9–37. DOI: 10.1515/cllt-2012-0002

Bibizadeh, R. E., Procter, R., Girvan, C., Webb, H., & Jirotka, M. (2023). Digitally un/free: The everyday impact of social media on the lives of young people. *Learning, Media and Technology*, 1–14. Advance online publication. DOI: 10.1080/17439884.2023.2237883

Bingham, A. J., Pane, J. F., Steiner, E. D., & Hamilton, L. S. (2016). Ahead of the curve: Implementation challenges in personalized learning school models. *Educational Policy*, *32*(3), 454–489. DOI: 10.1177/0895904816637688

Black, J. (2023). Past, present and tackling the future of artificial intelligence (ai) in education: Maintaining agency and establishing ai laws. *Open Journal of Social Sciences*, *11*(07), 442–464. DOI: 10.4236/jss.2023.117031

Bloom, L., & Lahey, M. (1978). *Language development and language disorders.* John Wiley & Sons, Inc. https://doi.org/DOI: 10.7916/D8QZ2GQ5

Bozkurt, A. (2023). Generative AI, Synthetic Contents, Open Educational Resources (OER), and Open Educational Practices (OEP): A New Front in the Openness Landscape. *Open Praxis, 15*(3), 178–184. DOI: 10.55982/openpraxis.15.3.579

Brown, H. D. (2007). *Principles of language learning and teaching* (5th ed.). Pearson Longman.

Bunt, H., Merlo, P., & Nivre, J. (Eds.). (2010). *Trends in parsing technology: Dependency parsing, domain adaptation, and deep parsing* (Vol. 43). Springer Science & Business Media. DOI: 10.1007/978-90-481-9352-3

Burke, B. (2016). *Gamify: How gamification motivates people to do extraordinary things.* Bibliomotion, Inc. DOI: 10.4324/9781315230344

Cardona, M. A., Rodríguez, R. J., & Ishmael, K. (2023, May 25). Artificial Intelligence and the Future of Teaching and Learning: Insights and Recommendations. Policycommons.net; Office of Educational Technology. https://policycommons.net/artifacts/3854312/ai-report/4660267/

Carolus, A., Koch, M., Straka, S., Latoschik, M. E., & Wienrich, C. (2023). MAILS - Meta AI literacy scale: Development and testing of an AI literacy questionnaire based on well-founded competency models and psychological change- and meta-competencies. *Computers in Human Behaviour: Artificial Humans, 1*(2), 100014. Advance online publication. DOI: 10.1016/j.chbah.2023.100014

Ceci, L. (2023, May 3). *Top language learning apps by downloads 2021.* Statista. https://www.statista.com/statistics/1239522/top-language-learning-apps-downloads/

Celik, I., Dindar, M., Muukkonen, H., & Jarvela, S. (2022). The promises and challenges of artificial intelligence for teachers: A systematic review of research. *TechTrends, 66*(4), 616–630. DOI: 10.1007/s11528-022-00715-y

Chalkidis, I., & Kampas, D. (2019). Deep learning in law: Early adaptation and legal word embeddings trained on large corpora. *Artificial Intelligence and Law, 27*(2), 171–198. DOI: 10.1007/s10506-018-9238-9

Chen, L. W., Watanabe, S., & Rudnicky, A. (2023). A vector quantized approach for text to speech synthesis on real-world spontaneous speech. arXiv preprint arXiv:2302.04215.

Chen, C. M. (2022). Personalized E-learning system with self-regulated learning assisted mechanisms for promoting learning performance. *Expert Systems with Applications, 41*(2), 225–238.

Chen, C. M., & Chung, C. J. (2008). Personalized mobile English vocabulary learning system based on item response theory and learning memory cycle. *Computers & Education, 51*(2), 624–645. DOI: 10.1016/j.compedu.2007.06.011

Chen, L., Chen, P., & Lin, Z. (2020). Artificial intelligence in education: A review. *IEEE Access : Practical Innovations, Open Solutions, 8*, 75264–75278. DOI: 10.1109/ACCESS.2020.2988510

Chen, X., Zou, D., Xie, H., & Cheng, G. (2021). Twenty years of personalized language learning: Topic modeling and knowledge mapping. *Journal of Educational Technology & Society, 24*(1), 205–222. https://www.jstor.org/stable/26977868

Chen, X., Zou, D., Xie, H., Cheng, G., & Liu, C. (2022). Two Decades of Artificial Intelligence in Education: Contributors, Collaborations, Research Topics, Challenges, and Future Directions. *Journal of Educational Technology & Society, 25*(1), 28–47.

Chiu, T. K. F., & Chai, C. S. (2020). Sustainable curriculum planning for artificial intelligence education: A self-determination theory perspective. *Sustainability (Basel), 12*(14), 5568. DOI: 10.3390/su12145568

Chomsky, N., Roberts, I., & Watumull, J. (2023, Mar 08). *Noam Chomsky: The false promise of ChatGPT: Guest essay.* Retrieved June 30, 2023, from https://www.nytimes.com/2023/03/08/opinion/noam-chomsky-chatgpt-ai.html

Choukaier, D. (2024). Integrating AI In English Language Pedagogy: Innovations And Outcomes In Teaching English As Second /Foreign Language *Educational Administration. Theory into Practice, 30*(5), 3811–3822. DOI: 10.53555/kuey.v30i5.3538

Chou, Y.-K. (2014). *Actionable Gamification: Beyond Points, Badges, and Leaderboards*. Octalysis Group.

Christians, G. (2018). The Origins and Future of Gamification. *Senior Theses*, 1–65. https://scholarcommons.sc.edu/senior_theses/254

Christoforou, M., Xerou, E., & Papadima-Sophocleous, S. (2019). Integrating a virtual reality application to simulate situated learning experiences in a foreign language course. In F. Meunier, J. Van De Vyver, L. Bradley, & S. Thouësny (Eds.), *CALL and complexity – short papers from EUROCALL 2019* (1st ed., pp. 82–87). Research-publishing.net. https://doi.org/DOI: 10.14705/rpnet.2019.38.990

Chun, D. M., Karimi, H., & Sañosa, D. J. (2022). Traveling by headset: Immersive VR for language learning. *CALICO Journal, 39*(2), 129–149. DOI: 10.1558/cj.21306

Chun, D., Kaplan-Rakowski, R., Ovsiannikova, U., Thrasher, T., & Yuan, Y. (2024 forthcoming). AI-mediated high-immersion virtual reality for language learning. In Lan, Y. J., Qi, G., & Chun, D. (Eds.), *AI-mediated language education in the metaverse era*. Springer.

Clancey, W. J. (1995) A tutorial on situated learning. In Self, J. (Ed.), *International Conference on Computers and Education (Taiwan)* (pp.49–70). AACE

Clark, D. (2020). *Artificial intelligence for learning: How to use AI to support employee development*. KoganPage.

Condon, W. (2011). Reinventing writing assessment: How the conversation is shifting. *WPA. Writing Program Administration, 34*(2), 162–183.

Connor, C. M., Mazzocco, M. M. M., Kurz, T., Crowe, E. C., Tighe, E. L., Wood, T. S., & Morrison, F. J. (2018). Using assessment to individualize early mathematics instruction. *Journal of School Psychology*, *66*, 97–113. DOI: 10.1016/j.jsp.2017.04.005 PMID: 29499792

Conway M, Hu M, Chapman W. (2019). Recent Advances in Using Natural Language Processing to Address Public Health Research Questions Using Social Media and Consumer-Generated Data. Aug;28(1):208-217. . Epub 2019 Aug 16. PMID: 31419834; PMCID: PMC6697505.DOI: 10.1055/s-0039-1677918

Cope, B., Kalantzis, M., & Searsmith, D. (2021). Artificial intelligence for education: Knowledge and its assessment in AI-enabled learning ecologies. *Educational Philosophy and Theory*, *53*(12), 1229–1245. DOI: 10.1080/00131857.2020.1728732

Correia, S. G., Lima, L. A. de O., Lourenço, E. M. da S. M., Filho, T. A. G., Melo, R. J. de, Manca, R. da S., Santos, A. M. dos, Abreu, A. V. N. de, Coelho, E. C. da S., & Santos, J. L. D. de M. (2024). Applicability of artificial intelligence in the teaching and learning process. *Seven Editora*, 651–661.

Costa, R. S., Tan, Q., Pivot, F., Zhang, X., & Wang, H. (2021). Personalized and adaptive learning: Educational practice and technological impact. *Texto Livre: Linguagem e Tecnologia*, *14*(3), 1–11. DOI: 10.35699/1983-3652.2021.33445

Crosthwaite, P., & Baisa, V. (2023). Generative AI and the end of corpus-assisted data-driven learning? Not so fast! *Applied Corpus Linguistics*, *3*(3), 100066. DOI: 10.1016/j.acorp.2023.100066

Dai, Y., & Wu, Z. (2023). Mobile-assisted pronunciation learning with feedback from peers and/or automatic speech recognition: A mixed-methods study. *Computer Assisted Language Learning*, *36*(5–6), 861–884. DOI: 10.1080/09588221.2021.1952272

Dang, T. P., & Boyd, W. A. (2014). Renovating early childhood education pedagogy: A case study in Vietnam. *International Journal of Early Years Education*, *22*(2), 184–196. DOI: 10.1080/09669760.2014.909306

Davis, F. D. (1989). Perceived usefulness, perceived ease of use, and user acceptance of information technology. *Management Information Systems Quarterly*, *13*(3), 319–340. DOI: 10.2307/249008

De la Vall, R. R. F., & Araya, F. G. (2023). Exploring the benefits and challenges of AI-language learning tools. *Int. J. Soc. Sci. Humanit. Invent*, *10*(1), 7569–7576. DOI: 10.18535/ijsshi/v10i01.02

Democratic Republic of Vietnam. (1946). S c l nh v đ t nh ng nguyên t c cơ b n c a n n giáo d c m i (The decree sets up the basic principles of the new education). Hanoi, Vietnam. Retrieved from https://thuvienphapluat.vn/van-ban/Giaoduc/Sac-lenh-146-dat-nguyen-tac-can-ban-nen-giao-duc-moi/36075/noi-dung.aspx

Dhimolea, T. K., Kaplan-Rakowski, R., & Lin, L. (2022). A systematic review of research on high-immersion virtual reality for language learning. *TechTrends*, *66*(5), 810–824. DOI: 10.1007/s11528-022-00717-w

Dicheva, D., Dichev, C., Agre, G., & Angelova, G. (2015). Gamification in education: A systematic mapping study. *Journal of Educational Technology & Society*, *18*(3), 75–88. https://www.jstor.org/stable/jeductechsoci.18.3.75

Diefenbach, D., López, V., Singh, K., & Maret, P. (2018). Core techniques of question answering systems over knowledge bases: A survey. *Knowledge and Information Systems*, *7*(3), 33–51. DOI: 10.1007/s10115-017-1100-y

Dincer, N., & Bal, S. (2024). A Qualitative Journey on Instructors' Perceptions of Artificial Intelligence in EFL Education. In Fang, P. (Ed.), *AI in Language Learning, Teaching and Assessment* (pp. 78–100). IGI Global., DOI: 10.4018/979-8-3693-0872-1.ch005

Dooly, M., Thrasher, T., & Sadler, R. (2023). "Whoa! Incredible!": Language learning experiences in virtual reality. *RELC Journal*, *54*(2), 321–339. DOI: 10.1177/00336882231167610

Dreimane, S. (2021). Gamification before its definitions – An overview of its historical development. *INTED2021 Proceedings*, 7187–7193. DOI: 10.21125/inted.2021.1434

Ebadi, S., & Azizimajd, H. (2024). Investigating the effects of speaking tasks in clubhouse on EFL learners' speaking and foreign language speaking anxiety. *Computer Assisted Language Learning*, •••, 1–33. https://doi-org.libproxy.library.unt.edu/10.1080/09588221.2024.2371381. DOI: 10.1080/09588221.2024.2371381

Edmett, A., Ichaporia, N., Crompron, N., & Crichton, R. (2023). *Artificial intelligence and English language teaching: Preparing for the future*. British Council.

Education, F. E. (2022, May 24). 85% Indians consider gamified apps as better language learning tool: Duolingo survey. Financial Express. https://www.financialexpress.com/jobs-career/education-85-indians-consider-gamified-apps-as-better-language-learning-tool-reveals-duolingo-survey-2536383/

Ekellem, E. (2024). Enhancing multicultural and multilingual education through problem-based teaching with conversational AI: A ChatGPT perspective. *TechRxiv*. DOI: 10.36227/techrxiv.170593903.35081891/v1

Ellis, R. (2021). A short history of SLA: Where have we come from and where are we going? *Language Teaching*, *54*(2), 190–205. DOI: 10.1017/S0261444820000038

Erekhinskaya, T., Tatu, M., Balakrishna, M., Patel, S., Strebkov, D., & Moldovan, D. (2020). Ten ways of leveraging ontologies for rapid natural language processing customization for multiple use cases in disjoint domains. *Open Journal of Semantic Web*, *7*, 33–51.

Essel, H. B., Vlachopoulos, D., Tachie-Menson, A., Johnson, E. E., & Baah, P. K. (2022). The impact of a virtual teaching assistant (chatbot) on students' learning in Ghanaian higher education. *International Journal of Educational Technology in Higher Education*, *19*(1), 57. DOI: 10.1186/s41239-022-00362-6

European Commission. (2018, April 25). *Artificial intelligence for Europe*. COM (2018) 237 final. https://eur-lex.europa.eu/legal-content/EN/TXT/?uri=COM%3A2018%3A237%3AFIN

Fernández, S., Gómez-Pérez, J. M., & Juristo, N. (2020). Ontologies in educational NLP applications: A systematic review. *Computers & Education, 143*, 103682.

Fernando, P. A., & Premadasa, H. K. Salinda. (2024). A systematic literature review. Educational Technology & Society, 27(2), 114–132. JSTOR. https://doi.org/DOI: 10.2307/48766166

Francisco, J., Flores, F., Del Este, U., & Rico, P. (2015). Using Gamification to Enhance Second Language Learning. https://files.eric.ed.gov/fulltext/EJ1065005.pdf

Fransson, G., Holmberg, J., & Westelius, C. (2020). The challenges of using head mounted virtual reality in K-12 schools from a teacher perspective. *Education and Information Technologies, 25*(4), 3383–3404. DOI: 10.1007/s10639-020-10119-1

Fryer, L. K., Ainley, M., Thompson, A., Gibson, A., & Sherlock, Z. (2017). Stimulating and sustaining interest in a language course: An experimental comparison of chatbot and human task partners. *Computers in Human Behavior, 75*, 461–468. DOI: 10.1016/j.chb.2017.05.045

Gelman, R. (2002). Cognitive development. In Kail, R. V. (Ed.), *Major reference works*. Wiley. DOI: 10.1002/0471214426.pas0212

Gentile, M., Ottaviano, S., Perna, S., & Allegra, M. (2023). Do we still need teachers? navigating the paradigm shift of the teacher's role in the AI era. *Frontiers in Education, 8*, 1161777. Advance online publication. DOI: 10.3389/feduc.2023.1161777

Godwin-Jones, R. (2022). Partnering with AI: Intelligent writing assistance and instructed language learning. *Language Learning & Technology, 26*(2), 5–24. 10125/73474

Golinkoff, R. M., & Hirsh-Pasek, K. (1999). *How babies talk: The magic and mystery of language in the first three years of life*. Dutton.

Gorozhanov, A. I., & Guseynova, I. A. (2020). Corpus analysis of the grammatical categories' constituents in fiction texts considering the linguo-regional component, Siberian Federal University. Humanities & Social Sciences, 13 (12).

Grant, P., & Basye, D. (2014). *Personalized learning: a guide for engaging students with technology*. International Society for Technology in Education.

Gruber, A., & Kaplan-Rakowski, R. (2020). Use experience of public speaking practice in virtual reality. In Zheng, R. (Ed.), *Cognitive and affective perspectives on immersive technology in education* (pp. 235–249). IGI Global., DOI: 10.4018/978-1-7998-3250-8.ch012

Grundmann, R. (2022). Using large text news archives for the analysis of climate change discourse: Some methodological observations. *Journal of Risk Research, 25*(3), 395–406. DOI: 10.1080/13669877.2021.1894471

Guillén-Yparrea, N., & Hernández-Rodríguez, F. (2024). Unveiling generative AI in higher education: Insights from engineering students and professors, *2024 IEEE Global Engineering Education Conference (EDUCON)*, Kos Island, Greece, pp. 1-5, DOI: 10.1109/EDUCON60312.2024.10578876

Hadley, G., & Charles, M. (2017). Enhancing extensive reading with data-driven learning. *Language Learning & Technology, 21*(3), 131–152.

Hall, C., & Bierman, K. (2015). Technology-assisted interventions for parents of young children: Emerging practices, current research, and future directions. *Early Childhood Research Quarterly, 33*, 21–32. DOI: 10.1016/j.ecresq.2015.05.003 PMID: 27773964

Hamari, J., Koivisto, J., & Sarsa, H. (2014). Does gamification work?—A literature review of empirical studies on gamification. *Proceedings of the 47th Hawaii International Conference on System Sciences*, 3025–3034. https://doi.org/DOI: 10.1109/HICSS.2014.377

Hammerschmidt-Snidarich, S. M., Edwards, L. M., Christ, T. J., & Thayer, A. J. (2019). Leveraging technology: A multi-component personalized system of instruction to teach sight words. *Journal of School Psychology, 72*, 150–171. DOI: 10.1016/j.jsp.2018.12.005 PMID: 30819460

Hanson, K., & Shelton, B. E. (2008). Design and development of virtual reality: Analysis of challenges faced by educators. *Journal of Educational Technology & Society*, *11*(1), 118–131. https://www.jstor.org/stable/jeductechsoci.11.1.118

Hartono, W., Nurfitri, N., Ridwan, R., Kase, E., Lake, F., & Zebua, Y. R. (2023). Artificial intelligence (AI) solutions in English language teaching: Teachers-students perceptions and experiences. *Journal on Education, 6*(1), 1452 -1461. https://jonedu.org/index.php/joe/article/view/3101

Healey, B. (2019). How children experience creative writing in the classroom. *Australian Journal of Language and Literacy*, *42*(3), 184–194. DOI: 10.1007/BF03652037

Heilman, M., Collins-Thompson, K., Callan, J., Eskenazi, M., Juffs, A., & Wilson, L. (2010). Personalization of reading passages improves vocabulary acquisition. *International Journal of Artificial Intelligence in Education*, *20*(1), 73–98. DOI: 10.3233/JAI-2010-0003

Hendrix, P., & Sun, C. C. (2020). A word or two about nonwords: Frequency, semantic neighborhood density, and orthography-to-semantics consistency effects for nonwords in the lexical decision task. *Journal of Experimental Psychology. Learning, Memory, and Cognition*, *47*(1), 157–183. DOI: 10.1037/xlm0000819 PMID: 31999159

Hieu, H. H., & Thao, L. T. (2024). Exploring the impact of AI in language education: Vietnamese EFL teachers' views on using chatgpt for fairy tale retelling tasks. *International Journal of Learning. Teaching and Educational Research*, *23*(3), 486–503. DOI: 10.26803/ijlter.23.3.24

Hinojo-Lucena, F.-J., Aznar-Díaz, I., Cáceres-Reche, M.-P., & Romero-Rodríguez, J.-M. (2019). Artificial intelligence in higher education: A Bibliometric study on its impact in the scientific literature. *Education Sciences*, *9*(1), 51. DOI: 10.3390/educsci9010051

Holmes, W., Bialik, M., & Fadel, C. (2019). *Artificial intelligence in education: Promises and implications for teaching and learning*. Center for Curriculum Redesign.

Holmes, W., Persson, J., Chounta, I., Wasson, B., & Dimitrova, V. (2022). *Artificial Intelligence and Education: A critical view through the lens of human rights, democracy and the rule of law*. Council of Europe.

Hooshyar, D., Yousefi, M., Wang, M., & Lim, H. (2018). A data-driven procedural-content-generation approach for educational games. *Journal of Computer Assisted Learning*, *34*(6), 731–739. DOI: 10.1111/jcal.12280

Hsieh, T.-C., Wang, T.-I., Su, C.-Y., & Lee, M.-C. (2024). A fuzzy logic-based personalized learning system for supporting adaptive English learning. *Journal of Educational Technology & Society*, *15*(1), 273–288. https://www.jstor.org/stable/10.2307/jeductechsoci.15.1.273

Hsu, C.-K., Hwang, G.-J., & Chang, C.-K. (2013). A personalized recommendation-based mobile learning approach to improving the reading performance of EFL students. *Computers & Education*, *63*, 327–336. DOI: 10.1016/j.compedu.2012.12.004

Huang, H. M., Rauch, U., & Liaw, S. S. (2010). Investigating learners' attitudes toward virtual reality learning environments: Based on a constructivist approach. *Computers & Education*, *55*(3), 1171–1182. DOI: 10.1016/j.compedu.2010.05.014

Huang, J. T., Li, J., Yu, D., Deng, L., & Gong, Y. (2020). Recent advances in deep learning for speech research at Microsoft. In *2013 IEEE International Conference on Acoustics, Speech and Signal Processing* (pp. 8604-8608). IEEE.

Huang, J., Saleh, S., & Liu, Y. (2021). A review on artificial intelligence in education. *Academic Journal of Interdisciplinary Studies*, *10*(3), 1–15. DOI: 10.36941/ajis-2021-0077

Huang, S.-L., & Shiu, J.-H. (2012). A user-centric adaptive learning system for e-learning 2.0. *Journal of Educational Technology & Society*, *15*(3), 214–225. https://www.jstor.org/stable/jeductechsoci.15.3.214

Huang, X., Zou, D., Cheng, G., Chen, X., & Xie, H. (2023). Trends, research issues and applications of artificial intelligence in language education. *Journal of Educational Technology & Society*, *26*(1), 112–131. DOI: 10.30191/ETS.202301_26(1).0009

Hulstijn, J. H., & Laufer, B. (2001). Some empirical evidence for the involvement load hypothesis in vocabulary acquisition. *Language Learning*, *51*(3), 539–558. DOI: 10.1111/0023-8333.00164

Hussain, R., Sabir, A., Lee, D., Zaidi, S. F. A., Pedro, A., Abbas, M. S., & Park, C. (2024). Conversational AI-based VR system to improve construction safety training of migrant workers. *Automation in Construction*, *160*, 105315. Advance online publication. DOI: 10.1016/j.autcon.2024.105315

Hwang, G. J., Xie, H., Wah, B. W., & Gašević, D. (2020). Vision, challenges, roles and research issues of Artificial Intelligence in Education. *Computers and Education: Artificial Intelligence*, *1*, 100001. DOI: 10.1016/j.caeai.2020.100001

Irfan, R., King, C. K., Grages, D., Ewen, S., Khan, S. U., Madani, S. A., Kolodziej, J., Wang, L., Chen, D., Rayes, A., Tziritas, N., Xu, C.-Z., Zomaya, A. Y., Alzahrani, A. S., & Li, H. (2015). A survey on text mining in social networks. *The Knowledge Engineering Review*, *30*(2), 157–170. DOI: 10.1017/S0269888914000277

Jiang, R. (2022). How does artificial intelligence empower EFL teaching and learning nowadays? a review of artificial intelligence in the EFL context. *Frontiers in Psychology*, *13*, 1049401. Advance online publication. DOI: 10.3389/fpsyg.2022.1049401 PMID: 36467167

Jones, R., Zhang, X., & Jacobsen, K. (2021). Challenges in ontology development and integration for educational applications. *Journal of the Association for Information Science and Technology*, *72*(10), 1245–1260.

Jordan, T. (2009). The ecology of games: Connecting youth, games and learning. *Information Communication and Society*, *12*(2), 291–293. DOI: 10.1080/13691180802552890

Jung, J., & Graf, S. (2008). An approach for personalized web-based vocabulary learning through word association games. *Proceedings of 2008 International Symposium on Applications and the Internet,* Finland, 325–328. IEEE. http://dx.doi.org/DOI: 10.1109/SAINT.2008.63

Jurafsky, D., & Martin, J. H. (2009). *Speech and language processing: An introduction to natural language processing, computational linguistics, and speech recognition.* Pearson Prentice Hall.

Kamrood, A. M., Davoudi, M., Ghaniabadi, S., & Amirian, S. M. R. (2021). Diagnosing L2 learners' development through online computerized dynamic assessment. *Computer Assisted Language Learning, 34*(7), 868–897. DOI: 10.1080/09588221.2019.1645181

Kannan, J., & Munday, P. (2018). New trends in second language learning and teaching through the lens of ICT, networked learning, and artificial intelligence. *Círculo de Lingüística Aplicada a la Comunicación, 76,* 13–30. DOI: 10.5209/CLAC.62495

Kapella, O., Schmidt, E., & Vogl, S. (2022). Integration of digital technologies in families with children aged 5-10 years: A synthesis report of four European country case studies. DigiGen Working Paper Series, No. 8. https://doi.org/DOI: 10.5281/zenodo.6411126

Kaplan-Rakowski, R. (2024). High-immersion virtual reality for pragmatics development. In Chapelle, C. A., Taguchi, N., & Kadar, D. (Eds.), *The encyclopedia of applied linguistics* (2nd ed.). Wiley-Blackwell.

Kaplan-Rakowski, R., Cockerham, D., & Ferdig, R. E. (2023). The impact of sound andimmersive experience on learners using high-immersion virtual reality and table: A mixed-methods study. *British Journal of Educational Technology, 55*(4), 1560–1582. DOI: 10.1111/bjet.13417

Kaplan-Rakowski, R., Dhimolea, T. K., & Khukalenko, I. S. (2023). Language teachers' beliefs about using high–immersion virtual reality. *Education and Information Technologies, 28*(10), 12505–12525. DOI: 10.1007/s10639-023-11686-9

Kaplan-Rakowski, R., Grotewold, K., Hartwick, P., & Papin, K. (2023). Generative AI and teachers' perspectives on its implementation in education. *Journal of Interactive Learning Research, 34*(2), 313–338. https://www.learntechlib.org/p/222363/. DOI: 10.70725/815246mfssgp

Kaplan-Rakowski, R., & Gruber, A. (2019). Low-immersion versus high-immersion virtual reality: Definitions, classification, and examples with a foreign language focus. *Proceedings of the Innovation in Language Learning International Conference 2019,* Florence, 552–555.

Kaplan-Rakowski, R., & Gruber, A. (2023). An experimental study on reading in high-immersion virtual reality. *British Journal of Educational Technology, 55*(2), 541–559. DOI: 10.1111/bjet.13392

Kaplan-Rakowski, R., Papin, K., & Hartwick, P. (2023). Language teachers' perceptions and use of extended reality. *CALICO Journal, 40*(1), 1–23. DOI: 10.1558/cj.22759

Kapp, K. M., Blair, L., & Mesch, R. (2013). *The gamification of learning and instruction fieldbook: Theory into practice.* John Wiley & Sons.

Kasneci, E., Sessler, K., Küchemann, S., Bannert, M., Dementieva, D., Fischer, F., Gasser, U., Groh, G., Günnemann, S., Hüllermeier, E., Krusche, S., Kutyniok, G., Michaeli, T., Nerdel, C., Pfeffer, J., Poquet, O., Sailer, M., Schmidt, A., Seidel, T., & Kasneci, G. (2023). ChatGPT for good? On opportunities and challenges of large language models for education. *Learning and Individual Differences, 103*, 102274. DOI: 10.1016/j.lindif.2023.102274

Kayalı, B., & Balat, Ş. (2024). Assessment, evaluation, and feedback in online education with artificial intelligence-supported tools. In Bansal, R., Chakir, A., Hafaz Ngah, A., Rabby, F., & Jain, A. (Eds.), *AI algorithms and ChatGPT for student engagement in online learning* (pp. 124–135). IGI Global., DOI: 10.4018/979-8-3693-4268-8.ch008

Kettler, T., Lamb, K., & Dekelaita-Mullet, D. (2019). *Developing creativity in the classroom: learning and innovation for 21st-century schools.* Routledge., DOI: 10.4324/9781003234104

Khaldi, A., Bouzidi, R., & Nader, F. (2023). Gamification of e-learning in Higher Education: A Systematic Literature Review. *Smart Learning Environments, 10*(1), 10. Advance online publication. DOI: 10.1186/s40561-023-00227-z PMID: 40478066

Kherazi, A., & Bourray, M. (2024). Gamification and m-learning: An innovative approach to sustainable language learning. E3S Web of Conferences, 477, 00066. .DOI: 10.1051/e3sconf/202447700066

Khukalenko, I. S., Kaplan-Rakowski, R., An, Y., & Iushina, V. D. (2022). Teachers' perceptions of using virtual reality technology in classrooms: A large-scale survey. *Education and Information Technologies, 27*(8), 11591–11613. DOI: 10.1007/s10639-022-11061-0 PMID: 35603316

Kim, S. K., & Webb, S. (2022). The effects of spaced practice on second language learning: A meta-analysis. *Language Learning, 72*(1), 269–319. DOI: 10.1111/lang.12479

Kinginger, C. (2002). Defining the zone of proximal development in US foreign language education. *Applied Linguistics, 23*(2), 240–261. DOI: 10.1093/applin/23.2.240

Klimova, B. F. (2014). Approaches to the teaching of writing skills. *Procedia: Social and Behavioral Sciences, 112*, 147–151. DOI: 10.1016/j.sbspro.2014.01.1149

Kohnke, L., Zhang, R., & Zou, D. (2019). Using mobile vocabulary learning apps as aids to knowledge retention: Business vocabulary acquisition. *Journal of Asia TEFL, 16*(2), 448–767. DOI: 10.18823/asiatefl.2019.16.2.16.683

Kolb, D. A. (1984). *Experiential learning: Experience as the source of learning and development*. Prentice-Hall, Inc.

Koraishi, O. (2023). Teaching English in the Age of AI: Embracing ChatGPT to Optimize EFL Materials and Assessment. [LET Journal]. *Language Education & Technology, 3*(1), 55–72.

Kramsch, C. (2014). Language and culture. *AILA Review*, *27*(1), 30–55. DOI: 10.1075/aila.27.02kra

Krashen, S. D. (1982). Principles and practice in second language acquisition. *Modern Language Journal*, *67*(2). https://www.sdkrashen.com/content/books/principles_and_practice.pdf

Krashen, S. D., & Terrell, T. D. (1983). *The natural approach: Language acquisition in the classroom*. Pergamon Press.

Krasselt, J., Dreesen, P., Stücheli-Herlach, P., Lemmenmeier, D., Cho, S., Rothenhäusler, K., & Fluor, M. (2023). Swiss-AL: platform for language data in applied sciences: on challenges in the field of language open research data. In 1st Conference on Research Data Infrastructure (CoRDI)-Connecting Communities, Karlsruhe, Germany, 12-14 September 2023 (Vol. 1). TIB Open Publishing. DOI: 10.52825/cordi.v1i.249

Kudugunta, S., Caswell, I., Zhang, B., Garcia, X., Xin, D., Kusupati, A., & Firat, O. (2024). Madlad-400: A multilingual and document-level large audited dataset. *Advances in Neural Information Processing Systems*, •••, 36.

Kumar, A., & Singh, M. (2020). Adaptive learning environments with ontologies: Towards a better understanding of learning styles. *Learning and Individual Differences*, *78*, 101832.

Lai, C., & Li, G. (2011). Technology and task-based language teaching: A critical review. *CALICO Journal*, *28*(2), 498–521. DOI: 10.11139/cj.28.2.498-521

Lampropoulos, G., Ferdig, R. E., & Kaplan-Rakowski, R. (2024). A social media data analysis of general and educational use of ChatGPT: Understanding emotional educators. *SSRN*. http://dx.doi.org/DOI: 10.2139/ssrn.4468181

Landers, R. N., Armstrong, M. B., & Collmus, A. B. (2017). How to Use Game Elements to Enhance Learning: Applications of the Theory of Gamified Learning. *Serious Games and Edutainment Applications*, 457–483. DOI: 10.1007/978-3-319-51645-5_21

Landers, R. N. (2014). Developing a Theory of Gamified Learning. *Simulation & Gaming, 45*(6), 752–768. DOI: 10.1177/1046878114563660

Landers, R. N., & Landers, A. K. (2014). An Empirical Test of the Theory of Gamified Learning. *Simulation & Gaming, 45*(6), 769–785. DOI: 10.1177/1046878114563662

Lave, J., & Wenger, E. (1991). *Situated learning: Legitimate peripheral participation*. Cambridge University Press. DOI: 10.1017/CBO9780511815355

Lee, A. (2019). Using virtual reality to test academic listening proficiency. *Korean Journal of English Language and Linguistics, 19*(4), 688–712. DOI: 10.15738/kjell.19.4.201912.688

Lee, D., Huh, Y., Lin, C.-Y., & Reigeluth, C. M. (2018). Technology functions for personalized learning in learner-centered schools. *Educational Technology Research and Development, 66*(5), 1269–1302. DOI: 10.1007/s11423-018-9615-9

Lee, D., Huh, Y., Lin, C.-Y., & Reigeluth, C. M. (2022). Personalized learning practice in U.S. learner-centered schools. *Contemporary Educational Technology, 14*(4), ep385. Advance online publication. DOI: 10.30935/cedtech/12330

Lee, S. M. (2023). The effectiveness of machine translation in foreign language education: A systematic review and meta-analysis. *Computer Assisted Language Learning, 36*(1–2), 103–125. DOI: 10.1080/09588221.2021.1901745

Leng, L., & Shan, G. (2019). Analysis and research on lexical errors in machine translation in Chinese and Korean translation. *International Journal of Frontiers in Engineering Technology, 1*(1), 30–37.

Li, C., Lin, L., Mao, W., Xiong, L., & Lin, Y. (2022). An automated essay scoring model based on stacking method. In 2022 IEEE 2nd International Conference on Software Engineering and Artificial Intelligence (SEAI), 248-252. IEEE. DOI: 10.1109/SEAI55746.2022.9832246

Li, F., Fan, S., & Wang, Y. (2022). Mobile-assisted language learning in Chinese higher education context: A systematic review from the perspective of the situated learning theory. *Education and Information Technologies, 27*(7), 9665–9688. DOI: 10.1007/s10639-022-11025-4

Lillard, P. P. (1972). *Montessori, a modern approach.* Schocken Books.

Lin, C. F., Yeh, Y.-C., Hung, Y. H., & Chang, R. I. (2013). Data mining for providing a personalized learning path in creativity: An application of decision trees. *Computers & Education, 68*, 199–210. DOI: 10.1016/j.compedu.2013.05.009

Linzen, T., & Baroni, M. (2021). Syntactic structure from deep learning. *Annual Review of Linguistics, 7*(1), 195–212. DOI: 10.1146/annurev-linguistics-032020-051035

Liu, D., Santhanam, R., & Webster, J. (2017). Toward Meaningful Engagement: A Framework for Design and Research of Gamified Information Systems. *Management Information Systems Quarterly, 41*(4), 1011–1034. DOI: 10.25300/MISQ/2017/41.4.01

Liu, H., Lai, C., & Xu, W. (2022). Leveraging ontologies for semantic web-enabled educational resources. *Educational Technology Research and Development, 70*(1), 371–390. PMID: 35125846

Liu, S., & Tian, A. (2023). The influence of Montessori education on children's personality development and the way of thinking. *Lecture Notes in Education Psychology and Public Media, 16*(1), 173–180. Advance online publication. DOI: 10.54254/2753-7048/16/20231141

Livingstone, S., Mascheroni, G., Dreier, M., Chaudron, S., & Lagae, K. (2015). *How parents of young children manage digital devices at home: The role of income, education and parental style.* EUKids Online, LSE

Lo, C. K. (2023). What is the impact of ChatGPT on education? A rapid review of the literature. *Education Sciences, 13*(4), 410. DOI: 10.3390/educsci13040410

Long, D., & Magerko, B. (2020). What is AI Literacy? Competencies and Design Considerations. *Proceedings of the 2020 CHI Conference on Human Factors in Computing Systems*. https://doi.org/DOI: 10.1145/3313831.3376727

Long, M. H. (1981). Input, interaction, and second-language acquisition. *Annals of the New York Academy of Sciences, 379*(1), 259–278. DOI: 10.1111/j.1749-6632.1981.tb42014.x

Louly, N.M. (2024). Application of AI tools in education - A conceptual framework. *Recent trends in Management and Commerce* 5(2), 1-7. https://doi.org/DOI: 10.46632/rmc/5/2/1

Luck, M., & Aylett, R. (2000). Applying artificial intelligence to virtual reality: Intelligent virtual environments. *Applied Artificial Intelligence, 14*(1), 3–32. DOI: 10.1080/088395100117142

Lu, X. (2014). *Computational methods for corpus annotation and analysis*. Springer. DOI: 10.1007/978-94-017-8645-4

Mabuan, R. A. (2024). ChatGPT and ELT: Exploring teachers' voices. [IJTE]. *International Journal of Technology in Education, 7*(1), 128–153. DOI: 10.46328/ijte.523

Magomadov, V. S. (2020). The application of artificial intelligence and Big Data analytics in personalized learning. *Journal of Physics: Conference Series, 1691*(1), 012169. Advance online publication. DOI: 10.1088/1742-6596/1691/1/012169

Makransky, G., Terkildsen, T. S., & Mayer, R. E. (2019). Adding immersive virtual reality to a science lab simulation causes more presence but less learning. *Learning and Instruction, 60*, 225–236. DOI: 10.1016/j.learninstruc.2017.12.007

Ma, L. (2021). An immersive context teaching method for college English based on artificial intelligence and machine learning in virtual reality technology. *Mobile Information Systems, 2021*(1), 2637439. Advance online publication. DOI: 10.1155/2021/2637439

Malone, T. W. (1981). Toward a Theory of Intrinsically Motivating Instruction. *Cognitive Science*, *5*(4), 333–369. DOI: 10.1207/s15516709cog0504_2

Marsh, J., Plowman, L., Yamada-Rice, D., Bishop, J., Lahmar, J., & Scott, F. (2018). Play and creativity in young children's use of apps. *British Journal of Educational Technology*, *49*(5), 870–882. DOI: 10.1111/bjet.12622

Medrouk, L., & Pappa, A. (2017). Deep learning model for sentiment analysis in multi-lingual corpus. In Neural Information Processing: 24th International Conference, ICONIP 2017, Guangzhou, China, November 14-18, 2017 [Springer International Publishing.]. *Proceedings*, *24*(Part I), 205–212.

Memrise. (2017). *Memrise - Learn a language. Meet the world.* Memrise. https://www.memrise.com/

Merriam-Webster. (2019). *Definition of GAMIFICATION.* Merriam-Webster.com. https://www.merriam-webster.com/dictionary/gamification

Mikheev, A., & Finch, S. (1997). A workbench for finding structure in texts. In *Fifth Conference on Applied Natural Language Processing*, 372-379. DOI: 10.3115/974557.974611

Minaee, S., Kalchbrenner, N., Cambria, E., Nikzad, N., Chenaghlu, M., & Gao, J. (2021). Deep learning—based text classification: A comprehensive review. *ACM Computing Surveys*, *54*(3), 1–40. DOI: 10.1145/3439726

Ministry of Education and Training Vietnam. (2009). Thông tư c a B Giáo d c và Đào t o s 17/2009 ngày 25 tháng 7 năm 2009: Ban hành chương trình giáo d c m m non (Circular number 17/2009 dated 25th July 2009 on Issuing the Preschool curriculum). Retrieved from https://luatvietnam .vn/giao-duc/thong-tu-17-2009-tt-bgddt-bo-giao-duc-va-dao-tao-44312 -d1.html

Ministry of Education and Training Vietnam. (2020). Thông tư 50/2020/TT-BGDĐT ban hành Chương trình làm quen v i ti ng Anh cho tr em m u giáo (Circular number 50/2020/TT/BGDDT on Issuing the English Familirisation Program). Retrieved from https://thuvienphapluat.vn/van-ban/Giao-duc/Thong-tu-50-2020-TT-BGDDT-Chuong-trinh-lam-quen-voi-tieng-Anh-danh-cho-tre-em-mau-giao-468715.aspx

Ministry of Education and Training Vietnam. (2022). *S li u th ng kê giáo d c m m non năm h c 2021 - 2022.* [Statistics on preschool education for the 2021-2022 academic year]. https://moet.gov.vn/thong-ke/Pages/thong-ke-giao-duc-mam-non.aspx?ItemID=8822

Mirzaei, M. S., Meshgi, K., & Nishida, T. (2020). A situation creation system to enable experiential learning in virtual worlds for developing cross-cultural competencies. In K.-M. Frederiksen, S. Larsen, L. Bradley, & S. Thouësny (Eds.), *CALL for widening participation: Short papers from EUROCALL 2020* (1st ed., pp. 233–239). Research-publishing.net. https://doi.org/DOI: 10.14705/rpnet.2020.48.1194

Mirzaei, M. S., Zhang, Q., Van der Struijk, S., & Nishida, T., (2018). Language learning through conversation envisioning in virtual reality: A sociocultural approach. *Future-proof CALL: Language learning as exploration and encounters-short papers from EUROCALL*, 207–213. http://dx.doi.org/DOI: 10.14705/rpnet.2018.26.838

Mohmed, H. E. F., & Elballat, D. B. (2024). The attitudes of faculty staff members and their assistants towards students' use of AI tools in scientific research: The attitudes of faculty staff members and their assistants towards students' use of AI tools in scientific research. [IJHS]. *International Journal of Humanities and Social Science*, *1*(1), 49–61. DOI: 10.69792/IJHS.24.1.5

Moisa, T., Ontanu, D., & Dediu, A. H. (2001). Speech synthesis using neural networks trained by an evolutionary algorithm. In Computational Science-ICCS 2001: International Conference San Francisco, CA, USA, May 28—30, 2001 Proceedings, Part II 1, 419-428. Springer Berlin Heidelberg. DOI: 10.1007/3-540-45718-6_46

Mondly. (2017). *Learn Languages Online for Free with Mondly - Get Fluent Now!* Mondly.com; Mondly Languages. https://www.mondly.com/

Montessori, M. (1967). *The discovery of the child.* Ballantine. (Work originally published 1948.)

Moorhouse, B. L., Yeo, M. A., & Wan, Y. (2023). Generative AI tools and assessment: Guidelines of the world's top-ranking universities. *Computers and Education Open*, *5*, 100151. DOI: 10.1016/j.caeo.2023.100151

Moybeka, A. (2023). Artificial intelligence and english classroom: the implications of ai toward efl students' motivation. *Edumaspul - Jurnal Pendidikan,* 7(2), 2444-2454. https://doi.org/.DOI: 10.33487/edumaspul.v7i2.6669

Mukhallafi, T. (2020). Using artificial intelligence for developing English language teaching/learning: An analytical study from university students' perspective. *International Journal of English Linguistics*, *10*(6), 40. DOI: 10.5539/ijel.v10n6p40

National Scientific Council on the Developing Child. (2007). The science of early childhood development. Retrieved from http://www.developingchild.net

Ng, D. T. K., Leung, J. K. L., Chu, K. W. S., & Qiao, M. S. (2021). AI literacy: Definition, teaching, evaluation and ethical issues. *Proceedings of the Association for Information Science and Technology*, *58*(1), 504–509. DOI: 10.1002/pra2.487

Ng, D. T. K., Leung, J. K. L., Su, J., Ng, R. C. W., & Chu, S. K. W. (2023). Teachers' AI digital competencies and twenty-first century skills in the post-pandemic world. *Educational Technology Research and Development*, *71*(1), 137–161. DOI: 10.1007/s11423-023-10203-6 PMID: 36844361

Nikken, P., & Jansz, J. (2014). Developing scales to measure parental mediation of young children's internet use. *Learning, Media and Technology*, *39*(2), 250–266. DOI: 10.1080/17439884.2013.782038

Nurmukhamedov, U., & Webb, S. (2019). Coverage and profiling: Lexical coverage in L2 reading and speed of lexical access during reading. *Applied Linguistics*, *40*(5), 841–865.

Nye, B. D., Graesser, A. C., & Hu, X. (2014). AutoTutor and family: A review of 17 years of natural language tutoring. *International Journal of Artificial Intelligence in Education*, *24*(4), 427–469. DOI: 10.1007/s40593-014-0029-5

Obari, H., Lambacher, S., & Kikuchi, H. (2020). The impact of using AI and VR with blended learning on English as a foreign language teaching. In K.-M. Frederiksen, S. Larsen, L. Bradley & S. Thouësny (Eds.), *CALL for widening participation: short papers from EUROCALL 2020 (pp. 253-258).* Research-publishing.net. https://doi.org/DOI: 10.14705/rpnet.2020.48.1197

OECD. (2019). *Providing quality early childhood education and care: Results from the Starting Strong Survey 2018. TALIS*. OECD Publishing., DOI: 10.1787/301005d1-

Open, A. I. (2024). ChatGPT (June 20 version) [Large language model]. https://chat.openai.com/chat

Pack, A., Barrett, A., Liang, H.-N., & Monteiro, D. V. (2020). University EAP students' perceptions of using a prototype virtual reality learning environment to learn writing structure. *International Journal of Computer-Assisted Language Learning and Teaching*, *10*(1), 27–46. DOI: 10.4018/IJCALLT.2020010103

Pahi, K., Hawlader, S., Hicks, E., Zaman, A., & Phan, V. (2024). Enhancing active learning through collaboration between human teachers and generative AI. *Computers and Education Open*, *6*, 100183. Advance online publication. DOI: 10.1016/j.caeo.2024.100183

Panagiotidis, P. (2021). Augmented and Mixed Reality in Language Learning. *European Journal of Education*, *4*(2), 28. DOI: 10.26417/501ibq23c

Park, M. (2018). Innovative assessment of aviation English in a virtual world: Windows into cognitive and metacognitive strategies. *ReCALL, 30*(2), 196–213. DOI: 10.1017/S0958344017000362

Parmaxi, A. (2020). Virtual Reality in Language Learning: A Systematic Review and Implications for Research and Practice. *Interactive Learning Environments, 31*(1), 172–184. DOI: 10.1080/10494820.2020.1765392

Pavlik, J. V. (2023). Collaborating with ChatGPT: Considering the implications of generative artificial intelligence for journalism and media education. *Journalism & Mass Communication Educator, 78*(1), 84–93. DOI: 10.1177/10776958221149577

Pedersen, I. (2023). The rise of generative AI and enculturating AI writing in postsecondary education. *Frontiers in Artificial Intelligence, 6*, 1259407. Advance online publication. DOI: 10.3389/frai.2023.1259407 PMID: 37635912

Peng, H., Ma, S., & Spector, J. M. (2019). Personalized adaptive learning: An emerging pedagogical approach enabled by a smart learning environment. *Smart Learning Environments, 6*(9), 9. Advance online publication. DOI: 10.1186/s40561-019-0089-y

Pérez-Paredes, P., Guillamón, C. O., & Jiménez, P. A. (2018). Language teachers' perceptions on the use of OER language processing technologies in MALL. *Computer Assisted Language Learning, 31*(5–6), 522–545. DOI: 10.1080/09588221.2017.1418754

Perkins, M. (2023). Academic integrity considerations of AI Large Language Models in the post- pandemic era: ChatGPT and beyond. *Journal of University Teaching & Learning Practice, 20*(2). Advance online publication. DOI: 10.53761/1.20.02.07

Petersen, G. B., Petkakis, G., & Makransky, G. (2022). A study of how immersion and interactivity drive VR learning. *Computers & Education, 179*, 104429. Advance online publication. DOI: 10.1016/j.compedu.2021.104429

Pham, S. T., Le, T. A., Nguyen, T. A., Dinh, T. H., & Ho, M. T. (2006). *60 năm Giáo d c M m non Vi t Nam* [60 years of Vietnamese Preschool Education]. Hanoi, Vietnam: Nhà xu t b n Giáo d c (Education Publisher).

Phan, H. T. T. (2012). Current curriculum and pedagogy reform in Vietnamese Early Childhood Education: A socio-historic interpretation. In Chan, P. W. K. (Ed.), *Asia Pacific education, diversity, challenges and changes*. Monash University Publishing.

Piaget, J. (1952). *The origins of intelligence in children.* International Universities Press. DOI: 10.1037/11494-000

Piaget, J. (1970). *The psychology of the child.* Basic Books.

Pikhart, M. (2020). Intelligent information processing for language education: The use of Artificial Intelligence in language learning apps. *Procedia Computer Science*, *176*, 1412–1419. DOI: 10.1016/j.procs.2020.09.151 PMID: 33042299

Plagiarize. 2024. In Merriam-Webster.com. Retrieved September 24, 2024, from https://www.merriam-webster.com/dictionary/plagiarize

Plowman, L., & McPake, J. (2013). Seven myths about young children and technology. *Childhood Education*, *89*(1), 27–33. DOI: 10.1080/00094056.2013.757490

Pokrivcakova, S. (2019). Preparing teachers for the application of AI-powered technologies in foreign language education. *Journal of Language and Cultural Education*, *7*(3), 135–153. DOI: 10.2478/jolace-2019-0025

Popenici, S., & Kerr, S. (2017). Exploring the impact of artificial intelligence on teaching and learning in higher education. *Research and Practice in Technology Enhanced Learning*, *12*(1), 22. Advance online publication. DOI: 10.1186/s41039-017-0062-8 PMID: 30595727

Poria, S., Cambria, E., Bajpai, R., & Hussain, A. (2017). A review of affective computing: From unimodal analysis to multimodal fusion. *Information Fusion*, *37*, 98–125. DOI: 10.1016/j.inffus.2017.02.003

Porter, B., & Grippa, F. (2020). A platform for AI-enabled real-time feedback to promote digital collaboration. *Sustainability (Basel)*, *12*(24), 10243. Advance online publication. DOI: 10.3390/su122410243

Porwol, L., Pereira, A. G., & Dumas, C. (2023). Transforming e-participation: VR-dialogue – building and evaluating an AI-supported framework for next-gen VR-enabled e-participation research. *Transforming Government*, *17*(2), 233–250. DOI: 10.1108/TG-12-2021-0205

Prior, D. D., Mazanov, J., Meacheam, D., Heaslip, G., & Hanson, J. (2016). Attitude, digital literacy and self- efficacy: Flown effects for online learning behavior. *The Internet and Higher Education*, *29*, 91–97. DOI: 10.1016/j.iheduc.2016.01.001

Rachels, J. R., & Rockinson-Szapkiw, A. J. (2018). The effects of a mobile gamification app on elementary students' Spanish achievement and self-efficacy. *Computer Assisted Language Learning*, *31*(1–2), 72–89. DOI: 10.1080/09588221.2017.1382536

Ramineni, C., & Williamson, D. M. (2013). Automated essay scoring: Psychometric guidelines and practices. *Assessing Writing*, *18*(1), 25–39. DOI: 10.1016/j.asw.2012.10.004

Ratner, A., & Ré, C. (2018). Knowledge base construction in the machine-learning era: three critical design points: joint-learning, weak supervision, and new representations. *ACM Queue; Tomorrow's Computing Today*, *16*(3), 79–90. DOI: 10.1145/3236386.3243045

Regan, P. M., & Jesse, J. (2019). Ethical challenges of edtech, big data and personalized learning: Twenty-first century student sorting and tracking. *Ethics and Information Technology*, *21*(3), 167–179. DOI: 10.1007/s10676-018-9492-2

Rithy, I. J., Shakil, H. H., Mondal, N., Sultana, F., & Shah, F. M. (2022). XTest: A Parallel Multilingual Corpus with Test Cases for Code Translation and Its Evaluation. In 2022 25th International Conference on Computer and Information Technology (ICCIT), 623-628. IEEE. DOI: 10.1109/ICCIT57492.2022.10055851

Roll, I., & Wylie, R. (2016). Evolution and revolution in artificial intelligence in education. *International Journal of Artificial Intelligence in Education, 26*(2), 582–599. DOI: 10.1007/s40593-016-0110-3

Şad, S. N., Konca, A. S., Özer, N., & Acar, F. (2016). Parental e-nvolvement: A phenomenological research on electronic parental involvement. International. *Journal of Pedagogies and Learning*, *11*(2), 163–186.

Saeli, H., Rahmati, P., & Koltovskaia, S. (2023). Learner engagement with written corrective feedback: The case of automated writing evaluation. *Journal of Response to Writing*, *9*(2), 1. https://scholarsarchive.byu.edu/journalrw/vol9/iss2/1

Safatian, F. (2023). Exploring the Effectiveness of Gamification in Mobile Language Learning Applications: A Mixed-Methods Study. *Education and Linguistics Research, 9*(1), 29–42. Researchgate. https://doi.org/DOI: 10.5296/elr.v9i2.21425

Samuel, N., Caporusso, N. & Ferman, D. (2022). A Peer-to-Peer Corpus for Conversational Agents for Long-Distance Relationships. Intelligent Human Systems Integration (IHSI 2022): Integrating People and Intelligent Systems, 22(22).

Sanchez, E. (2017). Competition and collaboration for game-based learning: A case study. In *Instructional Techniques to Facilitate Learning and Motivation of Serious Games* (pp. 161–184). Springer Nature. DOI: 10.1007/978-3-319-39298-1_9

Sarker, M. N. I., Wu, M., Cao, Q., Alam, G. M. M., & Li, D. (2019). Leveraging digital technology for better learning and education: A systematic literature review. *International Journal of Information and Education Technology (IJIET)*, *9*(7), 453–461. DOI: 10.18178/ijiet.2019.9.7.1246

Schmid, R., Pauli, C., Stebler, R., Reusser, K., & Petko, D. (2022). Implementation of technology-supported personalized learning—Its impact on instructional quality. *The Journal of Educational Research, 115*(3), 187–198. DOI: 10.1080/00220671.2022.2089086

Schmidt, T., & Strasser, T. (2022). Artificial intelligence in foreign language learning and teaching: A call for intelligent practice. *Anglistik, 33*(1), 165–184. DOI: 10.33675/ANGL/2022/1/14

Schwenk, H., & Gauvain, J. L. (2005). Training neural network language models on very large corpora. In *Proceedings of human language technology conference and conference on empirical methods in natural language processing*, 201-208. DOI: 10.3115/1220575.1220601

Sharadgah, T., & Sa'di, R. (2022). A systematic review of research on the use of artificial intelligence in English language teaching and learning (2015-2021): What are the current effects? *Journal of Information Technology Education, 21*, 337–377. DOI: 10.28945/4999

Sharma, R. C., & Bozkurt, A. (2024). Transforming Education With Generative AI: Prompt Engineering and Synthetic Content Creation. In www.igi-global.com. IGI Global. https://www.igi-global.com/book/transforming-education-generative/327460

Sharma, P., & Dash, B. (2023). AI and VR enabled modern LMS for students with special needs. *Journal of Foreign Language Education and Technology, 8*(1), 1–15.

Sharrab, Y., Almutiri, N. T., Tarawneh, M., Alzyoud, F., Al-Ghuwairi, A.-R. F., & Al-Fraihat, D. (2023). Toward smart and immersive classroom based on AI, VR, and 6G. *International Journal of Emerging Technologies in Learning, 18*(2), 4–16. DOI: 10.3991/ijet.v18i02.35997

Shemshack, A., & Spector, J. M. (2020). A systematic literature review of personalized learning terms. *Smart Learning Environments, 7*(1), 33. Advance online publication. DOI: 10.1186/s40561-020-00140-9

Shih, Y.-C., & Yang, M.-T. (2008). A collaborative virtual environment for situated language learning using VEC3D. *Journal of Educational Technology & Society, 11*(1), 56–68. https://www.jstor.org/stable/10.2307/jeductechsoci.11.1.56

Shute, V. J. (2008). Focus on formative feedback. *Review of Educational Research, 78*(1), 153–189. DOI: 10.3102/0034654307313795

Slavuj, V., Meštrović, A., & Kovačić, B. (2017). Adaptivity in educational systems for language learning: A review. *Computer Assisted Language Learning, 30*(1–2), 64–90. DOI: 10.1080/09588221.2016.1242502

Smiderle, R., Rigo, S. J., Marques, L. B., Peçanha de Miranda Coelho, J. A., & Jaques, P. A. (2020). The impact of gamification on students' learning, engagement and behavior based on their personality traits. *Smart Learning Environments, 7*(1). https://slejournal.springeropen.com/articles/10.1186/s40561-019-0098-x

Smith, L., & Patel, V. (2019). Enhancing education through ontologies and NLP. *Journal of Educational Technology & Society, 22*(3), 28–40.

Smith, N., Hoffmann, S., & Rayson, P. (2007). Corpus tools and methods today and tomorrow: Incorporating user-defined annotations. In *Corpus Linguistics Conference (CL2007).*

Son, J., Ružić, N. K., & Philpott, A. (2023). Artificial intelligence technologies and applications for language learning and teaching. *Journal of China Computer-Assisted Language Learning*. Advance online publication. DOI: 10.1515/jccall-2023-0015

Sougandh, T. G., Reddy, N. S., & Belwal, M. (2023). Automated Resume Parsing: A Natural Language Processing Approach. In 2023 7th International Conference on Computation System and Information Technology for Sustainable Solutions (CSITSS), 1-6. IEEE. DOI: 10.1109/CSITSS60515.2023.10334236

Srinivasan, V. (2022). AI & learning: A preferred future. *Computers and Education: Artificial Intelligence, 3*, 100062.

Sumakul, D. T., Hamied, F. A., & Sukyadi, D. (2022). Artificial intelligence in EFL classrooms: Friend or foe? *LEARN Journal: Language Education and Acquisition Research Network, 15*(1), 232–256.

Sung, G., Guillain, L., & Schneider, B. (2023). Can AI help teachers write higher quality feedback? Lessons learned from using the GPT-3 engine in a makerspace course. In Blikstein, P., Van Aalst, J., Kizito, R., & Brennan, K. (Eds.), *Proceedings of the 17th International Conference of the Learning Sciences - ICLS 2023* (pp. 2093–2094). International Society of the Learning Sciences., https://repository.isls.org//handle/1/10177 DOI: 10.22318/icls2023.904961

Su, P. H., Wu, C. H., & Lee, L. S. (2014). A recursive dialogue game for personalized computer-aided pronunciation training. *IEEE/ACM Transactions on Audio, Speech, and Language Processing*, *23*(1), 127–141. DOI: 10.1109/TASLP.2014.2375572

Sweeney, L. (2013). Discrimination in online ad delivery. *ACM Queue; Tomorrow's Computing Today*, *11*(3), 10–29. DOI: 10.1145/2460276.2460278

Sweller, J. (1988). Cognitive load during problem solving: Effects on learning. *Cognitive Science*, *12*(2), 257–285. DOI: 10.1207/s15516709cog1202_4

Sylva, K., Melhuish, E., Sammons, P., Siraj-Blatchford, I., & Taggart, B. (2004). The Effective Provision of Pre-School Education (EPPE) Project: Technical Paper 12 – The Final Report: Effective Pre-School Education. Institute of Education, University of London.

Tai, T. Y., & Chen, H. H. J. (2021). The impact of immersive virtual reality on EFL learners' listening comprehension. *Journal of Educational Computing Research*, *59*(7), 1272–1293. https://doi.org/https://doi.org/10.1177/0735633121994291. DOI: 10.1177/0735633121994291

Tan, D. Y., & Cheah, C. W. (2021). Developing a gamified AI-enabled online learning application to improve students' perception of university physics. *Computers and Education: Artificial Intelligence*, 2, 100032, https://www.sciencedirect.com/science/article/pii/S2666920X21000266?via%3Dihub

Tang, K.-Y., Chang, C.-Y., & Hwang, G.-J. (2023). Trends in artificial intelligence-supported e-learning: A systematic review and co-citation network analysis (1998–2019). *Interactive Learning Environments, 31*(4), 2134–2152. DOI: 10.1080/10494820.2021.1875001

Tao, J., Ferrão, S., Vitoria, F., & Silva, R. (2020). Gamification for Technology-Enhanced Language Learning (TELL) – Success factors of gamified language learning platform design. *Revista Iberoamericana de Informática Educativa, 31*, 54–69. Researchgate. https://www.researchgate.net/publication/342590083_Gamification_for_Technology-Enhanced_Language_Learning_TELL_-_Success_factors_of_gamified_language_learning_platform_design

Taylor, D. L., Yeung, M., & Bashet, A. Z. (2021). Personalized and adaptive learning. In Ryoo, J., & Winkelmann, K. (Eds.), *Innovative learning environments in STEM higher education* (pp. 17–34). Springer International Publishing., DOI: 10.1007/978-3-030-58948-6_2

The American Council on the Teaching of Foreign Languages (ACTFL). (2024). *The ACTFL proficiency guidelines 2024*. ACTFL. https://www.actfl.org/uploads/files/general/Resources-Publications/ACTFL_Proficiency_Guidelines_2024.pdf

Thompson, J., & Rains, S. (2022). *Chuck Coonradt: Data Creates a Culture of Growth - Blue Margin*. Www.bluemargin.com. https://www.bluemargin.com/ttd/forbes-grandfather-of-gamification-data-creates-a-culture-of-growth#:~:text=From%20this%20observation%2C%20Chuck%20started

Thormundsson, B. (2023, July 7). *AI corporate investment worldwide 2015-2022*. Statista. https://www.statista.com/statistics/941137/ai-investment-and-funding-worldwide/#statisticContainer

Thrasher, T. (2023). Meeting in the metaverse: Language learners' insights into the affordances of virtual reality. In D. Cockerham, R. Kaplan-Rakowski, W. Foshay & M. J. Spector (Eds.), *Reimagining education: Studies and stories for effective learning in an evolving digital environment* (pp. 179–194). Educational Communications and Technology: Issues and Innovations. Springer. https://doi.org/DOI: 10.1007/978-3-031-25102-3_17

Thrasher, T., Kaplan-Rakowski, R., Chun, D., & Sadler, R. (2023). Virtual reality: "Awesome", "OK", or "Not so good" for language learning? In B. Bédi, Y. Choubsaz, K. Friðriksdóttir, A. Gimeno-Sanz, S. Björg Vilhjálmsdóttir & S. Zahova (Eds.), *CALL for all Languages - EUROCALL 2023 Short Papers* (pp. 15–18). https://doi.org/DOI: 10.4995/EuroCALL2023.2023.16948

Thrasher, T., Kaplan-Rakowski, R., Ovsiannikova, U., Meyr, J., & Yuan, Y. (2024). "I can talk to Spanish speakers in Illinois!": Student perspectives on AI-avatar role plays in virtual reality. *WorldCALL2023: Conference Proceedings.*https://doi.org/DOI: 10.22492/issn.2759-1182.2023.18

Thrasher, T. (2022). The impact of virtual reality on L2 French learners' language anxiety and oral comprehensibility: An exploratory study. *CALICO Journal*, *39*(2), 219–238. DOI: 10.1558/cj.42198

Thurairasu, V. (2022). Gamification-Based Learning as The Future of Language Learning: An Overview. *European Journal of Humanities and Social Sciences*, *2*(6), 62–69. DOI: 10.24018/ejsocial.2022.2.6.353

Tica, L., & Krsmanović, I. (2024). Overcoming the Writer's Block? Exploring Students' Motivation and Perspectives on Using Chat GPT as a Writing Assistance Tool in ESP. *ELOPE: English Language Overseas Perspectives and Enquiries,* 21 (1), 129- 149 (316). https://doi.org/.DOI: 10.4312/elope.21.1.129-149

Toda, A. M., Klock, A. C. T., Oliveira, W., Palomino, P. T., Rodrigues, L., Shi, L., Bittencourt, I., Gasparini, I., Isotani, S., & Cristea, A. I. (2019). Analysing gamification elements in educational environments using an existing Gamification taxonomy. *Smart Learning Environments*, *6*(1), 16. Advance online publication. DOI: 10.1186/s40561-019-0106-1

Tolmasova, K. A. (2022). Using corpus linguistics in teaching leisure reading. *The American Journal of Social Science and Education Innovations*, *4*(04), 34–39. DOI: 10.37547/tajssei/Volume04Issue04-05

Tuomi, I. (2018). The impact of artificial intelligence on learning, teaching, and education. M., Cabrera, R., Vuorikari, & Y., Punie (Eds.), *Policies for the future*. Publications Office of the European Union.

U.S. Department of Education, Office of Educational Technology. (2023). *Artificial intelligence and future of teaching and learning: Insights and recommendations*. Washington, DC. Retrieved from https://tech.ed.gov

U.S. Department of Education, Office of Educational Technology. (November, 2010). Transforming American education: Learning powered by technology. National education technology plan 2010. https://www.ed.gov/sites/default/files/netp2010.pdf

UNESCO. (2022). *Recommendation on the ethics of artificial intelligence*. UNESCO. https://unesdoc.unesco.org/ark:/48223/pf0000381137

Urlaub, P., & Dessein, E. (2022). From disrupted classroom to human-machine collaboration? The pocket calculator, Google Translate, and the future of language education. *Journal of Linguistics and Language Teaching*, *14*(1), 45–59.

Vasavakul, T. (2000). Managing the young anarchists: kindergartens and national culture in postcolonial Vietnam. In Wollons, R. W. R. (Ed.), *Kindergartens and cultures: The global diffusion of an idea* (pp. 214–250). Yale University Press.

Vázquez, C., Xia, L., Aikawa, T., & Maes, P. (2018). Words in motion: Kinesthetic language learning in virtual reality. *In 2018 IEEE 18th International Conference on advanced learning technologies (ICALT)* (pp. 272–276). IEEE. https://doi.org/DOI: 10.1109/ICALT.2018.00069

Vera, F. (2023). Integrating Artificial Intelligence (AI) in the EFL Classroom: Benefits and Challenges. *Transformar,* 4(2), 66–77. Recuperado a partir de https://revistatransformar.cl/index.php/transformar/article/view/93

Viana, V., Menezes, D., & Mendes, M. (2011). Revelando sentidos na prática docente: A abordagem de corpus na análise do discurso. *DELTA. Documentação de Estudos em Lingüística Teórica e Aplicada, 27*(2), 175–217. DOI: 10.1590/S0102-44502011000200001

Vu, T. T. (2021). Early childhood education in Vietnam, history, and development. *International Journal of Child Care and Education Policy, 15*(3), 3. Advance online publication. DOI: 10.1186/s40723-020-00080-4

Vygotsky, L. (1978). *Mind in Society: The Development of Higher Psychological Processes.* Harvard University Press.

Wang, B., Rau, P.-L. P., & Yuan, T. (2023). Measuring user competence in using artificial intelligence: Validity and reliability of artificial intelligence literacy scale. *Behaviour & Information Technology, 42*(9), 1324–1337. https://ideas.repec.org/a/taf/tbitxx/v42y2023i9p1324-1337.html. DOI: 10.1080/0144929X.2022.2072768

Wang, D., Han, H., Zhan, Z., Xu, J., Liu, Q., & Ren, G. (2015). A problem solving oriented intelligent tutoring system to improve students' acquisition of basic computer skills. *Computers & Education, 81*, 102–112. DOI: 10.1016/j.compedu.2014.10.003

Wang, J., Hwang, G.-W., & Chang, C.-Y. (2021). Directions of the 100 most cited chatbot-related human behavior research: A review of academic publications. *Computers and Education: Artificial Intelligence, 2*, 100023. DOI: 10.1016/j.caeai.2021.100023

Wang, Y., Grant, S., & Grist, M. (2021). Enhancing the learning of multi-level undergraduate Chinese language with a 3D immersive experience - An exploratory study. *Computer Assisted Language Learning*, *34*(1–2), 114–132. DOI: 10.1080/09588221.2020.1774614

Warschauer, M. (2005). Sociocultural perspectives on CALL. In Egbert, J., & Petrie, G. (Eds.), *CALL research perspectives* (pp. 41–52). Lawrence Erlbaum.

Wei, C.-W., Kao, H.-Y., Lu, H.-H., & Liu, Y. C. (2018). The effects of competitive gaming scenarios and personalized assistance strategies on English vocabulary learning. *Journal of Educational Technology & Society*, *21*(3), 146–158. https://www.jstor.org/stable/26458514

Wibowo, G., Gunawan, I., & Sunuantari, M. (2024). Social network analysis# ChatGPT on social media. *International Journal of Innovative Research in Multidisciplinary Education*, *3*(07), 1178–1186. DOI: 10.58806/ijirme.2024.v3i7n02

Widlöcher, A., & Mathet, Y. (2012). The glozz platform: A corpus annotation and mining tool. In *Proceedings of the 2012 ACM symposium on Document engineering*, 171-180. DOI: 10.1145/2361354.2361394

Wilson, S., & Carson-Berndsen, J. (2011). The corpus analysis toolkit-analysing multilevel annotations. In Human Language Technology. Challenges for Computer Science and Linguistics: 4th Language and Technology Conference, LTC 2009, Poznan, Poland, November 6-8, 2009, Revised Selected Papers 4, 94-104. Springer Berlin Heidelberg.

Wong, J. (2000). "Applying" conversation analysis in applied linguistics: Evaluating English as a second language textbook dialogue [Electronic Version]. In *TESOL Convention, Vancouver, BC.*

Woo, J. H., & Choi, H. (2021). Systematic review for AI-based language learning tools. *arXiv preprint arXiv:2111.04455.* https://doi.org//arXiv.2111.04455DOI: 10.48550

Wu, T. T., Huang, Y. M., Chao, H. C., & Park, J. H. (2014). Personalized English reading sequencing based on learning portfolio analysis. *Information Sciences, 257*, 248–263. DOI: 10.1016/j.ins.2011.07.021

Xie, H., Chu, H.-C., Hwang, G.-J., & Wang, C.-C. (2019). Trends and development in technology-enhanced adaptive/personalized learning: A systematic review of journal publications from 2007 to 2017. *Computers & Education, 140*, 103599. Advance online publication. DOI: 10.1016/j.compedu.2019.103599

Xu, Y., Jia, R., Mou, L., Li, G., Chen, Y., Lu, Y., & Jin, Z. (2016). Improved relation classification by deep recurrent neural networks with data augmentation. arXiv preprint arXiv:1601.03651.

Xue, B., Green, R., & Zhang, M. (2023). Artificial Intelligence in New Zealand: Applications and innovation. *Journal of the Royal Society of New Zealand, 53*(1), 1–5. DOI: 10.1080/03036758.2023.2170165 PMID: 39439988

Xu, Y., Liu, X., Cao, X., Huang, C., Liu, E., Qian, S., & Zhang, J. (2021). Artificial intelligence: A powerful paradigm for scientific research. *Innovation (Cambridge (Mass.)), 2*(4), 100179. DOI: 10.1016/j.xinn.2021.100179 PMID: 34877560

Yang, H., & Zhu, K. (2022). Research on AI-assisted grading of math questions based on deep learning, Proc. SPIE 12174, *International Conference on Internet of Things and Machine Learning (IoTML 2021)*, 121740X (22 April 2022); DOI: 10.1117/12.2628649

Yang, C., Shu-liang, H., & Yong, Y. (2020). A practical teaching mode for colleges supported by artificial intelligence. *International Journal of Emerging Technologies in Learning, 15*(17), 195. DOI: 10.3991/ijet.v15i17.16737

Yang, H., Gao, C., & Shen, H. (2024). Learner interaction with, and response to, Ai-programmed automated writing evaluation feedback in EFL writing: An exploratory study. *Education and Information Technologies, 29*(4), 3837–3858. https://doi-org.libproxy.library.unt.edu/10.1007/s10639-023-11991-3. DOI: 10.1007/s10639-023-11991-3

Yang, Q. F., Lian, L. W., & Zhao, J. H. (2023). Developing a gamified artificial intelligence educational robot to promote learning effectiveness and behavior in laboratory safety courses for undergraduate students. *International Journal of Educational Technology in Higher Education, 20*(1), 18. DOI: 10.1186/s41239-023-00391-9

Yang, R., Cao, J., Wen, Z., Wu, Y., & He, X. (2020). Enhancing automated essay scoring performance via fine-tuning pre-trained language models with combination of regression and ranking. In *Findings of the Association for Computational Linguistics* (pp. 1560–1569). EMNLP. DOI: 10.18653/v1/2020.findings-emnlp.141

Ye, Y., & Kaplan-Rakowski, R. (2024). An exploratory study on practicing listening comprehension skills in high–immersion virtual reality. *British Journal of Educational Technology, 55*(4), 1651–1672. DOI: 10.1111/bjet.13481

You, X., Li, M., Xiao, Y., & Liu, H. (2019). The feedback of the Chinese learning diagnosis system for personalized learning in classrooms. *Frontiers in Psychology, 10*, 1751. DOI: 10.3389/fpsyg.2019.01751 PMID: 31611827

Yun, C.-O., Jung, S.-J., & Yun, T.-S. (2024). Interactive learning tutor service platform based on artificial intelligence in a virtual reality environment. In B. J. Choi, D. Singh, U. S. Tiwary, & W.-Y. Chung (Eds.), Intelligent Human Computer Interaction (pp. 367–373). Springer., , IHCI 2023.DOI: 10.1007/978-3-031-53827-8_32

Zawacki-Richter, O., Marín, V. I., Bond, M., & Gouverneur, F. (2019). Systematic review of research on artificial intelligence applications in higher education–where are the educators? *International Journal of Educational Technology in Higher Education, 16*(1), 1–27. DOI: 10.1186/s41239-019-0171-0

Zhai, X. (2022, December 27). ChatGPT User Experience: Implications for Education. Papers.*ssrn*.com. https://papers.ssrn.com/sol3/papers.cfm?abstract_id=4312418 DOI: 10.2139/ssrn.4312418

Zhang, K., Zhang, K., Zhang, M., Zhao, H., Liu, Q., Wu, W., & Chen, E. (2022). Incorporating dynamic semantics into pre-trained language model for aspect-based sentiment analysis. arXiv preprint arXiv:2203.16369. DOI: 10.18653/v1/2022.findings-acl.285

Zhang, H., Sproat, R., Ng, A. H., Stahlberg, F., Peng, X., Gorman, K., & Roark, B. (2019). Neural models of text normalization for speech applications. *Computational Linguistics*, *45*(2), 293–337. DOI: 10.1162/coli_a_00349

Zhao, L., Wu, X., & Luo, H. (2022). Developing ai literacy for primary and middle school teachers in china: Based on a structural equation modeling analysis. *Sustainability (Basel)*, *14*(21), 14549. DOI: 10.3390/su142114549

Zhaxybayev, D. O., & Barakhnin, V. B. (2022). Coordinate Indexing Algorithms Taking Into Account the Classification Signs-terms in the Subject Area. Computational nanotechnology, 9(1), 21-31.

Zhdanova, A. N., Kupriyanov, A. V., & Sherenkov, D. S. (2022). Morphological text analysis using neural networks. In *2022 VIII International Conference on Information Technology and Nanotechnology (ITNT)*, 1-4. IEEE.

Zhou, Z., Chen, J., Wu, J., & Wang, R. (2022). Sentiment Analysis Method for Agricultural Product Review Based on Corpus Characteristics and Deep Learning Model. In *2022 International Conference on Machine Learning and Intelligent Systems Engineering (MLISE)*, 423-430. IEEE. DOI: 10.1109/MLISE57402.2022.00091

Zimotti, G., Frances, C., & Whitaker, L. (2024). The future of language education: Teachers' perceptions about the surge of AI writing tools. *Technology in Language Teaching & Learning*, *6*(2), 1–24. DOI: 10.29140/tltl.v6n1.1136

Zou, D., Wang, M., Xie, H., Cheng, G., Wang, F. L., & Lee, L. K. (2021). A comparative study on linguistic theories for modeling EFL learners: Facilitating personalized vocabulary learning via task recommendations. *Interactive Learning Environments*, *29*(2), 270–282. DOI: 10.1080/10494820.2020.1789178

About the Contributors

Christina Nicole Giannikas holds a PhD in the field of Applied Linguistics. She is a consultant and founder of CG Education & Research Consultancy. She also works in Higher Education where she lectures courses in Applied Linguistics, is a teacher trainer for pre-service and in-service programs in Cyprus and beyond, and is a researcher for the Department of Rehabilitation Sciences at Cyprus University of Technology. She specializes in early language learning, age-appropriate digital pedagogies, digital literacies, assessment, and Teacher Education.

***

Dagmar Archan is a professor at CAMPUS 02 University of Applied Sciences in Graz, Austria, and Head of the Centre for Teaching Excellence at CAMPUS 02. Her doctoral thesis investigated the impact of Blended Learning on the teaching and learning of English for Specific Purposes in higher education. In 2019, she received the Ars Docendi State Award for Excellence in Teaching for the Blended Learning course discussed in her doctoral thesis. Dr Archan's research focuses on teacher education, digital literacy and the use of technology in teaching and learning, with a particular interest in AI in higher education. In recognition of its efforts to promote digital transformation for which the Centre for Teaching Excellence has been a driving force, CAMPUS 02 has been awarded the prestigious FIBAA (Foundation for International Business Administration Accreditation) Quality Seal of "Excellence in Digital Education" in March 2024.

Eunkyoung Elaine Cha is a doctoral student in the Learning, Design, and Technology program at the University of Georgia. Her research interests include technology-assisted language learning, extended reality (XR), artificial intelligence, and psychological factors in language learning. Her research goal is to support learners from diverse social and cultural backgrounds in having better experiences with second language acquisition. She earned her master's and undergraduate degrees from the University of Michigan and Ewha Womans University.

Prerna Choubey is a Ph.D. student in the Department of Learning Technologies at the University of North Texas. Her research interests include immersive learning technologies, cultural intelligence (CQ), and language learning. Prerna received master's and undergraduate degrees from the University of Washington and the University of Delhi. She is based in Seattle and works as a User Researcher for technology companies.

Huong Thi Bao Dinh obtained her PhD in Education from RMIT University, Australia, in 2015. She has been teaching a range of courses for both undergraduate and postgraduate students, and supervising MA and PhD students in English Studies. Her main areas of interest are ICT in English teaching and learning and TESOL Methodology.

Nabat Erdogan, Ph.D., is an Associate Professor in the Department of Educational Foundations and Literacy at the University of Central Missouri and has twenty-five years of experience in Teaching English to Speakers of Other Languages (TESOL) both in the United States and abroad. Dr. Erdogan earned her first Ph.D. in Linguistics from Azerbaijan University of Languages in 2008 and her second Ph.D. in Teaching English to Speakers of Other Languages (TESOL) and English from the University of Missouri - Kansas City in 2018. With her background in Linguistics, TESOL, and English, Dr. Erdogan's research and publications focus on comparative linguistics, applied linguistics, syntax, phonetics, pragmatics, second language literacy, and the use of generative Artificial Intelligence (AI) in language teaching and learning. Dr. Erdogan's award-winning book titled "Applied Linguistics for Teachers of Culturally and Linguistically Diverse Learners" combines linguistic theory and practice, and offers practical approaches and techniques of teaching English to English language learners.

Regina Kaplan-Rakowski is an Assistant Professor of Learning Technologies at the University of North Texas. She is also Vice President of the Computer-Assisted Language Instruction Consortium (CALICO). Her research interests include immersive learning technologies (e.g., virtual reality, augmented reality, mixed reality), emotional responses to learning technologies, artificial intelligence, and computer-assisted language learning. She serves on the Editorial Board of Educational Technology & Society (ET&S) and the Journal of Technology and Teacher Education (JTATE).

Christina Kitson, Ph.D., is an Associate Professor in the Department of English at UCM and has twenty years of experience in TESOL and has worked with refugee, immigrant, undergraduate, and graduate learners. With her background in TESOL, Applied Linguistics, technology, and assessment, Dr. Kitson adds areas of expertise and experience in program and curriculum development, pedagogical strategies, and assessment management and development designed to meet program and learner needs. Her research and publications focus on technology, applied linguistics, assessment, culture, policy, second language literacy, and the use of generative Artificial Intelligence (AI) in language teaching and learning. Dr. Kitson as part of the TESOL Inc. Research Council, conducted focus group interviews, analyzed survey results, and assisted with finalizing research reports and research studies from the collected data including the 2023-2027 TESOL Research Directions Report.

Ivana Krsmanović is a professor of applied sciences affiliated with the Faculty of Technical Sciences Čačak, University of Kragujevac, Serbia, where she also holds the position of Head of the Department for Humanities and Social Sciences. She is a recipient of the prestigious Joint Excellence in Sciences and Humanities (JESH) scholarship (2023), awarded by the Austrian Academy of Sciences, for research into aspects of Computer-assisted language learning. Dr Krsmanović's scholarly pursuits focus on English as a Foreign Language (EFL) instruction, Computer-assisted language learning, and Digital Humanities.

Hélder Fanha Martins currently holds the position of Full Professor at the Lisbon Accounting and Business School, part of the Polytechnic University of Lisbon (LABS-ISCAL). Furthermore, he is an Integrated Researcher affiliated with CETAPS at NOVA University of Lisbon. With a doctoral degree conferred by Nova University (UNL), Professor Martins has dedicated his research endeavours to the fields of Business Simulation Studies, Languages for Specific Purposes, and Computer-Assisted Language Learning. He serves on the editorial boards of multiple academic journals. Within LABS-ISCAL, he is responsible for overseeing the Department of Information and Communication Sciences and spearheads the International Business Simulation course.

Tuan Nhat Nguyen, PhD is Director of the International Education Center, home to transnational programs at Hanoi University. Nhat Tuan holds a PhD in Translation Studies, granted by Dublin City University (Ireland). His areas of expertise include translation studies, curriculum and syllabus development, TESOL and EMI. He can be contacted at tuannn@hanu.edu.vn

Yongluan Ye is a doctoral student at the Learning Technology Department of the University of North Texas and a seasoned educator. She also currently works as an instructional coach and federal grant coordinator at a K-12 school district, working with world language high school teachers and managing grant-related programs and materials. Before taking up the administrative role, Yongluan Ye had been a world language teacher for various age groups in different settings for over a decade. Her professional and personal interests led her to focus on virtual reality-assisted language learning.

Hümeyra Yener has been serving as English Language teacher since 2004 in different cities of Türkiye. She has MBA degree.

Serdar Yener has been serving as business professor in Sinop University since 2016. Besides he has ELT bachelor degree.

Index

A

C

D

E

F

G

I

L

M

N

O

P

S

U

W

www.ingramcontent.com/pod-product-compliance
Lightning Source LLC
LaVergne TN
LVHW062119200926
848484LV00007B/1713
9798369354773